PERSPECTIVES ON DEMOCRATIC CONSOLIDATION IN CENTRAL AND EASTERN EUROPE

EDITED BY
DIRK BERG-SCHLOSSER AND RAIVO VETIK

EAST EUROPEAN MONOGRAPHS, BOULDER
DISTRIBUTED BY COLUMBIA UNIVERSITY PRESS, NEW YORK

2001

EAST EUROPEAN MONOGRAPHS, NO. DLXXIII

ISBN 0-88033-471-1
Library of Congress Control Number 2001131429

Printed in the United States of America

Contents

III. Patterns of Performance and Consolidation

IV. Inter-regional comparative aspects

Preface

The papers presented in this book are the outcome of an international conference jointly organized by the Research Committee on "Democratization in Comparative Perspective" of the International Political Science Association and the Institute of International and Social Studies at Tallinn, Estonia in November 1998. Dirk Berg-Schlosser is chairman of the Research Committee and Raivo Vetik served as major local organizer.

This meeting has been made possible by the support of the Open Estonia Foundation and the Estonian Science Foundation together with a generous contribution by Kim Kwang-Woong who is also a member of the board of the Research Committee. To all these institutions and persons we want to express once again our sincere gratitude.

For their effective organization and cheerful hospitality in Tallinn we also want to thank Esta Ivalo and Tea Pohl. Stephen Fischer-Galati, a participant at the conference and editor of this series, has kindly offered to publish our proceedings in this important outlet.

Marburg, February 2000 Tallinn, February 2000

Dirk Berg-Schlosser Raivo Vetik

Introduction

DIRK BERG-SCHLOSSER

„AMONG THE GREAT VARIETY OF DEVELOPMENTS THAT HAVE OCCURRED IN THE TWENTIETH CENTURY, I DID NOT, ULTIMATELY, HAVE ANY DIFFICULTY IN CHOOSING ONE AS THE PREEMINENT DEVELOPMENT OF THE PERIOD: THE RISE OF DEMOCRACY".

Amartya Sen

The dramatic events of 1989/90 in Central and Eastern Europe have changed the world. The downfall of the Communist regimes, the dissolution of the Soviet bloc, the end of the Cold War and the changes towards more democratic and accountable regimes have not signalled the "end of history", as some observers assumed (see Fukuyama 1989), but rather a new beginning. This concerns not only the peoples living in this region, but, directly or indirectly, all of mankind. While these processes certainly give some reason for hope and a certain optimism compared to the previous period, as the quotation from Amartya Sen, the winner of the 1998 Nobel Prize for Economics, also implies, these changes and their continuing consequences are far from over and for those struggling to cope with them in their everyday lives the impact has been tremendous.

In fact, it is not only a transformation of the international world order and the domestic political regimes which has occurred, but also a profound economic transformation towards more capitalist elements on the national, regional and global levels with ensuing and still continuing domestic and world-wide turbulences. These changes are also transforming many social relations in the direction of greater personal autonomy and individualization, but also, in many cases, greater personal and social insecurity. Many people are adapting and learning fast, but quite a few are also left behind and become losers in this process.

Even though hardly any social scientist had foreseen this turn of events in any more precise way (see also von Beyme 1994, chapter 1), many of these dramatic changes have been well-researched and documented in the meantime. Our knowledge of these processes of political and economic transformation and, at in least in a number of instances, democratic consolidation has greatly increased and many aspects are by now better understood and the respective prevailing theoretical explanations not rarely had to be considerably modified. Among the vast number of studies, both by "Eastern" and "Western" scholars, if this distinction still has any meaning, only a few can be mentioned here. The most thorough and embracing book is probably the one by Juan Linz and Alfred Stepan (1996). Elite transformations have been covered by Dogan and Higley (1998) and, in greater detail in three "proto-typical" cases, Hollis (1999) for example. Institutional changes and the consequences for "constitutional engineering" have been discussed, amongst others, by Sartori (1994) and Agh (1998). The newly emerging party systems are treated by Kitschelt (1995) and Segert/Stöss/Niedermayer

(1997). The political cultural dimension at the "micro"-level which has now also become accessible by the established procedures of survey research is extensively documented by "Eurobarometer", the "New Democracies" and the "New Baltic Barometer" data (see, e.g., Plasser/Pribersky 1996, Barnes/Simon 1998, and, most importantly so far, Rose/Mishler/Haerpfer 1998). International aspects and, most significantly, the prospects with regard to the European Union and its possible enlargements are dealt with by Pridham, Herring and Sanford (1994) and Hyde-Price (1996). Summary accounts of all these processes and a discussion of their further perspectives can also be found in Merkel/Puhle (1999) and Diamond (1999).

Nevertheless, things are still very much in a state of flux and many of the occurring changes imply "building the ship at sea" in Elster's (1998) apt phrase. This entirely new challenge of simultaneous political, economic and social transformations and their international interactions and repercussions provide food for thought and common concerns for generations to come both in practical politics and the social sciences. In this regard, it is fortunate that a meaningful exchange of concepts and findings has now become possible between social scientists from Eastern Europe and other parts of the world. For this, the International Political Science Association (IPSA), the European Consortium for Political Research (ECPR), the European Science Foundation (ESF) and other similar organizations provide important fora and networks.

In the beginning, these dialogues still were characterized by a good deal of mutual uncertainty and, to some extent, suspicion. In most Eastern countries no independent, empirically oriented political science had existed before the changes of 1989/90. There had been some specialized institutes concerned with area studies and some compartmentalized historical and other divisions of the academies of science, but no research free from the dominating and mostly very orthodox Marxist doctrines and the respective party lines employing the tools of modern social science, as for example general population surveys, could be conducted (see, e.g., also Reich 1992, Pusic 1993). Participants at international congresses and, in particular, official representatives in the world-wide organizations usually were just party functionaries following the official doctrines.

In the meantime, together with the dramatic events around them, the skills and orientations of many social scientists, particularly form the middle and younger generations, have changed as well. For the first time a meaningful dialogue between equals in terms of epistemological backgrounds and methodological tools has become possible. This is not to say that "Western" behavioralist or other approaches have not been with problems of their own, and there has been a diversity of perspectives and schools of thought in other parts of the world as well. But for the first time these problems can be discussed openly and frankly from the different points of view by social scientists from many parts of the world including Eastern Europe.

A modest, but nevertheless significant forum in this regard has been provided by the Research Committee on "Democratization in a Comparative Perspective" of the International Political Science Association. This Research Committee, in the beginning as a separate "Study Group", was founded at the IPSA World Congress in Washington/D.C. in 1988, i.e. *before* the dramatic transformations of 1989 ff. The first chairpersons of this Study Group were Tatu Vanhanen and Dirk Berg-Schlosser. Apart from regular activities at the following IPSA world congresses (Buenos Aires 1991, Berlin 1994, Seoul 1997) a series of regional conferences was started (Abuja/Nigeria 1992, Rio de Janeiro 1995, Chandigarh/India 1996) which brought together scholars from all parts of the world. They discussed the respective chances and problems of further democratization in these regions in greater detail and attempted to draw some, at least preliminary, conclusions as to the historical, regional and cultural specificities, but also some of the more general aspects and the respective social forces at work and their future perspectives. Some of these activities have been documented in the respective conference proceedings (see Omoruyi/Berg-Schlosser/Sambo/Okwuosa 1994, Diniz 1996) and a large number of individual publications by the participants at these meetings. This Research Committee by now has become IPSA's largest in terms of individual members indicating their preferences concerning deductions of their membership fees.

The conference at Tallinn/Estonia in November 1998, from which this book emanates, has been the last in this series so far. It assembled some 40 scholars from 16 countries and, again, was an expression of the lively exchanges which now have become possible and for which the papers gathered in this volume served as the starting points. While the debates as such and the continuing contacts and discussions cannot be documented here, the overall quality of the papers, which have been revised to some extent after the conference, expresses both the diversity and the coherence of the different aspects and the respective approaches and points of view.

We have gathered them here under four general headings, one referring to the special historical, political-cultural, social-structural and socio-economic conditions of the region, the second covering a number of case studies, the third being concerned with some important cross-cutting aspects of these developments, and the fourth one providing a comparative perspective from the outside sharing some similar experiences. These papers, of course, are not the last word in these matters, but they carry forward the ongoing dialogues and demonstrate their important theoretical and empirical, but also, to some extent, practical-political contents.

The first one by Stephen Fischer-Galati, a nestor of contemporary East European history, gives an overview of the state of affairs in a greater number of countries. It points, in particular, to the international and even global implications of present developments. While, in his view, certain democracies may be considered "consolidated", there remains a strong dose of skepticism in his account. The second paper by Raivo Vetik is devoted to multiculturalism as a possible model for consolidation of democracy. He outlines the major historical, comparative and theoretical aspects of the phenomenon of multiculturalism and argues that multiculturalism is constantly gaining in importance in our day. The third paper by Laslo Sekelj, who is a member of the Hungarian minority in present-day Yugoslavia (Serbia), emphasizes the importance of the ethnic composition of the newly democratizing states and the significant role of parts of the old and the new elites in manipulating this factor in favour of their own more or less authoritarian control as in Mecir's Slovakia, Milosevic's Yugoslavia and Yeltsin's Russia. Other factors, such as socio-economic development, cultural-religious influences or the more recent political-institutional arrangements, are considered to be of less importance. The fourth chapter in this part by Tatu Vanhanen, a veteran of empirical political theory, critically examines his own previous assessments of the "distribution of power resources" and the level of democracy, as measured by the well-known indices developed by him. He concludes, even though his measures are admittedly rather crude, that, by and large, again they have shown to be significant predictors of current events. From this perspective he is relatively optimistic as to the future of democracy in the former socialist countries.

In the second part, dealing with particular cases, Vanhanen's approach is applied at a cross-regional level to the present state of affairs in Russia by Christopher Marsh. He demonstrates that there exists a great disparity in the degree to which Vanhanen's indices are distributed throughout Russia's regions. Not all of this diversity, however, points into the direction predicted by Vanhanen. Marsh remains nevertheless confident that continuing economic reforms positively affect the index of power resources and thus enhance the prospects of further democratization. The chapter by Jane Curry and Irena Pankow, a joint product of authors from different parts of the world, discusses some of the specificities of the Polish case, in particular the role played by Solidarnosz and its organisation as a uniquely enduring social movement both in the communist and post-communist periods. Somewhat paradoxically, as they convincingly demonstrate, the previous anti-regime and in this sense democratizing movement has failed to find its role as an effective democratic factor in the now pluralist political landscape, retaining some of its former organizational and ideological features. The contribution by Gabriella Ilonszki also deals with one of the relatively more successful cases. In her view Hungarian democracy can be considered to be consolidated in the sense that recent developments have now become irreversible comprising all major social and political forces in the country. This is also reflected by the working of parliament and the composition of its committees which she examines in greater detail.

The two subsequent chapters are concerned with the case of Estonia, one by a "close observer", Pami Aalto from Finland, and the other as again a "joint venture" by Jüri Ruus from Estonia. Aalto discusses again the ethnic factor from the perspective of the different Estonian and Russian identities and the respective political discourses and with regard to its geo-political international and comparative implications. Ruus documents the changes in the composition of the central political elites in the period of transition. Some parts of the old political nomenclatura now have been "recirculated" in other fields, in particular in newly established private businesses and companies. Others, mostly from the more intermediate and younger ranks in former times, have retained positions of political influence now with a strong "Estonian" national emphasis but, on the whole, accepting and actively contributing to the new democratic order. The final chapter by Lenka Rovna in this part addresses the role of external forces and in particular of the European Union as a factor contributing to further democratic consolidation in the case of the Czech Republic. She shows that the requirements on both sides are quite demanding, but that there is a strong desire in this country to come "back to Europe" both economically and politically.

The third part is concerned with some major cross-cutting aspects. The chapter by Jane Curry discusses the role of free media in the process of democratization. While the freedom of information and expression is a crucial element of democracy itself, the actual media structure in terms of ownership and political control may in effect distort their potentially positive influence enabling citizens to come to well-informed and reasoned judgements and to participate meaningfully in civil society and politics. As Jane Curry demonstrates, this is certainly still an under-researched and under-valued part of the processes of democratic transition and consolidation. But also the media structures in "Western" countries in terms of their sometimes sensationalist, populist, ethnocentric, or simply "soap" tendencies should be critically examined in this respect. Another important aspect concerning intermediate structures between the political sphere and the society at large are the newly emerging party systems. These are systematically compared by Algis Krupavicius from Lithuania in terms of the more common concepts and indicators developed by empirically-oriented political scientists in Western countries. On the whole, the new party systems have become increasingly stabilized, but electoral volatility remains relatively high and voter turnout may be declining, but the latter aspect is also true of some of the "established" West European democracies.

In another far-reaching comparative chapter Artur Gruszak from Poland assesses the performance of the new regimes in East Central Europe after almost 10 years. According to his account democratic governability can be shown to have been largely successful in the Czech, Hungarian and Polish cases, whereas Slovakia under Mecir lagged considerably behind. Only the recent change in government there may give cause to some more optimism, but, as he also points out, exceedingly high demands on governments and somewhat unrealistic expectations by the population at large may also be a factor impairing the further consolidation of democracy. – Harvard Hegre, Scott Gates, Nils Petter Gleditch and Tanja Ellingsen from Norway in another major joint research effort analyze the impact of democratization and the respective levels of democracy in terms of internal civil violence and international armed conflicts. On the basis of an (almost) world-wide data set they demonstrate the high probability of peaceful relations both within and among established democracies. The authoritarian states also exhibit a (repressive) domestic peace of sorts, whereas the middle category of recently democratizing countries or "semi-democracies" is the most conflict-prone, at least in the short term. In the longer run, however, the authors conclude that "a democratic civil peace is likely not only to be more just, but also more durable".

This relatively optimistic tone is shared by the non-European observers in the last part of this volume. Surinder Shukla from India discusses the difficulties of democratic survival in this relatively poor and "underdeveloped" and socially highly fragmented country. In spite of many obstacles a certain democratic consolidation has taken place. Some elements of this (relative) success may be meaningful for other countries in this region or under similar conditions in other parts of the world as well. Finally, Kim Kwang-Woong from South Korea presents a critical reflection on the administrative reforms of the new government under President Kim Dae Jung. As he shows, democratization also means administrative de-centralization and, to some extent, deregulation to bring government "closer to the people" and to make it more effective. In the reforms he discusses, at least some important steps in this direction have been taken. In the meantime, Kim himself has become a minister in the new government and now may be able to implement some of his ideas. This shows, incidentally, how close political science and practical politics may come. Better analysis and theory then can also mean better practice.

References

Agh, Attila (1998), The Politics of Central Europe, London: Sage.

Barnes, Samuel H. and János Simon (eds.) (1998), The Postcommunist Citizen, Budapest: Erasmus Foundation.

Beyme, Klaus von (1994), Systemwechsel in Osteuropa, Frankfurt/M.: Suhrkamp.

Diamond, Larry (1999), Developing Democracy – Toward Consolidation, Baltimore, Johns Hopkins.

Diniz, Eli (ed.) (1996), O Desafio da Democracia na América Latina, Rio de Janeiro: Instituto Universitário de Pesquisas do Rio de Janeiro (IUPERJ).

Dogan, Mattei and John Higley (eds.) (1998), Elites, Crises and the Origins of Regimes, Lanham/Md.: Rowman and Littlefield.

Elster, Jon (ed.) (1998), Institutional Design in Post-communist societies: Building the ship at sea, Cambridge: Cambridge UP.

Fukuyama, Francis (1989), "The End of History", National Interest, 16, pp. 3-18.

Hollis, Wendy (1999), The Influence of Communist Legacy on Democratic Transformation and Consolidation in Hungary, the Czech Republic and Romania, New York: Columbia UP.

Hyde-Price, Adrian (1996), The International Politics of East Central Europe, Manchester: Manchester UP.

Kitschelt, Herbert (1995), Party Systems in East Central Europe: Consolidation or Fluidity?, Glasgow: University of Strathclyde, Studies in Public Policy no. 241.

Linz, Juan J. and Alfred Stepan (1996), Problems of Democratic Transition and Consolidation, Baltimore: Johns Hopkins.

Merkel, Wolfgang and Hans-Jürgen Puhle (1999), Von der Diktatur zur Demokratie, Opladen: Westdeutscher Verlag.

Omoruyi, Omo, Dirk Berg-Schlosser, Adesina Sambo and Ada Okwuosa (1994), Democratisation in Africa, 4 vols., Benin City: Hima and Hima Ltd.

Plasser, Fritz and Andreas Pribersky (eds.) (1996), Political Culture in East Central Europe, Aldershot: Avebury.

Pridham, Geoffrey, Eric Herring and George Sanford (eds.) (1994), Building Democracy? – The International Dimension of Democratisation in Eastern Europe, Leicester: Leicester UP.

Pusic, V. (1993), "Intellectual Trends, Institutional Change and Scholarly Needs in Eastern Europe", East European Politics and Society, no. 1, pp. 1-13.

Reich, J. (1992), Abschied von den Lebenslügen – Die Intelligenz an der Macht, Reinbek: Rowohlt.

Rose, Richard, William Mishler and Christian Haerpfer (1998), Democracy and its Alternatives – Understanding Post-Communist Societies, Cambridge: Polity Press.

Sartori, Giovanni (1994), Comparative Constitutional Engineering, London: Macmillan.

Segert, Dieter, Richard Stöss and Oskar Niedermayer (eds.) (1997), Parteiensysteme in postkommunistischen Gesellschaften Osteuropas, Opladen: Westdeutscher Verlag.

Sen, Armartya (1999), "Democracy as a Universal Value", Journal of Democracy, vol. 10, no. 3, pp. 3-17.

I. GENERAL PRECONDITIONS AND PROBLEMS OF TRANSITION

Eastern Europe on the Eve of Y2K

STEPHEN FISCHER-GALATI

Ten years after the collapse of communism in Eastern Europe the road to democratization remains, realistically, paved with questionable intentions. And there are good reasons for that.

The assumption that the peoples' craving for democracy would overcome all obstacles to the restoration of the presumed democratic traditions of Eastern European states after half a century of totalitarianism of the right and of the left has proven to be less than accurate. So has been the presumption that the preconditions for expediting the restoration of democracy formulated primarily by the United States and, at least paid lip service to, by the "European allies" would be readily acceptable to and implemented by the post-communist governments of Eastern Europe. Thus the introduction of free market economies, privatization of state owned enterprises, restoration of party pluralism and of free elections, recognition and protection of the rights of minorities, the guaranteeing of freedom of speech, religion and assembly, and the corollary respecting of human rights, became a *sine qua non* for securing western aid, mostly financial, to facilitate the rapid transition to democracy.

The fallacy of this formula is that it ignored the political and historic realities of Eastern Europe. The prerequisites were used on a selective basis to further the specific, and basically incompatible aim of the main parties concerned with the evolution of post-communist Eastern Europe - the United States, Russia, and Germany and its primary acolyte in the European Union: France.

It is fair to say that the collapse of the communist order in Eastern Europe was attributable less to the people's "craving for democracy" or even to their deep-seated opposition to communism than to the collapfse of the Soviet Union and the corollary end of the Cold War. It is also fair to say that even if the United States claimed victory in that war, public interest in funding the democratization of Eastern Europe was limited. In fact, while supportive of democratization, the government of the United States expected that process to be led by Germany as a financially powerful western democracy. One should not exaggerate the significance of official statements applauding the anticommunism of Lech Walesa and Vaclav Havel, or those of the then Secretary of State James Baker hailing the restoration of "Albanian Party Pluralism," or even President Bush's reminding us of the "traditions of Ottoman democracy." The fact is that these declarations were motivated by political considerations only peripherally related to the post-communist evolution of Eastern Europe. In reality, the very notion of reviving the principles incorporated in the Marshall Plan of post-World War II gained no support from the executive and legislative branches of the US government. In short, by the early 1990s the "transition to democracy" in Eastern Europe was primarily a European problem.

If the notion of "making the world safe for democracy" was truly an essential part of American foreign policy in the twentieth century and if to many Americans the commitment to that goal, was, and continues to be, a legitimate mandate, it would be difficult to argue that the democratization of Eastern Europe was at best more than an imprecise desideratum of the politically-conscious American population, including the East European diaspora in the United States. And this is all the more true of the present "western democracies" in general and in particular of Germany which, it should be recalled, had not been entirely supportive of Washington's policies during the Cold War. If anything, by the early 1990s the "European allies" were intent on weakening America's influence in Europe.

On the other hand, most of the politically conscious population of Eastern Europe still regarded the United States as the liberator from communism, as the greatest, most powerful and wealthiest democracy, hoping that the repetition of the process of restoration of democratic orders in post-World War II western Europe would be repeated, again under American leadership, in post-Cold War Eastern Europe. However, these expectations were not to be realized, since it soon became apparent that the pattern for the evolution in the post-Cold War period was to be much closer to that of the post-World War I years than that identified with the Marshall Plan.

The equating of anti-communism with democracy was just as erroneous an assumption as that of the existence of democratic roots, if not necessarily democratic traditions, in the history of all countries of Eastern Europe prior to the years of Fascist and Communist totalitarianism. Whether this view, expressed primarily by the United States ,was cynical or naïve, it was *pro forma* shared by the "western democracies" and by parties interested in securing power or, at least, in changing the political order in Eastern Europe. It would be unfair to ascribe opportunism to all political leaders who assumed control of East European Governments after 1989 in the name of restoring and/or furthering the democratic traditions or aspirations of their people. But it would be absurd to assume that in so doing they would fail to seek legitimacy bases incompatible with the historic traditions and realities of their own countries. It would be equally absurd to assume that the policies of the external parties concerned with the future of Eastern Europe were to be guided by an *ad literam* enforcement of the enunciated principles of democratization. What was understood by all, however, was that the transition was to be to democracy and that all participants in the process would be at least "born again democrats."

It might seem that, despite the absence of genuine democratic traditions, there was a general predisposition toward democracy in Eastern Europe. It is doubtful, however, whether specific prerequisites primarily those related to minority rights, toleration of diversity, and other aspects at variance with national cultural traditions would be truly acceptable to political leaders and the people at large.

It may well be asked whether the adoption of the equivalent of the Marshall Plan would have altered the course of the transition to democracy. In all probability that course would have been somewhat different and the state of democratization more advanced than at present throughout Eastern Europe. But, in the absence of such commitments and also because of the transformation of the global economic system prior to, and especially, in the decade following the collapse of the communist regimes, democracy, as conceived in 1989 or as practiced in most of the west, is hardly consolidated anywhere in Eastern Europe. If anything, political instability is more the norm than the exception.

Contrary to politically-motivated claims, the so-called "consolidated democracies," Poland, Hungary and Czech Republic which were admitted to NATO and are front-runners in the race for membership in the European Union have not satisfied the rigid requirements set in 1989 in several major respects. It is true that the parliamentary systems are in place and functioning, that the economic prerequisites have been largely implemented, and that personal freedoms and basic human rights are guaranteed. It is also true that multi-party free elections have been the norm at all levels of government. However, the executors of these transformations and corollary implementation of pertinent laws and policies identified with the democratic state and society, have done little to educate the masses in the ways and spirit of democracy. This is at least partly explicable by the fact that the political class consists largely of members of conservative "historic" political parties of the pre-communist period, whose democratic credentials consist largely of opposition to communism, of new political parties whose leaders and adherents were formed under communist rule, of former members of the communist party who were either identified with or favouring "socialism with a human face" but also of bureaucrats, of military and security officers, of members of nationalist organizations, who either survived the old regime or resurfaced after 1989 or whose commitment to true democratization is questionable. It is also evident that most political organizations and government officials, and much of the population of the "consolidated" democracies are mostly socially and culturally conservative, less than tolerant of ethnic and religious diversity, more often than not authoritarian and nationalistic. And this is also true of the "non-consolidated" democracies of Eastern Europe.

"Consolidation", such as it is, was facilitated by factors specific to the evolution of communism in pre-1989 Hungary and Poland and, in all cases, by the political interests of Germany and, to a lesser extent, those of the United States.

The policies of Germany, if not necessarily based on traditional precedents and formulations such as "Mittel-Europa" and "Drang nach Osten," were to secure economic domination over Central Europe while encouraging Russia's economic development through investments. It is not that Germany was afraid of the resurgence of Russian militarism and imperialism in the aftermath of the Cold War; rather its policies were motivated by economic factors and historic spheres of influence. The former components of the Austro-Hungarian empire - Hungary, Czechoslovakia, Croatia, Slovenia and much of Poland - were natural targets for "democratization" by the reunited German state. Hungary, the Czech parts of pre-"velvet divorce" Czechoslovakia, Croatia, Slovenia and Poland were to be assisted whereas the non-Central European countries - Romania, Bulgaria, Albania and for that matter Serbia and Turkey, because of their geographic location, historic relations with Russia and presumed cultural, political and economic "underdevelopment" were to be treated in the manner contemptuously suggested by Bismarck as "bon pour l'Orient."

First Germany and later also its partners in various European organizations were lax in the enforcement of the criteria for democratization. They did however provide significant economic assistance thus insuring the relative economic viability of these states, and, at least, the adoption of democratic governance and institutions. However, Germany's recognition of Croatia's independence precipitated the dismemberment of Yugoslavia, as well as the disturbing Bosnian and Kosovo crises, and current political and military instability in Southeastern Europe. Germany has also shown remarkable tolerance of ethnic discrimination and nationalistic and chauvinistic polities by its protégés, while condemning similar policies by those states outside its immediate sphere of interest and overlooking its own policies of discrimination toward those from the "Orient." Thus, the authoritarian "democracy" of Tudjman's Croatia, Hungary's unabated irredentism, the all-pervasive regional discrimination against gypsies and the resurgence of an anti-semitic political right, are all indicative of the shallowness of the argument that true democratization is the criterion for recognizing the former communist countries as part of the democratic West and admitting them into the European Union and, eventually, NATO.

The German-dominated democratization of Eastern Europe has generally been endorsed and reinforced by the United States. Whereas American economic actions as such were of lesser importance in the "democratization" of Czechoslovakia, Poland, Hungary and, even less so, in that of Croatia and Slovenia, politically motivated factors were generally determinant.

Because of the limited economic importance of Eastern Europe for American investors, the primary interests of the United States have focused on global strategic considerations. It is fair to say that the United States does not wish to see the resurgence of totalitarianism in the former Soviet Union with the corollary renewal of possible nuclear races or confrontations. It is also true that an American military presence in Europe is regarded as essential for strategic and political considerations. The "European allies" overt actions designed to diminish America's preeminence in the global economic system, as symbolized by the adoption of the Euro as an alternative to the Dollar, are being accompanied by plans to reduce NATO's status to that of a protective military umbrella ultimately provided by the United States but controlled and managed by Europeans. This essentially ambiguous situation in which on the one hand the European members of NATO are in fact seeking to reduce the American political and economic presence in Europe while still ultimately seeking America's military protection and on the other, the American determination to maintain NATO as a credible military organization which requires American leadership and guarantees a meaningful presence in Europe, has clearly affected the process of democratization and, *nolens volens,* contributed to political instability in Eastern Europe.

America's support for the German-led "democratization" in Hungary, Poland and the Czech Republic is based primarily on pragmatic political considerations. The existence of a pre-World War II Czech democratic order together with the unquestionable commitment to democracy of Vaclav Havel are more than justificatory of the announced goals of American foreign policy. The major role played by the Polish-American communities in American domestic policies mandated American support of post-communist Poland and the overlooking of the fact that Lech Walesa's policies were never inspired by a genuine commitment to Western democratic values and principles and that, in fact, a resurgent ultra-conservative Polish Catholic church has been largely unsupportive of the democratization of the country.

Similarly, a meaningful presence in Eastern Europe, particularly in Hungary, made possible through the various programs and activities carried out by the foundations established by the prominent Hungarian-American financier George Soros, with the support of the US government, has been responsible for expediting Hungary's transition to democracy. The American policy, however, has also been influenced by a politically active Hungarian diaspora whose principal goal remains the invalidation of the provisions of the Treaty of Trianon of 1920 with corresponding alterations of the contemporary territorial status quo in Eastern Europe. As a consequence, the US government has lent a deaf ear to contemporary Hungarian revisionism manifested primarily through claims of Budapest's rights of extraterritorial protection of co-nationals wherever they may be located in Eastern Europe, and its toleration of Hungarian chauvinistic and nationalistic manifestations.

In view of all considerations, the US government has supported the admission of Hungary, the Czech Republic and Poland to NATO despite these nations' qualifications being inferior from a military standpoint to those of other nations whose membership has been denied.

The consonance of American and German policies has also been evident with respect to the "democratization" of Romania. In both instances the lack of economic interest, the desire not to challenge Russia's opposition to the expansion of NATO and, last but not least, the virulent opposition of the Hungarian and Romanian diasporas and their political organizations to the regime of Ion Iliescu, has resulted in the adoption of the official position of Romania's failing to meet the criteria for democratization. Whereas it is true that the left-wing Romanian government did in fact not adhere fully to the economic and political requirements imposed by the United States and its western allies, it is also true that democratization with respect to parliamentary governance, protection of human rights and guarantees of unlimited freedom of the press, religion and speech were granted immediately after the collapse of the regime of Nicolae Ceausescu. It is also true that after the elections of 1996, when the Iliescu regime was replaced by a coalition government of the Democratic Convention dominated by the historically democratic National Peasant Party, American and German policies toward Romania did not change. Granted that the new government has been very slow in reforming the economic system through rapid adoption of privatization and corollary encouragement of a genuine market economy, it is evident that the fundamental lack of interest in Romanian affairs, financial, political and strategic, by both NATO and the majority of the members of the European Union have contributed to the continuing deterioration of the economy and degradation of the people's standard of living, with a concomitant growth of social unrest.

Similarly, Bulgaria has been treated with equal indifference by the West and the United States with comparable results in economic development, living standards, and social problems.

As for Albania, the less said the better. James Baker's enthusiasm for the return of party pluralism evanesced as reality, rather than political opportunism and mythology, surfaced. The deplorable economic, political and social conditions were barely noted by the "democratizers" whose interest in that country may, however, undergo changes as a result of events and likely developments that the policies of the German-dominated European Union, of NATO and of the United States are likely to have to address in the near future.

The past, present and foreseeable problems related to the "democratization" of Eastern Europe are those concerning political issues involving Islam. The extended Bosnian crisis, the unresolved Kosovo problem, both bloody, violent and involving primarily nationalist Orthodox Serbia and Moslem Bosnians and, respectively, Albanians, had little to do with democratization. But, by their very nature, they became the focus and locus of divergent international interests transcending the strictly European context. The depiction of the Bosnian struggle for independence as an expression of the people's democratic aspirations, primarily by the government of the United States, is hardly tenable. Rather, the brutality of the Serbian forces involved in the repression of the Bosnians was rightly regarded as a violation of human rights obviously at odds with democratic principles. Similarly, it is the repression of the Albanian "freedom fighters" in Kosovo by the Serbian armed forces rather than the presumed democratic goals of the Albanian rebels that justifies NATO's intervention in the resolution of the Kosovo crisis. But, the crises, by involving Islamic military forces as opposed primarily to Serbian ones acting directly or indirectly under the direction of the nationalist, de facto communist, Yugoslav President Slobodan Milosevic, have exacerbated the rivalries and contradictions in the aims and policies of the European "democracies" and the United States despite common participation in NATO and presumed unity in promoting the democratization of Eastern Europe.

The European members of NATO supported military action in Bosnia at a time when that action was endorsed by the United Nations; moreover, when the European Union was at an early stage of development, American leadership in resolution of a European conflict was accepted. However, there was limited European enthusiasm for the American-sponsored peace negotiations resulting in the Dayton Accord. The Kosovo crisis in its present stage poses more intricate political problems. The consolidation of the European Union, the introduction of the Euro, opposition to American policies in the Near East, especially military actions unauthorized by the United Nations against Iraq, and the desire to have European problems settled by Europeans all contribute to the present European reluctance toward military action by an American-led NATO against Serbia. The invocation of the argument that such American-led action against a sovereign state without the express approval of the United Nations is very much in keeping with the political goal of having Europeans assume control of NATO, of enforcing the principle of "Europe for the Europeans," and ultimately of changing the nature of American-European relations from that of "The United States and our European allies" to "Europe (the European Union) and our American ally." This is not to say that American participation, at the behest of the European Union, is to be excluded or that the Europeans would not want to pursue democratization in Eastern Europe. But it is a clear signal that the United States is no longer to play a dominant role in NATO and more than a secondary role in the reshaping, or "democratization," of Eastern Europe. It is noteworthy in this context that the presence of American military bases in Turkey is tolerated only in that they are used for the implementation of American policies outside of Europe. The barring of Turkey, as an Islamic country, from membership in the European Union, at Germany's behest, is reflective of rising xenophobia not only in Germany against its Turkish population but also against the sizeable Islamic population in the western democracies.

Thus, ten years after the collapse of the communist regimes in Eastern Europe it may be politically convenient to speak of "consolidated democracies" but it is more realistic to state that the overall political, social and economic order in that part of Europe is hardly consolidated.

Politically all countries with the exception of Milosevic's Yugoslavia have adopted democratic institutions and generally the rule of law. But few of their leaders have abandoned nationalism as the primary factor in securing legitimacy and most have tolerated xenophobia, violations of the rights of minorities, and abuses of power. There has been little progress in encouraging the alteration of the traditionally rigid and dogmatic educational systems with a view to encouraging freedom of thought for the younger generations. In fact, political participation by the youth in the formulation of policies that would further democratization is severely circumscribed by generations of bureaucrats, politicians, and managers who had served or been active under communism or, even, under the pre-communist regimes.

Whereas nationalist and inter-ethnic and inter-religious conflicts remain major destabilizing actual or potential sources of conflict, the political instability resultant from intra-party rivalries and confrontations has also affected the implementation of the "transition to democracy." Realistically, for the West the key requirement was the transformation of the economic systems. Western insistence on the replacement of state-directed economies to market economies with corollary privatization, while rational for eventual attainment of democratic, capitalist societies and states was, in effect, inapplicable without significant financial assistance. It is fair to say that as a result of the economic policies of the Hungarian communist government of the 1980s the transition to a market economy was infinitely easier in that country than in the rest of the former communist states. In a way, even the rigid communist order in Czechoslovakia had adopted a more flexible economic policy than elsewhere and this was also true of the evolution of the Polish order during the post-Solidarity years. Thus, with significant economic assistance received by the "Mitteleuropa" states, "democratization" in the sense imposed by the west would proceed at a more rapid pace than in Romania, Albania or Bulgaria. Whether the Stalinist economic order of Ceausescu's Romania, or the rigid communist regimes of Zhivkov or Hoxha could have allowed relatively rapid transition to market economies even in the event of western financial assistance is uncertain. What is certain, however, is that in the absence of such assistance, the requirement for democratization was unlikely to be adopted in a rigorous and prompt manner.

It may well be asked whether the rapid adoption of market economies in any of the East European countries would have insured economic viability and, by raising the peoples' standards of living, encouraged the rapid democratization of those societies. The answer is probably no. After a decade of transition the median gross monthly salary in the "consolidated democracies" of Hungary, Poland and the Czech Republic are, respectively, $307, $343, and $330; this, in juxtaposition, to the corresponding median gross salaries of France and Germany of $1,000 and $3,000 respectively. It is fair to say that these three countries' economic well-being and, presumably, solid democratic credentials for being admitted to the European Union depend on continued economic support from Germany and the European Union, for surely, given the nature of the global economy, their economies could not be competitive with those of the Chinese People's Republic and of other non-European countries with lesser democratic credentials. By contrast, the median gross salary in Romania is $130 and in Bulgaria $120. These countries' economies are equally non-viable and non-competitive in the global economy and in the absence of any specific political or economic interest on the part of the European Union or the United States are less consolidated than those of Hungary, Poland and the Czech Republic. It is worth noting the obvious, however, that the median gross salaries in all countries of Eastern Europe are, at world prices, at best at the minimum subsistence level and, in the case of Romania and Bulgaria, at substantially below those levels. The potential consequences of these situations for the evolution of democracy in case of possible global economic or political changes require no critical comment.

In truth, however, there are several potentially major factors that would affect the future of Eastern Europe on the eve of Y2K. We are not unduly alarmed by the fears and dire predictions that the computer-generated crisis of January 2000 would result in a universal cataclysm. In fact, at least for Eastern Europe, the potential return of January 2000 to January 1900 may be a blessing rather than the end of the democratic world. First, the global economy is a stage in the development of capitalism in the revolutionary technological age. In this economy small nations, just as small companies, are dependent on the economies of scale directed by the capitalist giants. Even if the giants of world capitalism do periodically merge or collaborate with one another they remain in competition for leadership, control, and even supremacy of the global economic world. Whether the Euro will prevail over the dollar in Europe, whether the European Union will be able, in the longer run, to emerge supreme in Europe would depend on economic and political uncertainties characteristic of the evolution of the world economy and political orders. But in this competitive struggle the small nations of Eastern Europe with very limited resources and capital will invariably be at best minor players in the games affecting the evolution of the global economy. At this moment, with the virtual collapse of the Russian economy and Russian military power, the

United States' active participation in European affairs as the defender of America's European allies against the threat of Soviet militarism and communism has lost much of its rationale and popular support both in the United States and in Europe. And that influence and presence is likely to diminish further as long as Russia will be "stewing in its own juice." America's strategic interests in Europe are *nolens volens* likely to be safeguarded by European allies, at least for the time being, and its economic interests in Eastern Europe are now, as in the historic past, quite minimal. However, the European Union is still anxious to be able to secure America's military support in the event of a possible revival of Russian power. In fact, that possibility, while relatively remote on the eve of the twenty-first century, cannot be excluded.

The evolution of democracy in post-communist Russia has been fraught with major obstacles. The communists, albeit non-Stalinists, are still in control of parliament; extremist nationalists, while not politically dominant, are still encouraging xenophobic and anti-semitic manifestations by a disaffected Russian population part of which is not only supportive of the communists but is also remembering Stalin as a national hero. And, as President Boris Yeltsin, the authoritarian "democratizer" of Russian Federation is unlikely to survive both politically and physically in Y2K, the authoritarian nationalist General Lebed may well be Yeltsin's successor. Whereas Russian opposition to NATO's expansion in Europe or to proposed allied actions against Serbia in the Kosovo crisis may be ineffectual at this time, Moscow has made its position clear with respect to its continuing opposition to a western military presence in border states. And there is no reason to assume that in due course Russia will not reassert its opposition in a more determined manner.

Russia, moreover, has expressed its opposition to American policies in the Near and Middle East. It is true that the potential Russian veto of planned American military activities against Iraq in the United Nations Security Council prompted the circumventing of such action by the U.S.A. But it may be significant to note that the Russian position was supported by a leading member of the Council and of NATO: France. And it is also noteworthy that other members of NATO have adopted a similar position not only with respect to American policies in the Near and Middle East but also with respect to action against Serbia without the consent of the United Nations.

Thus, these divergences with respect to American policies are indicative of cooperation among Europeans, including the Russians, in matters related to common interests in general and, in the latter instance, to Russian concerns in Eastern Europe.

A related problem that is likely to affect the evolution of Eastern Europe is, as mentioned previously, the divergence of American and European policies toward the Islamic Near and Middle East. While paying lip service to American demands for enforcing the anti-Iraqi embargo and to condemnations of Islamic extremism and terrorism, France, Germany and other west European nations have cultivated Iranian leaders, supported UN resolutions condemning Israel's Palestinian policies, and have sought the easing of the embargo. Dependency on crude oil and the securing of markets rather than sympathy for Saddham Hussein or Khomeini's clerical successors are at the root of this cooperation but it would be difficult to argue that the democratization of Iran or Iraq were prerequisites theretofore. Moreover, it is quite likely that the European Union would tolerate a conservative Islamic, undemocratic government in Turkey were the fundamentalists to gain political power.

Whereas most of these uncertainty-producing factors are, if not dormant, at least impotent at this time, they are likely to affect the future evolution of Eastern Europe and of its "democratic consolidation". It is worth remembering that after the then voluntary advent of "isolationism" in the United States after World War I and its corollary leaving of Europe to the Europeans while allowing Russia to "stew in its own juice" in a period of global economic destabilization, the democratization of Eastern Europe subsided in short order. This is not to test the accuracy of the view that "history repeats itself" or of the opposite one that "only historians repeat themselves." But it is to say that the scenario of interwar Europe may be reconstructed under conditions that would fail to take into account the actual and potential factors present in today's, and most likely tomorrow's, world stage.

References

Agh, Attila. Emerging Democracies in East Central Europe and the Balkans. Cheltenham: Edward Elgar, 1998.

Berglund, Sten et al. Eds. The Handbook of Political Change in Eastern Europe. Cheltenham: Edward Elgar, 1998.

Bideleux, Robert and Taylor, Richard, Eds. European Integration and Disintegration : East and West. London and New York: Routledge, 1996.

Black, Stanley W., Ed. Europe's Economy Looks East: Implications for Germany and the European Union. Cambridge: Cambridge University Press, 1997.

Cottey, Andrew. East-Central Europe After the Cold War. New York: St. Martin's Press, 1995.

Csanadi, Maria. Party-states and their Legacies in Post-communist transformation. Cheltenham: Edward Elgar, 1997.

Dawisha, Karen and Parrott, Bruce, Eds. Politics, Power, and the Struggle for Democracy in South-East Europe. Cambridge: Cambridge University Press, 1997.

Goldman, Minton F. Revolution and Change in Central and Eastern Europe. New York: Sharpe, 1997.

Hollis, Wendy. Democratic Consolidation in Eastern Europe. Boulder and New York: East European Monographs, 1999.

Prifti, Pater R. Confrontation in Kosovo. Boulder and New York: East European Monographs, 1999.

Multiculturalism as a model for democratic consolidation

RAIVO VETIK

This chapter is devoted to the idea of multiculturalism and its relevance as a model for democratic consolidation in multi-ethnic countries. I will discuss historical, comparative and theoretical aspects of the phenomenon and conclude that multiculturalism is constantly gaining in importance in our day. At the end of the chapter, however, I bring up several internal difficulties that co-occur with the multicultural approach to societal organization.

National integration is one of the most important and most difficult elements in the ongoing democratic consolidation in many countries of Central and Eastern Europe. A similar process took place in the majority of Western European countries over a hundred years ago. The process involved homogenizing various social groups which had evolved from previous social systems, and this was carried through by means of the creation of a uniform language, common legal and educational systems and other such institutions. National integration in multiethnic countries of Central and Eastern Europe depends also in our day on a notable increase in homogeneity in the societies in question.

However, we must also bear in mind the particularities of the current situation. In Western Europe, national integration meant a relatively thorough assimilation of various cultural groups into a unified nation on the basis of one dominant group. At times this became quite a violent and painful process. The world has changed considerably over the last hundred years, and what was possible then may not be possible today. Recent global developments tend instead toward emphasizing differences and local identities. Therefore, comprehensive assimilation is not feasible in today's world. It is more realistic to try to find an optimal balance between the preservation of individual characteristics of various cultural groups and the tendency toward cultural homogenization in the national integration process. This balance is the key issue in a discussion of the relevance of multiculturalism as a possible model for democratic consolidation.

1. Historical perspective

Over the last decades, multiculturalism has become one of the major factors in contemporary politics. As a logical consequence, the notion of 'multiculturalism' has moved from the periphery to the center in the discourse of social science as well. Why have the issues of cultural difference and diversity become so important?

As a first approximation, it can be said that most modern states these days have multicultural populations. Due to the demographic changes that occurred after World War II, this applies also to traditional Western European nation-states. Less than 10% of all UN member states are ethnically homogeneous (Smith, 1995). In approximately one third of all countries in the world, no ethnic group exceeds 50% of the whole population (Cohen, 1993). In these conditions it is rather probable that cultural differences are expressed in politics as well.

However, the emergence of the issue of multiculturalism in global scope must be seen in the context of a polarization occurring between states: on the one hand there are wealthy western countries that are becoming increasingly richer, and on the other hand, poor developing countries whose relative poverty continues to grow. According to the UNDP global human development report of 1999, the income difference between the five richest and five poorest countries in the world has grown as follows during the last 40 years: in 1960, the income of the richest countries was thirty times that of the poorest countries, in 1990 the difference was 60-fold, and in 1997 it was 74-fold (Human Development Report 1999). One of the results of this difference is the extensive economic migration from the poor countries to the richer ones that has been characteristic of the whole post-World War II period. Migration has slowed down to a certain extent since the 1970s in connection with the new economic situation, but has continued in one way or another through today. Since the end of the 1980s, the former Communist world has also become a source of economic migration.

Consequently, a new internal policy problem has sprung up in the western world: what to do with the enormous number of migrants, who differ culturally to a great extent from the main population? What kind of rights should be given to these immigrants? To what extent is it possible to maintain their ethnic culture? Should their cultural differences be somehow institutionalized?

In a nutshell, the problem is that rich western countries are based on democratic principles and wish to remain democratic, yet the explosive growth in cultural heterogeneity has made accomplishing this aim problematic within the framework of the traditional liberal-democratic model. Historically, democracy emerged in a different context, as a result of modernization, which brought along remarkable social homogenization. In our day, analogous homogenization is impossible, which is why new ways must be found for making a society a coherent whole.

The problem of cultural diversity has been defined differently in different countries: the approaches of Germany and France may be considered as the two extremes of possible strategies to tackle the issue (Melotti, 1997). The goal of immigration policy in Germany has been to give the children of immigrants as much knowledge of the language, culture and homeland of their ancestors as possible. The goal of French policy, by contrast, has been to socialize immigrants through education into French culture as tightly as possible. This difference stems from the fact that in Germany aliens have been seen as guest workers who will eventually leave the country, whereas in France they have been considered to be an assimilating group.

It can be argued, however, that the alien policies in both Germany and France have in fact failed, because the Turks will not leave Germany and the Moslems will not become French. A change in policy is needed, and with the new citizenship law that allows dual citizenship, it can be said that Germany has taken the first step towards a change. An important broader lesson for other multiethnic countries to draw from these examples is that instead of choosing extremes on a scale of possible strategies, something in between should be preferred. One such possibility is the model of 'democratic multiculturalism'.

One more reason for the powerful emergence of the problematics of multiculturalism should be pointed out. The principal key phrase for the current stage of development is the information society. However, this stage brings along new concerns. Central among these is the confrontation between globalization and identity. Leading contemporary sociologist Manuel Castells eloquently describes this as "schizophrenia between function and meaning" (Castells, 1997). Globalization primarily concerns the instrumental dimension of human activity, upon which a social elite thrusts the integrative logic of its pragmatic interests. The wider public counter-reacts with its emotions, aspirations and identity. The information revolution and the rapid development of the world economy in the latter half of the 20th century are building up a network society which creates unprecedented opportunities, simultaneously destroying fundamental existing social and intellectual structures. The reason is that changes in identity are much slower to take effect. Hence a vacuum appears, filled by various forms of protest, contesting the integrative logic and the instrumentality of the network. The social bearers of protest will be groups and probably entire regions which are pushed ever further from the resources that facilitate coping in the 21st century, due to structural shifts in the movement of capital, information exchange and the labor market (Human Development Report 1999). The more people feel they are at the mercy of impersonal global forces, the greater is the need for something intimate and understandable, a need which is satisfied by ethnic and cultural identity. This need is turning into an important factor in internal politics, because minority cultures do not merely exist, but increasingly demand recognition as equal subjects in the framework of an expanding 'politics of recognition'.

2. Comparative perspective

The following forms of democracy are usually distinguished in the literature: liberal, consociational, and ethnic. Over recent years the list has been extended by the model of multicultural democracy. One example is the approach of van den Berghe (1999). This chapter proceeds from van den Berghe's definition, but the notion of 'multicultural democracy' is given a somewhat modified meaning. In order to explain the concept, I will compare multicultural democracy as a form of social organization with other forms of democracy. I am interested in what similarities and differences there are and which form of democracy is closest to multiculturalism.

Liberal democracy is the original form of democracy that presumes that power belongs to the people. Human and political rights belong to individuals, while the state is a neutral arbiter and guarantor of these rights. Civil society lies between the citizens and the state in the form of various interest groups which the state is independent of. Ethnic groups belong to civil society and are in no way bound to state power, which officially supports none of them and does not recognize them as important subjects in society.

The notion of consociational democracy was introduced by Arendt Lijphart to mark the polity of several multiethnic countries like Belgium, Switzerland and others (Lijphart, 1977). Its peculiarity lies in its recognition of the principle of group rights and collective representation, and in the proportional distribution of society's resources between officially defined ethnic, linguistic or religious groups. Offices in public institutions are also distributed on the same principle, although the state is, by definition, neutral towards different groups. People in a consociational democracy are recognized not only as citizens but also as members of specific groups, as their rights and obligations depend on this identity.

The notion of ethnic democracy was introduced by Sammy Smooha to mark those multiethnic countries that possess most of the characteristics of liberal democracy, but also institutionalize the political and cultural domination of one ethnic group in a given territory (Smooha, 1990). The notion of ethnic democracy is based on the example of Israel, but according to Smooha it is also applicable in some other cases. Thus, in the case of ethnic democracy, the state is not neutral but rather is intended, in the final analysis, to protect the culture and traditions of the titular nationality and to realize the political aspirations of that group. The state is seen as belonging to this group.

Where could multicultural democracy be positioned among the other forms of democracy mentioned above? As a first approximation, it lies somewhere between liberal and ethnic democracy. Multicultural democracy differs from liberal democracy in that it publicly recognizes ethnic heterogeneity and group rights, with one ethnic group as the titular nationality of the state, whom the state is named after. This group also gives the state its official language. The group's culture and way of life form the basis of a common communication field and societal cultural space. In other respects, multicultural democracy is similar to liberal democracy.

Further, multicultural democracy is similar to ethnic democracy in the sense that both recognize the existence of certain group rights. They differ in that multicultural democracy does not institutionalize the political domination of one group and does not claim that the state belongs to one group. Recognition of the substantive rights of the indigenous majority in multicultural democracy does not mean the discrimination of national or ethnic minorities, but rather is an expression of the fact that in a modern nation-state, the collective rights of different groups will inevitably vary, stemming from their different connections with the given country.

Finally, multicultural democracy differs from consociational democracy in that although it recognizes the ethnic heterogeneity of the state, it is institutionalized only culturally, not politically. Ethnic differences can, for instance, lay grounds for the cultural autonomy of ethnic minorities, but not for their territorial autonomy or federalism.

3. Theoretical perspective

The question for further theoretical investigation then is exactly what group rights are supported by democratic multiculturalism. In the social science literature, this problem has been discussed, for example, by Mati Heidmets and Marju Lauristin (Heidmets & Lauristin, 1998). They differentiate between political multiculturalism and political integration of minorities which takes place through individual and free cultural identification. The difference between these two approaches is a matter of principle. The model of political multiculturalism is supported, for example, by Juan Linz and Alfred Stepan in their book published in 1996. They claim in connection with Estonia and Latvia that democracy and the developmental logic of a nation-state are in conflict in the current stage of development of these nation-states (Linz & Stepan, 1996). In their opinion the solution lies in recognizing minorities as subjects possessing collective rights together with resulting possibilities for territorial autonomy, dual-language governance, etc. The contrasting model of cultural identification argues that the immigrant population does not form a national minority but a culturally different ethnic group whose members should be guaranteed equal participation in social life, together with the possibility of preserving their cultural characteristics. Multiculturalism in this approach does not mean collective political rights, but cultural diversity in a common societal cultural space that is supported by the majority. The notion of 'common societal cultural space' in this model is borrowed from Will Kymlicka (Kymlicka, 1995).

It is important to distinguish between two groups with different status – immigrants and national minorities - in the framework of the societal cultural space approach. National minorities formed complete and functioning societies in their historical homeland before being incorporated into a larger state. Examples are Native Americans, Finnish Lapps or the numerous northern nationalities in Russia. Immigrants, on the other hand, have voluntarily moved to another country due to economic or sometimes political reasons and do not constitute a native minority. Immigrants are, for instance, the Turks in Germany or the Pakistani in Norway. From a political theory perspective, in principle national minorities should possess the same group rights, including political rights, as the majority nationality. The group rights of immigrants, on the other hand, are usually tied to culture – the preservation of language, traditions, etc., in the private sphere. However, during the last decades there has been a general tendency in western countries to enlarge the group rights of both national and immigrant minorities. If historically many countries' attitudes towards national minorities have been rather dominating and negative, now important steps have been taken in the direction of recognizing even their territorial rights. As examples, we can mention the Canadian policy towards Quebec and England's policy towards Scotland and Wales. Further, though only a few decades ago it was assumed that immigrant minorities should assimilate to the mainstream society as quickly as possible, now cultural diversity is supported and actual steps are taken to institutionalize these differences as well. For example, in Canada the police has adjusted its uniform requirements to allow policemen of Sikh nationality to wear a turban on duty according to their religious traditions.

For further investigation of the implications of the multiculturalist approach to social diversity, it is useful to link the notion to a wider conception of society. Subsequently we will analyze two forms of liberalism – procedural and substantive – and show that the first one tends to support group rights and the second tends to reject them.

Immanuel Kant's concept of individual autonomy, according to which every person has a right to define for him or herself what is good, can be considered the basis of a procedural theory of society. Since different people have different views, the procedural theory derives, from the principle of autonomy, the idea that the state itself should not formulate one substantive viewpoint that everyone ought to follow. It is important to note that Kant's moral philosophy as a whole remains on formal grounds. His moral philosophy proceeds from his overall philosophical disposition as well as the desire to achieve the certainty characteristic of natural sciences in philosophy. In Kant's view this would be possible in moral philosophy only in a formalistic system. If substantial arguments were to be produced as well, then their scientific essence would be lost, as they cannot be universal. Later liberalism (for instance, Ronald Dworkin and John Rawls) has developed several procedural theories of society proceeding from Kant's standpoint. Together these constitute the dominating trend in contemporary social philosophy as well.

Liberalism based on Kant presumes individualism, social homogeneity and the neutrality of the state. From this starting point, the co-existence of different cultures on one territory is problematic in and of itself. One can refer to John Stuart Mill, a classical author of liberalism, according to whom "free institutions are next to impossible in a country made up of different nationalities". Thus, as culture is a group phenomenon in its essence, multiculturalism is inevitably an uncomfortable notion for classical liberalism.

There is another trend in the framework of liberal theory that does not rest upon the procedural, but the substantial definition of the social good. This has emerged during the last decades precisely in connection with the aforementioned problem – the inability of classical liberalism to adequately conceptualize issues connected with group rights. This trend is exemplified by the approach of Charles Taylor. In the well-known article, 'The Politics of Recognition', he discusses the way in which the identity of one culture depends on its dialogic relations with others (Taylor, 1994). He distinguishes between monologic and dialogic ideals of culture and opines that not only culture but also an individual is dialogic in nature, as the identity of a person develops only in dialogue with others (that can at times also be a contest). It is worth pointing out that with the notion of dialogue Taylor refers to the works of Mikhail Bahtin. One of Bahtin's most famous students was Juri Lotman, and we can use several of Lotman's ideas to further develop the idea of the dialogic nature of culture. For instance, Lotman has claimed that any intellectual mechanism presupposes two languages and a dialogue between them. The ideal of one absolute language is an abstraction that emphasizes one side of reality but does not correspond to reality as a whole. Lotman sees an analogy in the structure and functioning of culture, human consciousness and text, with the dialogic character of each being primary (Lotman, 1983).

The dialogic approach to culture places the phenomenon of multiculturalism on new ground. On the assumption that any culture is dialogic, it can be argued that multiculturalism is the normal form of cultural existence. Multiculturalism is not the exception but the rule – without multiculturalism, there is no culture. It is important to note that such an approach brings the possible practical problems connected with multiculturalism into a new light. It turns out that we are not dealing with a phenomenon that could or should be completely eliminated. According to the monologic approach (represented by procedural liberalism), multiculturalism is a deviation from the norm, but according to the dialogic approach, multiculturalism is rather a resource. This does not mean that multiculturalism cannot cause problems. Multiculturalism is both a potential resource and a problem, but the dialogic approach constructs it as normal and thus as not requiring elimination. Monologic cultural discourse, on the contrary, constructs multiculturalism as a deviation from the norm and presumes that the solution lies in its elimination. To conclude, the dialogic approach changes the emphasis and thus helps to accommodate possible conflicts related to multiculturalism.

We encounter both procedural and substantive approaches in various countries. A procedural orientation is most obvious in the USA, the archetype country of individualism. The USA is already historically an immigrant country, and the process of Americanization has taken place mainly through individual assimilation. We might add that the most critical attacks on multiculturalism as a model of society come from American authors, the latest famous example being Arthur Schlesinger's controversial book 'The Disuniting of America' (Schlesinger, 1992).

The most evident example of procedural orientation is Quebec, a society with strong collective goals and liberal values at the same time. 'It is axiomatic for Quebec governments that the survival and flourishing of French culture in Quebec is a good' (Taylor, 1994). On the other hand, diversity is also respected in Quebec and adequate safeguards for fundamental rights have been created. Certainly there are tensions and difficulties in pursuing these objectives together, 'but such a pursuit is not impossible, and the problems are not in principle greater than those encountered by any liberal society that has to combine, for example, liberty and equality, or prosperity and justice' (Taylor, 1994).

Thus, the multicultural model of democracy is based on substantive liberalism. An interesting theoretical approach explaining the notion of multiculturalism is proposed by John Rex. His theory is based on the differentiation of public and private spheres in society (Rex, 1996). According to Rex, to define multiculturalism as a form of social organization, it is important to determine how homogeneous or different the main cultural groups are in these two spheres and what kind of policy the state implements in this regard. Combining these two distinctions, four logical possibilities are created:

(a) society that is unitary in the public sphere but tolerant regarding differences in the private sphere;
(b) society that is unitary in the public sphere and promotes unity also in the private sphere;
(c) society that promotes difference and differential rights in both the public and private sphere;
(d) society that promotes difference and differential rights in the public sphere but unity in the private sphere (Rex, 1996).

Version (a) represents multiculturalism, (b) represents the French model of assimilation, (c) describes colonialism and (d) is characteristic of the southern states in the USA before the civil rights movement (Rex, 1996). Thus, according to Rex's theory, the proportion of unity-difference in both the public and private sphere is the most important variable in defining multiculturalism. Difference should be promoted in the private sphere, because it enriches the overall cultural arena. In the public sphere, however, homogeneity should dominate, as this provides the coherence necessary for the normal functioning of society.

The problem with such an approach, however, is that several important social phenomena belong to both spheres. For example, education gives a person instrumental competence, but at the same time teaches moral values that are characteristic of a certain culture. The same applies to language – on the one hand, it is an instrument that is needed in order to manage society, while on the other, it is a bearer of a certain intellectuality. Thus, although public and private spheres are distinguishable, they nevertheless influence one another. Therefore, no single recipe exists for creating a democratic model of multiculturalism in all multiethnic countries. As different problems arise in different countries, the proportion between unity and difference in public and private spheres should be defined differently as well.

4. Open questions

It is important to stress that multicultural democracy as a form of social organization is not an idyll, but also contains internal difficulties (Melotti, 1997). At the end of the chapter, I would like to formulate a few problems in connection with multiculturalism as a form of society. In a sense, these are 'eternal questions' that might not have a final answer at all. But this does not mean that answers should not be explored.

One can ask: does multiculturalism foster the engendering of negative stereotypes? When does multiculturalism develop into ethnocentrism (Schlesinger, 1992)? Let us discuss different interpretations of Estonian history by the different ethnic groups living in this country. Does loyalty to the Estonian state presume that the events of 1940 are considered as an occupation, and not as Estonia's voluntary unification with the Soviet Union? It must be noted that the whole foundation of the Estonian state rests on the former standpoint. The education of many non-Estonians, however, took place in the period when history was taught according to the latter view. The question above is directly related to another one: what should be the non-Estonians' conception of themselves? Should the state aspire to make them comprehend themselves following the official doctrine? If we follow this approach to a logical conclusion, it would seem that those who came here during the Soviet period are illegal immigrants. However, this conclusion would create new problems. According to Gordon, the conformation of ethnic dignity is necessary for successful national integration (Gordon, 1964). This means it is important that the self-comprehension of non-Estonians be positive.

The homogenization of society and the preservation of cultural differences are processes that can conflict. In this regard it should be asked: how does the preservation of differences influence the formation of a common cultural space in a society? Preservation of differences tends to strengthen the existing identity, whereas national integration presumes development and change of existing identities. Is it correct that multiculturalism strengthens the ties within an ethnic group and weakens outward ties?

Recognition of the equal value of different cultures fulfills a basic human need for recognition. At the same time, all societies inevitably contain ethnic prejudices and stereotypes. These negative phenomena actually perform positive functions in society as well. American psychoanalyst Vamik Volkan has written a book arguing that human beings have a psychological need for the existence of an enemy (Volkan, 1988). In a recent survey in the USA, 29% of Black respondents thought it true or possibly true that the AIDS virus was invented by racist conspirators to kill Blacks (Schlesinger, 1992). The negative image of the outgroup in this case plays a certain role in building the integrity of the internal group. Can we do without that? If not, what of the prospects of multiculturalism?

To what extent is the dispute over the possibility of multiculturalism actually a dispute over political power? This aspect is often stressed in the political science literature. How does the question of power influence the comprehension of multiculturalism in post-communist countries? Is support for, or opposition to, multiculturalism based on considerations that are mainly connected with the public interest as a whole or with some narrow political interests?

The questions posed refer to a few problems related to multiculturalism. But they already indicate that it is a complex phenomenon that requires particular attention and responsibility on behalf of decision-makers. A simplified party-political or naïve-optimistic approach to the issue can cause huge damage to the whole society for a long period of time.

5. Conclusion

Most contemporary societies are multicultural. While in a cultural sense heterogeneity is a resource, it can cause various problems socially and politically. To function normally, a certain coherence is necessary in society, in order to create a common field of communication and common societal cultural space. These are usually based on the language and culture of the titular nationality. At the same time, a question arises about the rights of minority groups. It should be admitted that the understanding of majority and minority groups can diverge in this respect. This divergence derives from their different historical relationships to the country, their different cultural and other traditions as well as different aspirations. A useful approach for tackling the problem is to distinguish between private and public spheres. In the private sphere the preservation of differences between different groups is positive, as it enriches the overall cultural arena. At the same time, a certain amount of homogeneity should exist in the public sphere. In our day the question is no longer set against a view in ethno-policy where the alternatives are either national purity or complete blending. Instead, the ability to remain yourself while in the process of changing is becoming a key to successful development. In a democratic multicultural model of society, this applies to both the majority and minority cultures.

References

van den Berghe, Pierre L., 'Multicultural Democracy: Can It Work?', paper presented in the conference 'Multiculturalism and Democracy in Divided Societies', University of Haifa, March 17-18, 1999.

Castells, Manuel, *The Information Age: Economy, Society and Culture, vol. II, The Power of Identity*, Blackwell 1997.

Cohen, Ronald, 'Conclusion: Ethnicity, the State, and Moral Order', in Judith Toland, ed., *Ethnicity and the State*, Transaction Publishers, London, pp. 231-258.

Gordon, Milton M., *Assimilation in American Life*, Oxford University Press 1964.

Heidmets Mati & Marju Lauristin, 'Sissejuhatus: mitmekultuurilise Eesti valikud', in *Mitmekultuuriline Eesti: väljakutse haridusele,* Tartu Ülikool 1998. pp.7-20.

Human Development Report 1999, Oxford University Press 1999.

Kymlicka, Will, *Multicultural Citizenship. A Liberal Theory of Minority Rights,* Oxford 1995.

Lijphart, Arend, *Democracy in Plural Societies*, Yale University Press 1977.

Linz, Juan & Alfred Stepan, 'When Democracy and the Nation-State Are Conflicting Logics: Estonia and Latvia', in Juan Linz & Alfred Stepan (eds.), *Problems of Democratic Transition and Consolidation: Southern Europe, South America, and Post-Communist Europe,* Johns Hopkins University Press.

Lotman, Juri, 'Assimetria i dialog', in *Trudy po znakovym sistemam,* no. 16, Tartu 1983.

Melotti, Umberto, 'International Migration in Europe: Social Projects and Political Cultures', in Tariq Modood & Pnina Werbner, eds., *The Politics of Multiculturalism in the New Europe*, Zed Books 1997, pp. 73-92.

Rex, John, Ethnic minorities in the modern nation state: working papers in the theory of multiculturalism and political integration, MacMillan Press 1996.

Schlesinger, Arthur M., Jr, *The Disuniting of America. Reflections on a Multicultural Society*, W.W.Norton & Company 1992.

Smith, Anthony D., *Nations and Nationalism in a Global Era,* Polity Press 1995.

Sammy Smooha, 'Minority Status in an Ethnic Democracy: the Status of Arab Minority in Israel', in *Ethnic and Racial Studies*, vol.13, No.3, 1990, pp.389-413.

Taylor, Charles, The Politics of Recognition, in Amy Gutman, ed., *Multiculturalism,* Princeton University Press 1994, pp.25-74.

Volkan, Vamik, *The Need to Have Enemies and Allies*, Jason Aronson Inc., London 1988.

National-state and Success of Democratic Transformation in Former European Communist States

LASLO SEKELJ

1. Introduction

The main idea of this chapter is that the difference in the level of implementation of political democracy and the restructuring of economy in former European communist states is structurally connected with their ethnic composition. From this point of view, any operative political system is the combined outcome of three hierarchical levels of decision-making:

1) Who "we" are at the most fundamental level, i.e. decisions on identity, citizenship, and the territorial as well as cultural and social boundaries of the nation state (patriotism, honor).
2) Constitution or the institutional framework of the 'regime': rules, procedures and rights (reason).
3) Who gets what, when, and how in terms of political power and economic resources (interests) (Offe, 1992:11).

Unchallenged equal status of all subjects in terms of the "national" citizenship is the necessary pre-condition of the basic consensus on social norms and values, as well as on the institutional framework of the state, which is the *conditio sine qua non* of the democratic regime. Due to this fact, in Eastern Europe where the ethnic and non-political dimension of nationality (and statehood) is traditionally dominant the mode of identification of the "we-group" is - so far - a dominant factor how the rules, procedures, and rights inside the institutional framework are created together with the consciousness about what are one's personal and group interests. In the process of economic and political transformation, the linkage between patriotism, reason and interests is highly open to manipulation and determined by the ethnic composition of the particular state.

2. General characteristics of the transformation process

Academic criticism of "real socialism" was primarily motivated by the intellectuals' concern for human rights as a basic value of liberal democracy. In the 1980's, this concern was expanded to include the concept of civil society. However, the fall of "real socialism" has not automatically led to the triumph of liberal democracy and its values in Eastern, Central, and Southeastern Europe.

The former socialist countries have taken their separate paths to the realm of "real capitalism". However, they have in the first stage (1989-1993) the following characteristics in common:

1) Scant participation by citizens in the political process.
2) Absence of a conscientious electorate and elections in which the individual merits of candidates are the surest way to public office.
3) Manipulation and suppression of the interests of particular groups and social strata by political elites based on the idea of ethno-nationalist homogenization.
4) Threats to individual freedoms, particularly to the rights of minorities in multi-ethnic states, such as former Yugoslavia.
5) Civil society guaranteeing individual freedoms remains a distant ideological ideal rather than a pragmatic agenda. Political transformation has stopped at the macro-level even where it is a success story (in Hungary, Poland, Czech Republic and Slovenia). There is no functional democracy at the macro level (organized interests) or direct and local democracy (micro level). Politics has hindered this deepening and widening process of democratization in many ways. There is no civil society manifested through the activities of organized interests. "Parties have considered them major enemies from the very beginning, since they have been their most important rivals in the power and influence game." (Agh, 1994: 209-210). There are no social pacts so characteristic for the South European transitions.
6) Modernization attempts create market systems at odds with ideas of social citizenship and a social-democratic welfare state.
7) The process of individualization as the basis of a liberal *Weltanschauung* and the whole set of liberal institutions is shrouded in mystification of the old and new collectivist ideologies, pre-modern institutions, and the traditional legacy.
8) Contradictions, which existed between the reality and practice of the "real-existing socialism", ended in the collapse of the communist system. However, the collapse of communism has not automatically led to democratization. So far, a new authoritarianism based on nationalism has emerged in parts of former Communist Europe. This New Authoritarianism has emerged in Eastern, Central and Southeastern Europe as the immediate result of the collapse of communism.

Communist totalitarianism has been replaced by ethnic totalitarianism, and national homogenization has succeeded class homogenization. This is what destroyed the Soviet Union and Yugoslavia and dissolved Czechoslovakia. In Albania, Romania and to a large extent in Bulgaria as well, it has simply substituted the former authoritarian power. In Hungary and Poland, it has taken the form of populism whose political power - due to the ethnic composition of these states - seems to be on the definite wane after the latest round of elections.

3. The New Authoritarianism

This New Authoritarianism does not simply continue the nationalistic and chauvinistic traditions of Eastern, Central and South-Eastern Europe. It is, largely, an impotent expression of the failure of populist demagoguery to solve the crisis of modernization. I am going to demonstrate this with examples from the second post-communist elections in Serbia (December 1993) and Hungary (May 1994).

Serbian elections were held at a time of rampant inflation (in billions percent), misery of the general populace, and economic and social degradation and disintegration. Everyone knew this was the result of ruling party policies. However, voters in Serbia had already fallen prey to a campaign of national homogenization; in their view, the issue of the 1993 elections was not the efficiency of the ruling party's policies, but the creation of a national state. The creation of "nation-states" on ethnically non-homogenous lands is under way all over former Yugoslavia; this process resembles the creation of nation-states in other parts of Europe in the latter half of the last and the first half of this century, and it proceeds along roughly the same lines as the decolonization in Africa and Asia did. Serbs thus voted for the very political party that broke the world hyperinflation record, reduced GNP to one third of that in 1989, produced an enormous unemployment rate of 30%, and so on. (Posarac, 1995: 330). The Serbian opposition likes to believe that election results in Serbia have to do exclusively with the fact that the ruling Socialist Party and its leader Slobodan Milosevic have total control over state television. However, one needs to know that Serbia, unlike Hungary, in those days had several private television stations favorable to the opposition.

Five months after the elections in Serbia, Hungary held its second post-communist elections, too. The ruling conservative coalition used a pattern of manipulation identical to Slobodan Milosevic' s in Serbia. State television was put at the service of the government and its re-election campaign; just like Milosevic, the government tried to substitute the economic and social issues by the issue of national interests. Instead of dealing with unemployment and a 30% inflation rate, it proceeded to focus the voters' attention on the issue of the Hungarian minorities in Romania, Serbia and Slovakia.

Unlike in Serbia, nationalist manipulation did not pay off in Hungary. People voted for the party (Socialist) which they believed capable of taking on the economic issues. All the political parties that ran on a nationalist platform suffered a catastrophic electoral defeat. In Hungarian elections, the decisive factor turned out to be 30% inflation and 15% unemployment. In Serbia, 30% unemployment and a much higher inflation were not enough to change the government. In the Hungarian case, civic consciousness determined the outcome of the elections. In the Serbian case, national consciousness, as a product of the New Authoritarianism, did the same.

The Yugoslav case represents all the negative features of the transformation process at its extreme. The price of abolishing one type of authoritarian regime called "communism" was the abolition of not only the state and political community, but also of the civilized relations and citizenry.

4. Types of Transformation Processes

The gap between the normative liberal and democratic agenda and the reality of political transformation can be summarized in the following 13points (Holmes, 1997: 16-21):

1. assertion of independence and the rise of nationalism;
2. near absence of a culture of compromise;
3. high expectations of leaders;
4. cynicism towards and/or mistrust of political institutions;
5. rejection of teleologism and grand theories;
6. an ideological vacuum;
7. moral confusion;
8. temporality;
9. dynamism;
10. instability;
11. a widespread sense of insecurity;

12. unfortunate timing;

13. legitimization problems.

Describing the limits of the ongoing democratization process in the former European communist states, I do not want to deny the obvious fact that there are crucial differences between particular states and societies in terms of success or failure of the transformation process. Generally speaking, there have been two different attempts to transcend the crisis of modernization through two different types of transformation models. In terms of the introduction of a market economy and political democracy in pluralist society, one has succeeded and the other has failed. One can speak of a success story in the transformation of the former collectivist communist society in the former German Democratic republic (GDR), Hungary, Poland, Slovenia and the Czech Republic; all became homogenous nation-states (national states of the titular nationality in the full meaning of that term) after the turmoil of World War II. At the time of transition from communism, all were mono-ethnic nation- states where, contrary to the historic mainstream in this part of Europe, the vast majority of the population shared the identity of the Nation and the State. In other words, when the transformation process started in Hungary, Poland, the Czech Republic and Slovenia, more than 92% of the citizens shared the (titular) nationality and literally all citizens a feeling of being a part of the very same political community - a very uncommon feature east of the river Elbe between the Baltic, Mediterranean and Caspian seas in the past 100 years.

When one compares different ways in which the process of democratization has been affecting mono-ethnic and multi-ethnic states, the apparently inevitable conclusion is that the functioning of democracy exacerbates the relationship between ethnic, religious and other collectivist commitments. Hungary and the former Yugoslavia are, again, obvious test cases. We are thus coming to the main thesis of this chapter: there are two basic different types of states, and a third one, which is a dynamic mixture of the two:

1. First Basic Type. Hungary, Poland, the Czech Republic, GDR and Slovenia: the transformation process is likely to be a success story. They are all strictly Nation-States in the Anglo-Saxon sense of the term, without significant minorities, and what is much more important, at the moment of regime change nobody questioned the continuity or the legacy of the State. The objective pre-condition for the constitution of the Polish, Slovenian, Czech, German, and the Hungarian political community - the unquestionable, overwhelming consensus on "who 'we' are", on the most fundamental level of the community, i.e. decisions on identity, citizenship, and the territorial as well as cultural and social boundaries of the nation state.

2. Type. Former Yugoslavia (except Slovenia), Russia, Belarus, Ukraine, Moldavia, the Commonwealth of the Independent States (CIS) republics and Albania: transformation process has hitherto lagged way behind the states in Type 1. They are all either multi-ethnic or multi-confessional states or have significant ethnic and/or religious minorities. Contrary to the states of basic type 1, the continuity and the legacy of the State is in doubt here. All the pre-conditions for the basic consensus on the most fundamental question "who we are" were non-existent, i.e. the identity, citizenship, territorial, cultural and social boundaries of the particular state. There were not one political community but many, based exclusively on the national identity in a strict ethnic (in sense of blood and origin) and non-political sense. In short, states of this basic type were and still are, in all the basic features that should constitute the most fundamental features of a community, a total contradiction to the states of basic type 1.

3. Mixed Type. Slovakia, and the Baltic republics. The problems of transformation and, in particular, of democratization are similar to those in Type 2 due to a similar ethno-nationalistic bias, but external factors are propelling developments in the other (positive) direction. After the last round of elections in Bulgaria and Romania and, more clearly, in Slovakia, those three countries seem to be moving away from Type 2 and towards a real process of pluralization, democratization and marketization. Especially at the beginning of the transformation process they shared all the basic features of the basic type 2 states, with one difference: namely no political actor, inside or outside, objected or doubted the legacy and continuity of the State. The question was about the form of the state (decentralization). The most fundamental question about "who 'we' are" was focused only to the titular nation and one (decisive) minority: the Russian in Baltic, the Hungarian in Romania and Slovakia, the Turks in Bulgaria.

I argue that there are two paradigmatic models of implementing social, economic, political, cultural and ethnic pluralism in former European communist countries. The first comes from mono-ethnic states such as Hungary and Poland; the second is associated with multi-ethnic and multi-confessional societies and countries such as former Yugoslavia and all its successor states, with the exception of Slovenia. Before I proceed, however, I would like to underline two main features of the transformation process: (1) In the long-term, change is inevitable in every state and society concerned; (2) the process - as the very meaning of the word implies - is something in motion, and this has been proved by Bulgaria, Romania and Slovakia since the last elections (1996-1998).

My thesis is that the ethnic composition of the state is the decisive factor determining success or failure, in creating a pluralist, individualist and market-oriented society. The latter is a prerequisite for effectively solving the crisis of modernization in former European communist countries. It is within this context that I view, on the one hand, the successful first-step transition in the Hungarian, Czech, Polish and Slovenian cases and, on the other, the total failure of transition in former Yugoslavia - mono-ethnic Slovenia excepted. The multi-ethnic and multi-confessional character of Yugoslavia is, in this respect, exemplary. It should be noted that multi-ethnicity and religious diversity *per se* are not insurmountable obstacles to modernization. However, they do seem to determine the mode and speed of the process, in the aftermath of the death of communism. Judging by their comparative economic and social structures and egalitarian value systems, Yugoslavia and Hungary should have had a comparatively difficult transition from state socialism to pluralism. The only significant distinction in the realm of ideology lay in radically different prospects in manipulating the friend-enemy paradigm on an ethnic basis. And that is my point. Not the ethnic geography *per se* is the functional or causal factor here but its connection to the behavior of the communist nomenclatures in the 1980's.[1] Namely, regardless of the type of society, political elites have a significant degree of autonomy, as R. Dahl has noted (Dahl, 1992: 21). Another essential functional characteristic of political elites in the formerly communist countries is that, at the beginning of the transformation process, they invariably resorted to nationalism as a means of their legitimacy. In the countries of basic type 2, they have succeeded in retaining power throughout the period of political and economic transformation primarily owing to this particular means of manipulation. Ethno-nationalism as a legitimacy basis and the unbroken continuity of political elites are linked in Croatia, the FR of Yugoslavia, Bosnia and Herzegovina, Macedonia and most CIS countries. Romania, Slovakia, Bulgaria and the Baltic states (type 3) are similar in respect of this relationship, but since transformation is a dynamic process and they are themselves a transitive form between the two basic types of discontinuity of elites, are much more pronounced than in the case of countries of the basic type 2.

5. In search of the independent variable

The above mentioned common features of the transformation process have been shared by all former European communist states only in the first stage of this process generally until 1993, until the second post-communist elections or until the end of "destructive", first stage economic reforms - where they were implemented at all:

Table 1. ***Transformation process – (status in 1999)***

Established **Basic Type 1**	"pains of growth": **Basic Type 2**	in motion and mixture: **Basic Type 3**
Hungary	FR Yugoslavia	Slovakia
Poland	Croatia	Baltic states
Czech Rep.	Macedonia	Bulgaria
GDR*	Russia	Rumania
Slovenia	Ukraine	
	Moldavia	
	Belarus	
	CIS States	
	Albania	
	Bosnia and Herzegovina	

*GDR being directly incorporated into FRG and the EU is a very specific case

If one compares the state of the transformation process with the ethnic composition of former European communist states one will find a total identity between the "established" column, Basic Type 1, and the "mono-national" column in Table 2, and between "pains of growth", Basic Type 2, and "multi-national" or "decisive minority" columns in Table 2.

The size of the majority or of the other nation(s) is of secondary importance. What counts is that relations between those nationalities are not based on civic solidarity and togetherness of the citizenry, i. e. not all ethnic groups identify with the state as their own political community. It is also of particular importance to differentiate between two types of non-mononational states: multi-national and the national state with decisive minority. Today only the Russian Federation is a multi-national state *de iure and de facto.* Serbia is multinational *de facto*, Croatia ceased to be a multinational state both *de iure* since 1991 and *de facto* since 1995. The difference might be of importance in the constitutional framework: in the multinational states a certain nation or nations used to have a privileged position toward the national minorities like the Serbs in Croatia or in Bosnia and Herzegovina before they became established ethno-democracies, Croatia in 1991 and Bosnia and Herzegovina in 1992: it used to be constitutionally their (Serbs from Croatia and the Serbs from Bosnia-Herzegovina) national state as well. In most CIS states the Russian minority has a very privileged position. In that sense they are also multi-national states.

Table 2. ***Countries by ethnic composition***

Mono-National	Multi-national	Decisive minority
Hungary	Ex-Yugoslavia	Baltic states
Poland	Russia	Slovakia
Czech Rep.	Moldavia	Bulgaria
GDR	Ukraine	Rumania
Slovenia	Serbia	Albania
	Croatia	Belarus
	CIS States	Macedonia
	Bosnia and Herzegovina	Montenegro

My assertion that the ethnic characteristic of the particular state is the major cause of the success or delay of transformation into pluralistic and democratic societies is based on empirical evidence. And this issue is not completely new in Europe. In the late 19th century faced with the Irish question and the latent nationalistic eruption in three continental empires, particularly the Austro-Hungarian, some Liberals, like J.S. Mill, argued that the values essential to free institutions could not exist when the inhabitants of a country were not, and did not feel to be members of an identical political community. "Free institutions are next to impossible in a country made up of different nationalities. Among a people without fellow-feeling, especially if they read and speak different languages, the united public opinion, necessary to the working of representative government, cannot exist" (Mill, 1861: 360-364).

The second obstacle is class division, which in the second half of this century has been overcome - at least at the level of feelings - as the crucial barrier for full and equal citizenship in the Western industrial nations. Even east of the river Rhine, not class but the nation was decisive in the failure of liberal institutions in the inter-war period - when the majority of these nations became independent and were directed on the path of authoritarianism and dictatorship through politics of biased ethno-nationalism - and this seems to be again the main point of difference in the ongoing transformation process. Social citizenship inside the monoethnic national state might be possible in East, Central and Southeast Europe, but nationality as equal membership in the political community for all regardless of a subgroup's ethnic and/or religious origin is a much more problematic task in all ethnically non-homogenous states in this part of Europe. And this issue has originally nothing to do with the communist past.

One may argue that certain other issues are determining the outcome of the transformation process. Especially material (economic) development and a number of spiritual factors such as civilization, religion or political culture. Table 3 summarizes material development:

Table 3. ***Degree of material development (in 1990)***

High	Medium	Undeveloped	Ext.undeveloped
GDR	Hungary	Macedonia	Albania
Czech Rep.	Ex-Yugoslavia	Rumania	Moldavia
Slovenia	Croatia	Ukraine	Belarus
	Serbia	Montenegro	CIS States
	Slovakia	Russia	
	Poland	Bulgaria	
	Baltic republics	Bosnia and Herzegovina	

There is only a limited linkage between Tables 1 and 3. Namely, all three relatively developed former European communist countries: the German Democratic Republic (GDR), the Czech Republic and Slovenia have performed very well in the course of the transformation process. However, two other success stories - Hungary and Poland - are not in that group. Estonia, which has been evaluated similarly by the EU Commission regarding marketization, even belongs to the group which was a step behind in 1989-1990. One might argue that in terms of material development and the quality of the economy, in particular, the recent situation (1997) would be different from that eight years ago. All members of the 'established' cluster from Table 1 would now form a separate 'high' subgroup in Table 3, Serbia and, perhaps, Croatia would loose ground, etc. However, all this results from, rather than determines the transformation process.

Economic reforms in the sense of a real change to a market economy, privatization, deregulation of export and import (including foreign investments), decline of state investment in production and labor force employment, and creation of the rule of law in practice as the most important pre-condition for a market economy were implemented first in the former German Democratic Republic, Czech Republic, Slovenia and followed - not without hesitations - in Hungary, Poland and eventually by Estonia as well. At the opposite side are all the basic group II states with all kind of particularities, from Albania to Russia, via FR Yugoslavia and Bulgaria, but these are all nuances not real differences of the same deep structural crisis which remained unsolved. State or mixed property, inflation or hyperinflation, the essence remained the same: limited market, regulated economy, obstacles for foreign trade and foreign investments for the sake of control over the economy in the hands of the ruling elite (in most cases the old communist oligarchy in the new nationalist costume). The point is that if one political force challenges the power, the rulers' answer has an ethno-nationalist bias. And to produce this situation is very easy in all societies in transformation: "Only a developed market economy produces the social structural conditions for stable democracy and makes it possible to form compromises within the framework of what is perceived a positive-sum-game. But the introduction of a market economy in the post-socialist societies is a 'political' project, which has prospects of success only if it rests on a strong democratic legitimization. And it is possible that the majority of the population finds neither democracy nor a market economy a desirable perspective" (Offe, 1992:17). In non-homogenous states it is even easier to mislead the population, with the nationalistic bias and to prolong the inevitable marketization up to the economic collapse. The result is total economic disaster when the economic transformation (reform) starts, like in the Bulgarian and Romanian cases, which soon will be followed by Slovakia. This is the most important reason why I argue that the transformation process is inevitable, and why the number of basic group 3 states is growing after 7-8 years lost and the misery being not only economic but general.

6. Different spiritual backgrounds

Samuel Huntington (1993: 22-49) used the argument of the contrast between West and East which arguably divided two different civilizations. This dividing line follows the boundaries of Christianity, which means that the success of the transformation is based on the particular (Western) Christian tradition.

Some authors have resorted to basically the same argument, but using the legacy of the Austro-Hungarian Monarchy as point of reference *vis-à-vis* two other empires, the Russian and the Ottoman. Let us look at the next two tables, which describe the difference between Western and Eastern Churches (Table 4), the socio-political impact of religion on society (Table 5).

Table 4. ***Western and Eastern Churches***

Western Christianity	Orthodoxy
Poland	Russia ## ###
Hungary	Belarus
Slovakia #	Ukraine ##
Czech Rep.	Montenegro## ###
Croatia ##	Serbia## ###
Slovenia	Macedonia ###
Baltic states##	Bulgaria###
GDR	Romania # ##
	Moldavia # ##
	Armenia
	Georgia ###

Titular nation divided
Minority(ies) of other ethnic origin and type of Christendom
Large Muslim minority

Obviously, the differentiation based on the border between Western and Eastern Christianity or the Austro-Hungarian Monarchy and the two other empires is relevant to our subject. All established transformation societies belong by tradition to Western Christianity, and several belonged to the Double Monarchy as well. However, they all (Czech Republic, Poland, Hungary, GDR and Slovenia) where the object of almost total "ethnic cleansing" during and immediately after World War II and by this fact they became mono-ethnic or national states in the Anglo-Saxon notion of this term. Also, a good part of Poland was once part of the Russian Empire. On the other hand, Moldavia, Bosnia and Herzegovina, and parts of Romania and Ukraine were also part of Austro-Hungary. This might be a good argument against overstating the importance of the Double Monarchy for the ongoing transformation process, but not automatically against the crucial importance of the dividing line within Christianity itself.

A second problem is Bosnia, which has a relative (not absolute) Muslim majority, followed by Orthodox Serbs and, third, Catholic Croats. One could classify Bosnia-Herzegovina alongside the second European state with Muslim majority, Albania, and thus as belonging to a different civilization - which is precisely what Huntington does.

In the narrow sense of this argument, however, there are certain problems. First, what does Western Christianity mean, especially in the context of the sociological analysis of the transformation process? What about the differentiation between Catholicism and Protestantism, especially concerning the process of political, economic and cultural modernization?

The gap between a Catholic Croat and a Lutheran Estonian (or Catholic Croat and Catholic German) is much wider than that between the Orthodox Serb and the Catholic Croat. The single success of modernization in Southeastern Europe, to date, Greece, utterly invalidates the presumption that Eastern Christianity or former Turkish rule are *per se* crucial to the success or temporary failure of democratization, pluralization and marketization. I will go even further: I doubt if religion or religious heritage might be the most important factor in the above-mentioned process in societies where religion has a very limited socio-political role and impact:

Table 5. ***Socio-political impact of religion in 1989-1990***

high	**medium**	**low**	**irrelevant**
Poland	Slovakia	Czech Rep.	Albania
Croatia	Baltic republics	Bulgaria	Serbia
Bosnia-Herz. #.	Slovenia	Macedonia#	Russia
		Rumania	Montenegro
		Moldavia	Belarus
	other CIS States	Ukraine	
		GDR	
		Hungary	

Religion identified with the nation misused through nationalistic manipulation for ethno-national purposes.

Political culture is another factor that might influence the ongoing transformation process. There are obvious differences in the result of the political process - and in that sense, in political culture - between countries of Basic Type 1 and Basic Type 2. Assuming that there is a clash of civilizations or division in Christianity, the "friends" of Double Monarchy are using differences in political culture between the Czech Republic, Hungary, and Poland, on the one hand, and Serbia, Montenegro, Albania, etc., on the other, as an important argument for their position. Yet is the difference in political culture due to religion or to foreign domination only? Obviously not. Let us examine, in Table 6, the state of affairs in 1945, prior to the communist seizure of power:

Table 6. ***Type of political tradition and regime before 1945***

DEMOCRATIC:			**DICTATORSHIP:**	
developed	limited	small	authoritatian	auth. plus
Czech Rep.	Slovakia	Slovenia	all CIS states	Slovakia
	Serbia	Croatia	Albania	Croatia
	Macedonia	Bosnia-	Baltic states	Hungary
	Poland	Hungary	Poland	GDR
			Bulgaria	
			Rumania	
			ex-Yugoslavia*	

* Some states appear in two different columns because of their change of regime. Contrary to Serbia, the entire political spectrum in Slovenia, Croatia and Bosnia in 1918-1941 was reduced to one party, which was the sole representative of the Nation and not of any specific Weltanschauung.

Similarly the degree of (non-) legitimacy of the communist seizure of power alone cannot explain the issue - recent differences in political culture between Type 1 and Types 2 and 3:

Table 7. ***Legitimacy of the communist seizure of power***

Legitimate	Illegitimate	
	Comm. with roots	rootless#
Russia ##	Czech Republic	Poland
Ex-Yugoslavia ###	Slovakia	Rumania
	Bulgaria	Hungary
	Albania	Baltic states
		Moldavia
		CIS states
		GDR

Only by virtue of Soviet occupation.
Russia (1917) on the assumption of the legitimacy of the revolution.
In the Yugoslav case, the legitimacy of the communist seizure of power is based on the country's liberation from the occupation and elections in 1945.

A far more important factor for understanding recent differences in political culture is that the national composition of the relevant states was decisive in allowing or undermining the possibility of nationalist manipulation and the emergence of the New Authoritarianism. In this context, this means that the multi-ethnic and multi-confessional composition of the state was the main obstacle in the 1970's and 1980's to the birth of civil society, a liberal opposition and, possibly, of a reformist-communist fraction in the communist oligarchy. The last point is crucial for understanding another political process: the attempt to transform the former ruling oligarchy into the new political elite of the respective society. Where this happened - in Hungary, Poland and, partly, in Slovenia - communism was overruled by the liberal opposition and the reformist- communist fraction, in contrast to its immanent breakdown like in Serbia and all other Basic Type 2 countries.

Table 8. ***Communism overruled by liberal opposition or nationalism***

LIBERAL OPPOSITION		NATIONALISM	
consolidation	secession	breakdown	secession
Hungary*	Slovenia*	FR Yugoslavia	Baltic states
Czech Repub		Albania	Ukraine
Poland		Bulgaria	CIS
GDR		Rumania	Croatia
Slovakia		Macedonia**	Moldavia
		Russia	
		Soviet Union	
		Ex-Yugoslavia	

* Significant role of the reformed communists

** Macedonia formally seceded from the former Yugoslav state, but this was an unwilling secession.

Some additional explanation is needed: there would be no secession without a breakdown of the Soviet Union and Yugoslavia. In Albania, FR Yugoslavia (Serbia and Montenegro), Croatia, Macedonia, Belarus, Ukraine, Russia, CIS states and prior to the 1996 elections, in Bulgaria and Rumania, one can speak - for the time being - only about certain changes, but hardly about a change of regime. All these regimes share some features of modern representative democracy, but the overall socio-political system is neither democratic nor liberal. Some authors are using the term "illiberal democracies" to describe this kind of regime, but I think the notion "ethno-democracies" is more suitable. Slovenia, the Baltic states and to a certain degree Slovakia have two things in common: (1) communism overthrown by the liberal opposition and reformist communists; (2) secession. Let us now compare Table 8 with Table 9: what happened in 1989-1990 with those in power:

Table 9. ***Who is in Power (1997)***

Reformed Comm/ Liberal Democrats	Nationalists #	Nationalists and Ex-Comm. ##
Hungary	Baltic Repub. Yugoslavia	Russia
Poland	Bosnia-Herz.	Ukraine
Czech Repub.	Croatia	Slovakia**
Slovenia		FR Yugoslavia
GDR	Bulgaria*	Albania
	Romania*	Mazedonia
		Moldavia
		Belarus
		Georgia and oth. CIS States

Nationalists of the anti-Communist legitimization;

Nationalists and ex-communist means nationalist of communist origin such as Milosevic in Serbia. Both share an authoritarian or manipulative (based on the nation and friend-enemy notion) type of political order.

*Romania and Bulgaria are marked with an asterisk (*) as political systems in transformation from Basic Type 2 to Basic Type 1, including the governing coalition and general framework of politics. They are literally societies in transition.

** It is very hard to describe the ruling coalition in Slovakia. It is a coalition of all three patterns mentioned in this table.

Before drawing any conclusions, let us consider the type of recent governments in post-communist countries:

Table 10. ***Type of government (1996)***

Parliamentarian	Mixture	Strong Presidency
Hungary	Slovenia	Russia
GDR	Bulgaria Bosnia-Herz.	Serbia
Slovakia	Poland	Moldavia
Czech Repub.	Albania	Baltic states
		Croatia
		Belarus
		Georgia and oth. CIS States
		Ukraine
		Macedonia

Tables 1, 2, 8 and 9 are almost identical, whereas the others show hardly any relationship. Thus the type of recent government seems to be as irrelevant to the outcome of the transformation process as the political culture and type of regime prior to the communist seizure of power. Yet, there is definitely a direct link between the post-1945 ethnic composition, the immediate success of the transformation process, and the fact that the ruling communist oligarchy was overthrown by the liberal opposition and reformist communists (no country of Basic type 2 in this category). On the other hand, there is a direct link between multi-ethnic composition of the state, lost years in terms of marketization, pluralization and democratization of society, the immanent breakdown of the communist regime and recent ethno-nationalist and/or national-communist authoritarian rule. One may even expand the argument to cover the earlier past: in Hungary, Poland, the Czech Republic, and the GDR, there was first democratic resistance within the communist party (1953, 1956, 1968) and, after the change in paradigm of resistance, in civil society with citizens creating movements to demand democratization and respect for individual rights. The notion of civil society - as used in Central and Eastern Europe - never had much to do with the usage of this term by classical authors like Ferguson, Locke, etc. To speak of civil society - in Poland, the Czech Republic and Hungary, and only there was this language really spoken - was instead to express a twofold opposition. The first dimension was opposition to authority, the second was that in which civil society was used in contradistinction to 'the nation', understood in hereditary, ethnic terms. Vaclav Havel in Czech Republic, Adam Michnik and Jacek Kuron in Poland, Janos Kiss in Hungary, to name some of the most prominent, "challenged the traditionally dominant ethnic conception of the nation with a non-ethnic, political concept. By promoting civil society rather than ethnic community, they were not only proposing a wholly different way of defining "us" and "them", but also suggesting a different way of looking at the past and the future" (Smolar, 1996: 24-25). The ruling communist oligarchy was not able to suppress or suspend the democratic communist movements and, later, the civil society dissidents with ethno-nationalistic manipulation and friend-enemy policies - whereas in the mono-ethnic state, there is no real ground for such an appeal. This served as a basis for developing a different political culture (to a certain degree) and a permanent opposition to communism from the liberal position - contrary to the multi-ethnic states, such as all countries in the Southeastern and Eastern Europe, where the ethno-nationalist appeal of the rulers had a sufficient basis, together with the friend-enemy interethnic policies, to satisfy the needs of the national communist and, eventually, the post-communist elites. The ethnic composition of the state thus became in the first stage of transition an important, in some cases even the most important factor, while in other (mono-ethnic) ex-communist countries democracy has become "the only game in town". This is the case with political regimes in Hungary, Poland, the Czech Republic and Slovenia. They are consolidated democracies in a behavioral, attitudinal and constitutional sense as it is used by mainstream Western political science, for example by Linz and Stepan (1996: 5-7). By contrast, in FR of Yugoslavia (Serbia and Montenegro), Croatia, Russia, Belarus, Bosnia and Hercegovina, etc. there is no basic consensus on the citizenship, state (patriotism), and due to this fact about institutional framework of the regime and on the articulation and aggregation of interests. Thus, on the one hand, in the countries of basic type 2 we have autocrats and nationalists (usually both) with ethno-nationalism as the legitimacy basis of the ruling elite and also as its most important instrument of political manipulation. On the other hand, in the countries of basic type 1, we find the ruling political elite whose proponents have successfully participated in the democratic competition where both left or right wing democrats participate and where the legitimacy basis is in the very process of transformation, i.e. pluralism, the rule of law, democracy and market economy. Simultaneously, in these homogenous national states, **and only there**, a counter-elite rooted in civil society already emerged during communist rule, and this process was eventually accompanied by the public establishment of a reform-oriented faction within the communist party and the ruling oligarchy. This counter-elite did not create a civil society, but rather, the emergence of a counter-elite was possible only where there was a civil society already in existence (Winderl, 1994:623). Only where civil society existed in the communist world did a politically and functionally relevant reform wing within the nomenclature emerge. That is why in countries which underwent the first stage of transformation (i.e. states of the basic type 1), researchers - despite the change of regime - note a "relative stability in personnel and a rather significant change in institutional structure" (Szelenyi and Szelenyi, 1995: 625). Nevertheless, there occurred one very significant change: namely in personnel composition at the top of the political elite. And this was the case not only in the basic type 1 states, that very change created a pre-condition for the beginning of the transformation process in basic type 2 states as well. By contrast, in countries with an ethno-nationalist political matrix, this essential institutional change was missing at the very outset of the transformation process, as was the change in real value (authoritarianism *versus* pluralism) orientation of the political elites.

Notes

1 And this is what differentiates my argument from the many case-studies were the significance of the ethnic factor is mentioned or even stressed, but only in particular perspective of the relevant case study. On the other hand, in studies like Vachudova and Snyder (1997) or Elster, Offe, Preuss, (1998) "ethnic geography" as universal factor is mentioned but not interrelated with the (successful) struggle of the old political elite to retain its **political** power through manipulation, creating a most successful tool: the biased ethno-nationalism, nationalism based on the notion of the other as the enemy **including and excluding from the political community** based exclusively on a pre-modern (blood, origin) and non-political notion of the nation

References

Agh, Attila. 1994. "The Premature Senility of the Young Democracies: The Central European Experience". In: Dieter Segert, (ed.). Konfliktregulierung durch Parteien und politische Stabilitaet in Ostmitteleuropa. Frankfurt a/M. etc.1994. 205-221.

Dahl, Robert. 1992. "Why All Democratic Countries Have Mixed Economies," in: Szoboszlai Gyoergy, ed., Flying Blind: Emerging Democracies in East-Central Europe, Budapest: HPSA. 9-26.

Elster, Jon; Offe, Claus; Preuss, Ulrich K with Frank Boenker, Ulrike Goetting, Friedbert W. Rueb. 1998. Institutional Design in Post-communist Socıties. Cambridge, etc.: Cambridge University Press.

Holmes, Lesli. 1997. Post-Communism: An Introduction. Cambridge: Polity Press. 1997.

Huntington, Samuel, P. 1993. "The Clash of Civilizations?". Foreign Affairs. 1993, Summer. 72(3): 22-49

Linz, Juan J. and Stepan, Alfred. 1996. Problems of democratic transition and consolidation: Southern Europe, South America, and post-communist Europe. Baltimore: Johns Hopkins University Press. 1996.

Mill, John Stuart. 1861. Consideration on Representative Government. In: On Liberty, Utilitarianism and Representative Government. London: 1960.

Offe, Claus. 1992. "Capitalism by Democratic Design?" In: Gy. Lengyel, C. Offe, and J.Tholen eds. Economic Institutions, Actors and Attitudes. Budapest: UES; 1992. 11-22.

Posarac, Aleksandra. 1995: "Pauperizacija stanovni{tva u Srbiji - jedan od osnovnih vidova potisnutosti civilnog dru{tva". In: V. Pavlovi}, ed. Potisnuto civilno dru{tvo. Beograd: EKO centar. 1995: 329-368.

Smolar, Aleksander. 1996. "From Opposition to Atomization: Civil Society After Communism". Journal of Democracy. 1996, January. 7(1): 24-38.

Szelenyi, Ivan and Szelenyi, Szonya. 1995. "Circulation or reproduction of elites during the postcommunist transformation of Eastern Europe." *Theory and Society*, 24: 4: 613-628.

Vachudova, Milada Ana and Snyder, Tim. 1997. "Are Transitions Transitory? Two Types of Political Change in Eastern Europe Since 1989." East European Politics and Society. Winter 1997. 11(1): 1-35

Winderl, Thomas. 1994. "Machteliten im Systemwechsel: Über Wandlung und Kontinuität osteuropäischer Eliten." *Südosteuropa*, 43: 11-12: 613-627.

Predictions of Democracy Revisited

TATU VANHANEN

1. Introduction

In my book *Prospects of Democracy: A study of 172 countries* (1997), I made predictions on the chances of democracy in various countries. The predictions were based on the situation in 1993. Now, five years later, it is interesting to review those predictions in order to see to what extent later developments have supported or contradicted them. First, however, I shall introduce my theoretical explanation of democracy briefly and compare it to some other theoretical explanations. The clarification of theoretical premises is necessary because predictions are derived from a theory that explains in what conditions democratization is expected to take place and what are the causal factors of democratization.

My resource distribution theory of democratization is based on evolutionary arguments. Politics is regarded as a forum of the general struggle for existence. In this struggle the central question concerns the distribution of scarce resources. The permanent scarcity of some important resources and the need to distribute them by some means explains the necessity of politics in human societies. Politics evolved in the struggle for scarce resources within and between human societies. People compete and fight for political power because power can be used to further their own interests in this struggle. By power I mean the ability to compel or persuade others to do something what they would not otherwise do. This ability to compel or persuade others rests on the possibility of sanctions. If the resources used as sources of power are concentrated in the hands of one group, this group is potentially the most powerful group. If the resources to be used as sanctions are distributed widely among several groups, it is reasonable to expect that power becomes distributed among several groups, too. I assume that this relationship is regular across all cultural variations. Those controlling the most effective power resources have better chances to get power than those whose power resources are meagre or who are without any significant power resources. These arguments let me hypothesize that *the concentration as well as distribution of political power depends on the degree of resource distribution.*

This "Darwinian" interpretation of politics provides a theoretical explanation for the necessity of the relationship between resource distribution and the distribution of political power. Because politics is a part of the general struggle for existence, in which people tend to use all available resources, the distribution of political power becomes dependent on the degree of resource distribution. There is a causal link between resource distribution and power distribution, although this link does not need to be unilinear from resource distribution to power distribution. This link is reciprocal to some extent because power can be used and is used to get more resources. I assume, however, that the distribution of resources is a more independent variable than the distribution of political power because some important aspects of resource distribution are outside the scope of conscious politics. In other words, some important changes in resource distribution take place independently from political power. When such independent changes in resource distribution have accumulated, they can cause changes in power distribution. They are underlying currents that undermine existing power structures. The variation of political systems from the rule of the few to the rule of the many follows from this regular relationship between resource distribution and the distribution of political power. In societies where relevant power resources are concentrated in the hands of the few, political power tends to become concentrated in the hands of the few, too, and in societies where important power resources are distributed widely, political power tends to become widely distributed, as well. We can derive a Darwinian explanation of democracy and democratization from these arguments. My basic hypothesis is that *democratization takes place under conditions in which power resources have become so widely distributed that no group is any longer able to suppress its competitors or to maintain its hegemony*.

Briefly stated, this is my evolutionary resource distribution theory of democratization (see Vanhanen 1990, 1992, 1997). The degree of resource distribution is assumed to be the common causal factor of democratization. It is possible to test this theory by formulating empirical variables to measure some crucial aspects of the hypothetical concepts democratization and power resources.

I have used two electoral indicators to measure two crucial dimensions of democracy — competition and participation (cf. Dahl 1971, 1—9). The smaller parties' share of the votes cast in parliamentary or presidential elections, or both, is used to indicate the degree of competition. It is calculated by subtracting the percentage of the votes received by the largest party from 100. The remainder represents the share of the smaller parties. The percentage of the population who actually voted in the election concerned is used to measure the degree of electoral participation. These two basic indicators (competition and participation) are combined into an *Index of Democratization* (ID) by multiplying the two percentages and by dividing the outcome by 100. This means that ID gets high values only if the values of both basic variables are high. This method to combine the two basic variables is based on the assumption that both of them represent equally important dimensions of democratization and that a high level of electoral participation cannot compensate for the lack of competition, or vice versa (for the definition of political variables, see Vanhanen 1990, 17—24; 1993, 1997, 34-38). I assume that these two simple electoral variables are enough to measure major differences between political systems from the perspective of democracy, although they cannot take into account all important aspects of democracy. Further, I assume that the combination of them (ID) is a more valid measure of democratization than either of them separately. Therefore I use ID as my principal dependent variable and as the operational substitute for the hypothetical concept democratization.

It is very difficult to find reliable and valid empirical variables to measure resource distribution because so many different types of resources can be used in the struggle for power. It is simply not possible to know all relevant power resources and even more difficult to measure their distribution. I came to the conclusion that the best strategy would be to focus on some crucial types of power resources, which can be assumed to be relevant in all societies. I think that economic and intellectual power resources are relevant in all societies. So I attempted to measure some aspects of the distribution of economic and intellectual power resources. The following six variables were used to measure the relative distribution of these resources:

(1) The urban population as a percentage of the total population.

(2) The non-agricultural population as a percentage of the total population.
(3) The number of students in universities and equivalent degree-granting institutions per 100,000 inhabitants.
(4) The literate population as a percentage of the adult population.
(5) The area of family farms as a percentage of the total area of holdings.
(6) The degree of decentralization of non-agricultural economic resources.

My basic assumption is that each of these variables measures, directly or indirectly, some important aspects of economic and intellectual power resources. The higher the values of these variables, the higher the relative distribution of power resources. However, I am not particularly interested in the separate explanatory power of these variables because they are intended to measure the hypothetical ´resource distribution´ from various perspectives. Therefore I combined them into an *Index of Power Resources* (IPR). It was done by first combining the six original explanatory variables into three sectional indices (IOD, IKD, and DER) and then by multiplying them and by dividing the outcome by 10,000. In addition, I formulated an alternative version of this index, the *Index of Power Resources and Structural Imbalance* (IPRI), in which the discrepancy between the three sectional indices is taken into account. It is based on the assumption that a country in which some power resources are relatively widely distributed has better chances to establish and maintain democracy than a country for which all three sectional indices indicate the concentration of power resources. IPR is my principal explanatory variable and operational substitute for the hypothetical concept of ´power resources´, although it is sometimes necessary to refer to IPRI, too. My assumption is that the higher the value of IPR, the more widely politically relevant power resources are usually distributed in a society and the more favourable social conditions are for democratization (for explanatory variables, see Vanhanen 1997). It is clear that these variables are only imperfect measures for resource distribution, but they are the only ones I have for this purpose. These variables cannot take into account local variations in the types of relevant power resources; they do not take into account the use of external power resources and outside interventions; and they do not measure the distribution of the means of violence. Despite these and other defects, I dare to assume that they measure, although roughly, crucial differences between societies in the distribution of power resources. Therefore, it is plausible to hypothesize that *the Index of Democratization (ID) is positively correlated with the Index of Power Resources (IPR) and that all countries tend to cross the threshold of democracy at about the same level of IPR.*

I tested my evolutionary resource distribution theory of democratization by empirical evidence in several comparative studies. The latest study includes 172 states of the period 1991-93 and 967 decennial units of analysis of the period 1850—1980.

2. Other Theories of Democratization

Researchers have presented various theoretical explanations of democracy and democratization. In this connection, I refer briefly only to some of them. Karl A. Wittfogel (1957/1963) found that despotic power of rulers in hydraulic societies was based on the ownership and control of the means of production. The same group, the state managerial bureaucracy, which controlled the strategic means of production, was also the politically ruling class. It used power to further its own interests. Consequently, a multicentered society — in which private property is strong and large bureaucratized complexes, like Big Government, Big Business, Big Agriculture, and Big Labour, mutually check each other — would form a natural basis for democracy. William Kornhauser (1959) traced the origin of democracy to pluralist society. His important insight is that the "major guarantee against the aggrandizement of power by elites is the existence of a plurality of groups that are equal enough in power to generate genuine competition for leadership on the several levels of political society" (p. 236). These two theoretical explanations emphasize the importance of resource distribution.

Daniel Lerner (1958/1964) sought explanation for the emergence of democracy from modernization. He assumed that modernization follows the same sequences everywhere. It begins with urbanization, is followed by literacy and media participation, and finally is crowned by political participation. Seymour Martin Lipset (1959) presented the same idea on the crucial importance of socio-economic development in a slightly different form. He hypothesized that "the more well-to-do a nation, the greater the chances that it will sustain democracy." Lipset repeats his hypothesis in a revised edition of *Political Man* (1983) and refers to many social scientists whose empirical studies have confirmed the positive relationship between economic development and democracy (cf. Diamond and Marks 1992; Lipset, Seong and Torres 1993; Lipset 1994). Such an explanation implies that democratic attitudes and beliefs serve as intervening mechanisms between economic development and democracy. It should be noted that Lipset stresses, in addition to economic development, the significance of political culture, legitimacy, and suitable institutions as conditions of democracy. Samuel P. Huntington (1997) emphasizes the significance of economic development. He says that "an extremely high correlation exists between levels of democracy and levels of economic development," and continues that setting aside the oil-rich states as special cases, "all the wealthiest countries in the world, except Singapore, are democratic, and almost all the poorest countries in the world, with the notable exception of India and perhaps one or two others, are not democratic" (p. 5). I have attempted to show by my comparative studies that the principal explanatory factor is not the level of economic development or wealth but the degree of resource distribution. It means that democracy is possible also in poor countries in which some crucial power resources are sufficiently distributed among competing groups.

Larry Diamond (1992) reinterpreted Lipset's thesis on the relationship between socio-economic development and democracy and tested it by new empirical evidence. He used GNP per capita to measure the level of socio-economic development and the results of Freedom House's annual survey of political rights and liberties to measure the level of democracy in a comparison group of 142 states in 1990. The cross-tabulation of data indicated, once more, a strong relationship between economic development and democracy. Then he found that this relationship becomes even stronger when the Human Development Index (HDI) constructed by the United Nations Development Program (1991) is used as the development indicator. The HDI had a substantially higher correlation (0.71) with the combined index of political freedom than GNP (0.51). Diamond reformulated Lipset's thesis: "The more well-to-do the people of a country, the more likely they will favor, achieve, and maintain a democratic system for their country." He emphasizes that the level of socio-economic development is the most important variable in determining the chances of democracy and that this relationship is causal in at least one direction: "Higher levels of socio-economic development generate a significantly higher probability of democratic government" (Diamond 1992; see also Lane and Ersson 1994, 214—16).

Several researchers have emphasized that it is impossible to explain democratization by any single causal factor. Robert A. Dahl stresses in his studies that several factors should be taken into account in explanations of democracy. He listed seven sets of conditions of democracy or polyarchy in his book *Polyarchy* (1971) and assumed that if all of them were favorable for polyarchy, a country had very good chances to establish and maintain polyarchy, and vice versa. In a later study *Democracy and its Critics* (1989), Dahl connects the chances of democracy to definable environmental conditions, but not to any single dominant explanatory factor, although he emphasizes the significance of the dispersion of the means of violent coercion, of the dynamic pluralist society, and of cultural homogeneity in particular. All the conditions listed by Dahl may be relevant for democracy, but the problem is how to operationalize them and how to weight the relative significance of different conditions.

In the twenty-six nation comparative study *Politics in Developing Countries* (1990), Larry Diamond, Juan J. Linz and Seymour Martin Lipset "seek to explain whether, why, and to what extent democracy has evolved and taken root in the vastly different cultural and historical soils of these countries" (p. 1). Just like Dahl, they assume that many different factors can facilitate or obstruct the establishment and survival of democratic institutions. They listed the following facilitating and obstructing factors: legitimacy and performance, political leadership, political culture, social structure and socioeconomic development, associational life, state and society, political institutions, ethnic and regional conflicts, the military, and international factors (pp. 9—34). However, their list of factors does not constitute a theory of democratization. It would be very difficult to operationalize those factors, to measure them, and to weight their relative significance.

Samuel Huntington's conclusion on the possibility to find a coherent theoretical explanation for democratization is equally pessimistic in his book *The Third Way* (1991). He argues that the "causes of democratization differ substantially from one place to another and from one time to another." He explains the third wave of democratization since the 1970s by referring to many different factors, including the declining legitimacy of nondemocratic rule, economic development, the role of Western Christianity, external actors, demonstration effects or snowballing, and the significance of political leaders, but he does not make any attempt to operationalize these factors into measurable indicators (see also Huntington 1996). Therefore, it is impossible to know to what extent they might explain democratization or the lack of democratization in particular cases. My point is that there must be some common factor behind democratization because central characteristics of human nature do not vary from "one place to another and from one time to another".

There are many other interesting comparative studies of democracy, but it is not possible to introduce them in this connection (see, for example, Arat 1991; Hadenius 1992; Rueschemeyer et al. 1992; Held 1993; Olson 1993; Pinkney 1993; Sorensen 1993; Berg-Schlosser and DeMeur 1994; Parry and Moran 1994; Midlarsky 1997).

My resource distribution theory of democratization differs from the other theoretical explanations discussed above in some respects. Because the explanatory principles of my theory are derived from the Darwinian theory of evolution, they are assumed to apply to all human societies across cultural, ethnic, geographical, and developmental differences. Consequently, it was possible to formulate universal propositions concerning the factors affecting democratization. The explanatory factors of other theories and models are expressed in less universal form. Besides, I would like to argue that my hypothetical concept 'power resources' covers and explains several explanatory factors used in other theories. Let us take the Lerner-Lipset hypothesis. Economic and intellectual resources become usually more widely distributed when the level of socio-economic development rises. It implies that resource distribution may be the underlying factor that explains the positive correlation between socio-economic development and the level of democracy. Kornhauser's pluralist and Wittfogel's multicentered societies provides a favorable environment for democratization because power resources are divided among the many and not concentrated in the hands of the few in such societies.

Are there differences in the explanatory power of these theories and how can we measure such differences? I think that it is justified to evaluate theories on the basis of their explanatory power and parsimony. A theory that explains a significant part of the dependent phenomenon is more useful than a theory that explains less of the dependent phenomenon. A hypothesis that can be tested by relatively few simple indicators is more useful than a hypothesis that needs many complicated indicators. Besides, a hypothesis which can be operationalized and tested by empirical evidence is more useful than a hypothesis the concepts of which cannot be operationalized. Testable theories and hypotheses are scientifically more useful than untestable ones. From this perspective, there are significant differences between the theories and hypotheses discussed above.

Most of the theories of democratization seem to be untestable. Kornhauser's idea is good, but he did not indicate how we could measure the degree of pluralism in a society. The same applies for Wittfogel's multicentered society. Dahl's model of explanatory factors includes variables that are impossible to operationalize, although it also includes variables that can be operationalized. Another problem is that Dahl has not explained how we could evaluate the relative significance of his seven different explanatory factors. Diamond, Linz and Lipset's (1990) list of explanatory factors includes many different variables. Most of them are such that it is impossible to operationalize them. It would be even more difficult to combine them and to weight their relative significance. Therefore it is not possible to test the explanatory power of their model.

Lerner-Lipset's socio-economic hypothesis is testable and it has been tested by empirical evidence since the 1960s. The results have nearly always supported the hypothesis on the positive correlation between the level of socio-economic development and the level of democracy (see Lipset 1983, 469—76; 1995; Diamond 1992). Because GNP per capita has been used as the major indicator of socio-economic development and because it is regarded to be the dominant explanatory variable (see Lipset, Seong and Torres 1993, 156), I shall compare the explanatory powers of GNP per capita and my IPR. Diamond's reformulated Lipset hypothesis, in which the level of human development is used as the principal explanatory factor, provides another testable theory. UNDP's Human Development Index (HDI) is Diamond's explanatory variable. In the end, Lerner-Lipset's original socio-economic hypothesis and Diamond's reformulated human development hypothesis seem to be the only ones that can be tested by empirical data and compared with my resource distribution hypothesis. In the following test, GNP per capita, HDI, and IPR will be used as the alternative explanatory variables and my Index of Democratization (ID) in 1993 and the Freedom House Survey Team's ratings of political rights and liberties (RL) in 1991 as the alternative dependent variables. The 172 countries of my study are used as the units of analysis (Vanhanen 1997). Nearly all data on GNP per capita are from *World Development Report 1993* and *Human Development Report 1993*. Data on the Human Development Index (HDI) are from *Human Development Report 1993*. Data on IPR and ID are from my recent study (Vanhanen 1997) and data on RL-91 from Freedom House's *Freedom in the World 1991—92*. The results of correlation analysis are given in Table 1.

Table 1. ***Intercorrelations of three explanatory and two dependent variables in the comparison group of 172 countries in 1990—93***

Variables	GNP per capita-91	HDI-90	IPR-91	ID-93	RL-91
GNP per capita		0.623	0.798	0.571	-0.480
Human Development Index (HDI)			0.702	0.664	-0.590
Index of Power Resources (IPR)				0.768	-0.650
Index of Democratization (ID)					-0.781
Political rights and liberties (RL)					

The most interesting correlations are between the explanatory and dependent variables. They indicate to what extent the explanatory powers of the three alternative explanatory factors differ from each other. The results show that GNP per capita explains 33 percent of the variation in ID-93 and 23 percent of the variation in RL-91, whereas HDI explains 44 and 35 percent respectively and IPR 59 and 42 percent (i.e. the squared values of the correlations given above). GNP is thus the weakest and IPR the strongest explanatory variable. HDI is between them.

3. Predictions on the Prospects of Democracy

Relatively strong correlations between explanatory and dependent variables provide an empirical basis to make predictions on the prospects of democracy in individual countries. However, researchers using Lipset's or Diamond's explanatory variables have not presented any detailed predictions. It is understandable because it would be difficult to determine any minimum level of GNP per capita or of HDI above which countries would be expected to become democracies. The results of regression analysis (Figure 1) disclose that it is impossible to establish any threshold of GNP per capita under which democracy would be impossible. Figure 2 discloses that nondemocracies have been frequent until a very high level of HDI.

Because the level of democratization (ID) is more strongly correlated with IPR than with GNP per capita or HDI, this relationship provides a significantly better basis for predictions. Figure 3 illustrates the results of regression analysis in which ID-93 is used as the dependent variable and the Index of Power Resources (IPR) as the explanatory variable. There are numerous deviating cases, but most countries are clustered around the regression line. Therefore I used the results of regression analysis to predict the chances of democracy in individual countries.

Figure 1. ***The results of regression analysis of ID-93 on GNP per capita in 1991 in the cross-sectional comparison group of 172 countries in 1993***

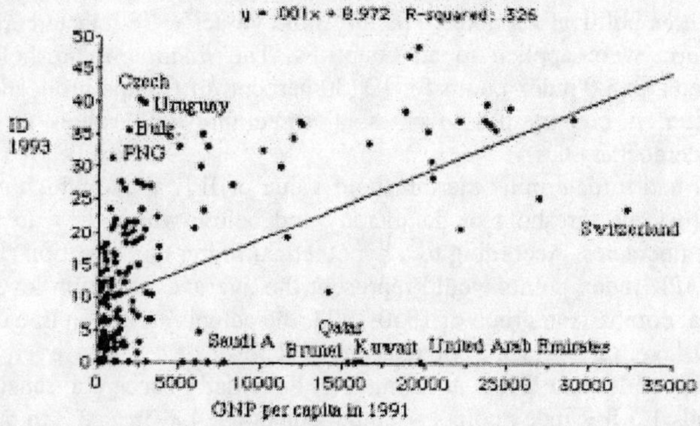

Figure 2. ***The results of regression analysis of ID-93 on HDI-90 in the cross-sectional comparison group of 172 countries in 1993***

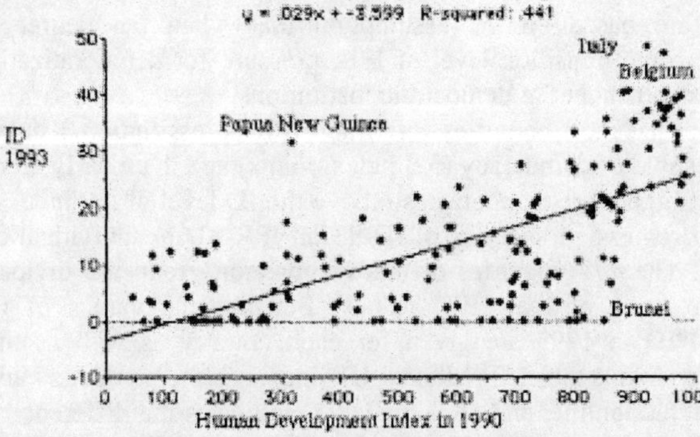

Figure 3. ***The results of regression analysis of ID-93 on IPR-90 in the cross-sectional comparison group of 172 countries in 1993***

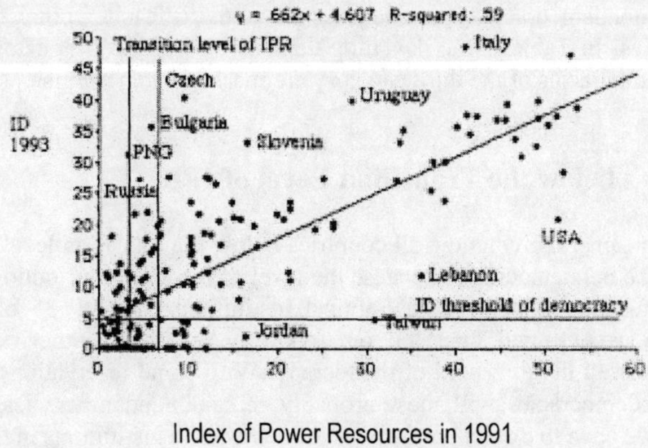

There is no natural borderline between democracies and nondemocracies in Figure 3. How to determine which political systems are democracies and which are non-democracies? I decided to determine minimum criteria of democracy by using the values of the three political variables. The threshold values were selected arbitrarily, but the same criteria were applied to all countries. The minimum threshold values of democracy used are: 5.0 index points for ID, 30 percent for Competition, and 15 percent for Participation. A country has to cross all three threshold values in order to be regarded as a democracy.

Similarly, I had to determine the threshold value of IPR above which countries are expected to cross the threshold of democracy and below which they are expected to remain nondemocracies. According to a hypothetical regression equation (ID est. = 0 + 1.0xIPR), 5.0 IPR index points would represent the average transition level of IPR. In the longitudinal comparison group of 1850-1993, the actual regression line of ID on IPR crosses the ID level of 5.0 index points at the IPR level of 4.8. However, because the correlation between ID and IPR is not complete, I decided to accept a transition level of IPR that extends 1.5 IPR index points around the average 4.8 (from 3.3 to 6.3 IPR index points). Consequently, countries below 3.3 IPR index points were expected to be nondemocracies, and countries above 6.3 IPR index points were expected to be democracies. So the transition level of 3.0 IPR index points was assumed to separate nondemocracies from democracies. My predictions on the prospects of democracy in single countries are based on the assumption that when the degree of resource distribution rises to the transition level of IPR, pressure for democratization increases and leads to the establishment of democratic institutions.

Figure 3 shows that most countries for which IPR is less than 3.3 index points are below the ID threshold of democracy (5.0 index points) and that nearly all countries for which ID is 6.3 or higher are democracies (above the ID level of 5.0 index points). The detailed results of regression analyses of ID-93 on IPR-91 for individual countries are given in Table 2. The 172 countries of this comparison group are divided into three categories on the basis of their IPR values. Besides, the values of Competition, Participation, and ID in 1993 are given for each country as well as the results of regression analysis. In this table, "Predicted: ID" indicates the predicted value of ID, i.e. its value at the regressionline, and "Residual: ID" indicates the difference between the actual value of ID and its predicted value. It is the vertical distance from the actual value of ID to the regression line. The three categories clarify my predictions. The countries below 3.3 IPR index points are expected to be nondemocracies. I cannot make any predictions for the countries at the transition level of IPR because they can be either democracies or nondemocracies. The countries above 6.3 IPR index points are expected to be democracies. In Table 2, the deviating democracies of the first category and the deviating nondemocracies of the third category are marked by an asterisk (*).

3.1. Countries below the Transition Level of IPR

According to my general prediction, all countries below the transition level of IPR (3.3) are expected to be nondemocracies because the level of resource distribution is assumed to be too low to support democratic political institutions. In fact, 35 of them were nondemocracies as expected in 1993, but, contrary to the hypothesis, eight other countries had crossed the threshold of democracy. With some reservations, I predicted that the 35 nondemocracies will most probably remain nondemocracies in the near future and that we have to expect breakdowns of democratic institutions in the eight

Table 2. ***The results of regression analysis of ID on IPR in the longitudinal comparison group of 1,139 observation units of the period 1850-1993 for the subgroup of 172 contemporary countries in 1993, which are divided into three IPR categories.***

	Country/Region	C-93	P-93	D-93	IPR	Residual:ID	Predicted: ID	
1. IPR below 3.3 (countries below the transition level of IPR)								Deviating democracies *
1	Afghanistan	0	0	0	2.5	-3.3	3.3	
2	Angola	23	18	4.1	2.2	1.0	3.1	
3	Azerbaijan	6	52	3.1	2.1	0.1	3.0	
4	Bangladesh	49	28	13.7	2.5	10.4	3.3	*
5	Belarus	19	34	6.5	2.0	3.5	3.0	
6	Benin	56	22	12.3	2.1	9.3	3.0	*
7	Bhutan	0	0	0	0.6	-1.9	1.9	
8	Burkina Faso	33	11	3.6	0.6	1.7	1.9	
9	Burundi	13	17	2.2	1.1	-0.1	2.3	
10	Cambodia	27	22	5.9	0.4	4.1	1.8	
11	Chad	0	0	0	2.1	-3.0	3.0	
12	Comoros	39	25	9.7	2.5	6.4	3.3	*
13	Djibouti	19	15	2.8	2.3	-0.4	3.2	
14	Eq. Guinea	1	20	0	2.8	-3.6	3.6	
15	Ethiopia	0	0	0	2.3	-3.2	3.2	
16	Gambia	36	25	9.0	1.8	6.2	2.8	*
17	Guinea	24	17	4.1	1.3	1.6	2.5	
18	Guinea-Biss.	0	0	0	2.0	-3.0	3.0	
19	Kazakhstan	3	50	1.5	2.2	-1.6	3.1	
20	Korea, North	0	25	0	1.1	-2.3	2.3	
21	Kyrgyzstan	5	48	2.4	1.8	-0.4	2.8	
22	Laos	0	45	0	2.6	-3.4	3.4	
23	Liberia	0	0	0	1.9	-2.9	2.9	
24	Malawi	0	0	0	1.7	-2.7	2.7	
25	Mali	33	9	3.0	1.6	0.3	2.7	
26	Mosambique	0	0	0	1.0	-2.2	2.2	
27	Namibia	21	24	5.0	2.2	1.9	3.1	
28	Nepal	46	26	12.0	0.9	9.8	2.2	*
29	Niger	43	27	11.6	1.2	9.2	2.4	*
30	Oman	0	0	0	3.1	-3.8	3.8	
31	Rwanda	0	40	0	1.1	-2.3	2.3	
32	Senegal	42	15	6.3	2.6	2.9	3.4	*
33	Sierra Leone	0	0	0	1.9	-2.9	2.9	
34	Solomon Is.	55	33	18.1	1.4	15.6	2.5	*
35	Somalia	0	0	0	1.9	-2.9	2.9	
36	Sudan	0	0	0	1.7	-2.7	2.7	
37	Tajikistan	6	50	3.0	1.7	-0.3	2.7	
38	Tanzania	2	21	0.4	2.4	-2.9	3.3	

39	Togo	2	28	0.6	3.0	-3.1	3.7
40	Turkmenistan	5	50	2.5	0.8	0.4	2.1
41	Uganda	0	0	0	1.9	-2.9	2.9
42	Uzbekistan	9	50	4.5	1.9	1.6	2.9
43	Vietnam	0	53	0	2.7	-3.5	3.5

2. IPR 3.3 - 6.3 (countries at the transition level of IPR)

44	Albania	32	24	7.7	4.2	3.1	4.6
45	Botswana	35	20	7.0	5.9	1.1	5.9
46	Brunei	0	0	0	3.9	-4.4	4.4
47	Bulgaria	60	59	35.4	5.9	29.5	5.9
48	Cameroon	55	21	11.5	5.3	6.1	5.4
49	Cape Verde	29	29	8.4	5.1	3.1	5.3
50	Central A.R.	53	23	12.2	3.3	8.3	3.9
51	China	0	0	0	3.5	-4.1	4.1
52	Congo	44	35	15.4	6.0	9.4	6.0
53	Cote d'Ivoire	12	19	2.3	4.7	-2.7	5.0
54	Cuba	0	33	0	4.4	-4.8	4.8
55	Gabon	49	33	16.2	6.3	10.0	6.2
56	Guatemala	41	9	3.7	3.8	-0.6	4.3
57	Haiti	0	0	0	4.2	-4.6	4.6
58	Honduras	47	30	14.1	5.0	8.9	5.2
59	India	55	32	17.6	5.4	12.1	5.5
60	Kenya	55	21	11.5	3.8	7.2	4.3
61	Lesotho	12	14	1.7	4.2	-2.9	4.6
62	Madagascar	38	29	11.0	4.8	5.9	5.1
63	Mauritania	26	23	6.0	3.3	2.1	3.9
64	Moldova	16	50	8.0	3.4	4.0	4.0
65	Nigeria	0	0	0	4.9	-5.1	5.1
66	Pakistan	52	13	6.8	3.5	2.7	4.1
67	Papua N.G.	80	39	31.2	3.3	27.3	3.9
68	Paraguay	57	24	13.7	4.7	8.7	5.0
69	Russia	60	45	27.0	4.6	22.1	4.9
70	Sao Tome	32	29	9.3	4.7	4.3	5.0
71	Swaziland	0	0	0	3.8	-4.3	4.3
72	Ukraine	38	57	21.7	4.0	17.2	4.5
73	United Arab E.	0	0	0	6.1	-6.0	6.0
74	Vanuatu	59	37	21.8	5.6	16.1	5.7
75	Yemen	29	10	2.9	4.4	-1.9	4.8
76	Zaire	0	0	0	5.4	-5.5	5.5
77	Zambia	25	15	3.7	5.7	-2.0	5.7
78	Zimbabwe	12	27	3.2	3.5	-0.9	4.1

3. IPR above 6.3 (countries above the transition level of IPR)

Deviating nondemocracies *

79	Algeria	0	0	0	8.0	-7.4	7.4	*
80	Argentina	44	49	27.0	33.4	0.6	26.4	
81	Armenia	41	45	18.4	7.0	11.7	6.7	
82	Australia	55	59	32.4	49.0	-5.6	38.0	
83	Austria	59	60	35.4	40.1	4.0	31.4	
84	Bahamas	45	43	19.3	26.4	-1.8	21.1	
85	Bahrain	0	0	0	12.1	-10.5	10.5	*
86	Barbados	50	47	23.5	21.6	5.9	17.6	
87	Belgium	76	62	47.1	52.8	6.3	40.8	
88	Belize	45	32	14.4	12.3	3.8	10.6	
89	Bolivia	50	21	10.5	9.6	1.9	8.6	
90	Brazil	62	33	20.5	13.6	8.9	11.6	
91	Canada	59	48	28.3	52.1	-12.1	40.3	
92	Chile	42	48	20.2	26.4	-0.9	21.1	
93	Colombia	49	16	7.8	15.8	-5.4	13.2	
94	Costa Rica	49	44	21.6	20.0	5.2	16.4	
95	Croatia	49	54	26.5	13.1	15.3	11.2	
96	Cyprus	57	48	27.4	25.3	7.1	20.3	
97	Czech R.	66	61	40.3	9.7	31.6	8.7	
98	Denmark	63	63	39.7	49.3	1.5	38.2	
99	Dom. Rep.	64	26	16.6	13.8	4.8	11.8	
100	Ecuador	57	37	21.1	15.3	8.2	12.9	
101	Egypt	12	20	2.4	8.7	-5.6	8.0	*
102	El Salvador	51	20	10.2	10.6	0.8	9.4	
103	Estonia	59	30	17.7	10.4	8.5	9.2	
104	Fiji	57	32	18.2	12.6	7.3	10.9	
105	Finland	63	58	36.5	45.5	1.1	35.4	
106	France	63	49	30.9	47.4	-5.9	36.8	
107	Georgia	43	46	19.8	6.6	13.4	6.4	
108	Germany	63	59	37.2	42.4	4.1	33.1	
109	Ghana	24	19	4.6	7.0	-2.1	6.7	*
110	Greece	53	66	35.0	34.1	8.1	26.9	
111	Guyana	47	38	17.9	6.8	11.4	6.5	
112	Hungary	57	48	27.4	12.4	16.7	10.7	
113	Iceland	61	61	37.2	51.3	-2.5	39.7	
114	Indonesia	16	25	4.0	10.1	-5.0	9.0	*
115	Iran	31	30	9.3	7.8	2.0	7.3	
116	Iraq	0	0	0	8.6	-7.9	7.9	*
117	Ireland	61	49	30.0	37.6	0.5	29.5	
118	Israel	65	53	34.4	41.7	1.9	32.5	
119	Italy	70	69	48.3	41.0	16.3	32.0	
120	Jamaica	40	26	10.4	13.8	-1.4	11.8	
121	Japan	67	38	25.5	37.4	-3.8	29.3	
122	Jordan	22	9	2.0	16.5	-11.8	13.8	*
123	Korea, South	60	50	30.0	38.8	-0.4	30.4	
124	Kuwait	19	2	0.4	9.7	-8.3	8.7	*
125	Latvia	51	21	19.5	10.5	1.2	9.3	
126	Lebanon	73	16	11.7	36.3	-16.8	28.5	
127	Libya	0	0	0	8.3	-7.7	7.7	*

128	Lithuania	47	50	23.5	10.4	14.3	9.2	
129	Luxembourg	68	55	37.4	41.2	5.2	32.2	
130	Macedonia	49	25	12.2	12.3	1.6	10.6	
131	Malaysia	48	31	14.9	10.4	5.7	9.2	
132	Maldives	8	28	2.2	9.7	-6.5	8.7	*
133	Malta	48	69	33.1	33.9	6.4	26.7	
134	Mauritius	52	53	27.6	12.0	17.2	10.4	
135	Mexico	44	24	10.6	15.9	-2.7	13.3	
136	Mongolia	42	49	20.6	7.0	13.9	6.7	
137	Morocco	39	11	4.3	9.4	-4.2	8.5	*
138	Myanmar	0	0	0	7.7	-7.2	7.2	*
139	Netherlands	64	60	38.4	53.5	-2.9	41.3	
140	New Zealand	65	57	37.0	49.3	-1.2	38.2	
141	Nicaragua	45	37	16.6	10.4	7.4	9.2	
142	Norway	63	57	35.9	50.4	-3.1	39.0	
143	Panama	48	45	21.6	11.4	11.6	10.0	
144	Peru	53	31	16.4	17.9	1.6	14.8	
145	Philippines	67	35	23.4	15.1	10.7	12.7	
146	Poland	53	37	19.6	17.5	5.1	14.5	
147	Portugal	39	53	20.7	20.8	3.7	17.0	
148	Qatar	0	0	0	10.0	-8.9	8.9	*
149	Romania	55	50	27.5	8.0	20.1	7.4	
150	St. Lucia	43	43	18.5	11.8	8.2	10.3	
151	St. Vincent	34	40	13.6	10.8	4.1	9.5	
152	Saudi Arabia	0	0	0	8.2	-7.6	7.6	*
153	Singapore	39	28	10.9	21.6	-6.7	17.6	
154	Slovenia	56	59	33.0	16.7	19.1	13.9	
155	South Africa	52	6	3.1	9.5	-5.5	8.6	*
156	Spain	61	60	36.6	44.5	2.0	34.6	
157	Sri Lanka	49	32	15.7	10.5	6.4	9.3	
158	Suriname	31	21	6.5	11.4	-3.5	10.0	
159	Sweden	62	63	39.1	45.7	3.6	35.5	
160	Switzerland	79	30	23.7	38.8	-6.7	30.4	
161	Syria	17	40	6.8	11.0	-2.9	9.7	*
162	Taiwan	20	23	4.6	31.1	-20.0	24.6	*
163	Thailand	39	16	6.2	12.9	-4.9	11.1	
164	Trinidad & T.	55	41	22.5	21.6	4.9	17.6	
165	Tunisia	10	26	2.6	11.9	-7.7	10.3	*
166	Turkey	58	21	12.2	21.4	-5.2	17.4	
167	UK	58	58	33.6	46.6	-2.6	36.2	
168	USA	53	39	20.7	51.5	-19.1	39.8	
169	Uruguay	62	64	39.7	28.5	17.0	22.7	
170	Venezuela	71	27	19.2	24.3	-0.4	19.6	
171	W. Samoa	45	28	12.6	7.6	5.5	7.1	
172	Yugoslavia	46	45	20.7	16.0	7.3	13.4	

deviating democracies. However, it should be noted that these predictions are based on the assumption that the level of resource distribution remains approximately the same. If the level of resource distribution (IPR) rises significantly in a country, its chances to establish democratic institutions would improve. In the following, I shall briefly describe what has happened to deviating democracies until now (November 1998) and whether the other 35 countries are still nondemocracies as expected. This review of political developments in the period 1994-98 is principally based on information provided by *Political Handbook of the World 1997*; *Chronicle of Parliamentary Elections,* years 1993-1997; and *Keesing's Record of World Events*, years 1994-1998.

Let us start from the group of deviating democracies. In the case of **Bangladesh**, I hesitated to predict the failure of democracy because the country is a deviating democracy only on the basis of IPR, not on the basis of IPRI. The relatively high level of Family Farms increased the country's IPRI value. Democratic institutions survived in Bangladesh, although opposition groups several times launched legislative boycotts (see Banks et al. 1997; Chronicle 1997). **Benin** has also remained a deviating democracy. My explanatory variables are unable to explain the emergence and survival of democracy in a country like Benin. I noticed in my book that a hegemonic system would be in better balance with a low degree of resource distribution in Benin. In the case of **Comoros**, I predicted a significant decrease in the level of democratization. There was a violent coup in September 1995 and a French military intervention in October 1995. Democratic institutions collapsed, but they were re-established through presidential and parliamentary elections in March 1996. However, Comoros was not able to cross the threshold of democracy because the Competition variable remained below the 30 percent threshold (Keesing's 1996: 40988; Chronicle 1995-1996). **Gambia** was the most persistent deviating democracy from its independence in 1965 until the military coup on July 22, 1994. The coup leader, Lt. Yahya Jammeh legalized his position through a competitive presidential election on September 26, 1996. He won by 56 percent of the votes (Banks et al. 1997). Competitive legislative elections were held in January 1997. President Jammeh's party won 73 percent of the seats (Keesing's 1997, 41434; Chronicle 1997). Gambia's political system became re-democratized, although it crossed the Competition threshold of democracy only slightly. **Nepal** has remained a stable democracy since the parliamentary elections of 1991. It is a clearly deviating democracy on the basis of IPR, but not on the basis of IPRI. Therefore I did not predict a breakdown of its democratic system. Besides, I noted that some power resources may be more widely distributed in Nepal than my variables indicate. **Niger** crossed the threshold of democracy in the 1993 presidential and parliamentary elections and became a deviating democracy. I predicted a significant decrease in the level of democratization. In fact, democratic institutions collapsed as a consequence of a violent military coup on January 27, 1996, but a democratically elected government was re-established through a presidential election in July 1996 and parliamentary elections in November 1996. The coup leader, Gen. Maïnassara, was elected president by 52 percent of the votes, and his party won 71 percent of the seats in legislative elections (see Banks et al. 1997, 616-17; Chronicle 1995-1996). Political violence has continued in Niger. Therefore, the nature of its democracy is questionable. **Senegal** crossed the threshold of democracy in the 1993 parliamentary and presidential elections. It is a much more stable democracy than Niger because the previous dominant party (Socialist Party) remained in power. Besides, on the basis of regression analysis, it is only a slightly deviating case (residual 2.9). **Solomon Islands** is the most deviating democracy in this category. I noticed that its low IPR value predicts the breakdown of democratic institutions, but some local factors may be more favourable for democracy. Its IPRI value is just above the lower limit of transition level. However, I expected a significant decrease in the level of democracy. It has not happened (see Chronicle1997).

IPR values predicted failures of democracy in these eight countries that were deviating democracies in 1993. In fact, democratic institutions collapsed in three of them as a consequence of violent coups, but Gambia and Niger were able to re-cross the threshold of democracy, whereas Comoros remained below the minimum criteria of democracy. Bangladesh, Nepal, and Solomon Islands are not completely deviating cases because their IPRI values are at the transition level. Benin has remained a surprisingly stable deviating African democracy since 1991. Senegal is only a slightly deviating democracy.

Let us next examine what has happended in the 35 nondemocracies of this category since 1993. **Afghanistan** and **Bhutan** are still without any elected government. Civil war continues in **Angola**. President Aliyev dominates in **Azerbaijan,** he was elected by 99 percent of the votes in 1993. **Belarus** is dominated by President Lukashenko, who was elected by 80 percent of the votes on July 10, 1994. Because IPRI value for Belarus is high enough for democratization, I predicted that democratic institutions will become stabilized in Belarus. It has not yet taken place. The privatization process has been slower than I expected. The process of democratization has started in **Burkina Faso**, but the country was not able to cross the minimum threshold of democracy in the National Assembly elections on May 11, 1997 (see Chronicle1997). Attempts of democratization failed in **Burundi**, in which a new military coup took place in July 1996 (see Banks et al. 1997). Politics in **Cambodia** has been so violent that the country cannot be regarded as a democracy, although new parliamentary elections were held on July 26, 1998 (Keesing's 1998, 42400-401). Before elections, in July 1997, the second prime minister Hun Sen had ousted the first prime minister Ranariddh by a coup d'etat (see Keesing's 1997, 41733-34). After many years of civil wars, **Chad** started the process of democratization by competitive presidential elections in 1996 and legislative elections in 1997, but it was not able to cross the Competition threshold of democracy (see Banks et al. 1997; Chronicle 1997). **Djibouti** has remained a nondemocracy. President Aptidon's party Popular Rally for Progress with the allied Front for the Restoration of Unity and Democracy won all the seats in the National Assembly elections in December 1997. **Equatorial Guinea** has remained below the threshold of democracy. President Obiang was re-elected in February 1996 by 98 percent of the votes (see Banks et al. 1997). In **Ethiopia**, the process of democratization is just beginning. The Ethiopian People's Revolutionary Democratic Front, dominated by the Tigre People's Liberation Front, won more than 90 percent of the seats in the legislative elections on May 7, 1995. Most opposition parties boycotted the elections.

Guinea crossed the threshold of democracy on June 11, 1995, with the legislative elections, in which the President's ruling Party for Unity and Progress was credited with 62 percent of the seats (Chronicle 1994-1995). President Lansana Conte himself had been elected in 1993 by 52 percent of the votes. So Guinea became a new deviating democracy. **Guinea-Bissau** entered into the category of democracies through competitive legislative elections on July 3, 1994. The ruling party's share of the seats decreased to 62 percent (see Banks et al. 1997; Chronicle 1994-1995). However, democracy in Guinea-Bissau collapsed in June1998 when some elements of the army rebelled and established a "transitional government". The rebellion continued throughout the summer 1998 (see Keesing's 1998, 42323, 42380-81, 42430). **Kazakhstan** remained below the threshold of democracy because of President Nazarbayev's dominant position. He obtained a 95 percent mandate for the extension of his presidential term to December 2000 by a referendum on April 29, 1995 (see Banks et al. 1997). **North Korea** has remained as a stable nondemocracy. In **Kyrgyzstan**, President Akayev was re-elected on December 24, 1995, by 71.6 percent of the votes (Banks et al. 1997). The country remained slightly below the threshold of democracy. Because of a slow process of privatization, economic power resources have remained concentrated in the hands of the government. The complete dominance of the Lao Patriotic Front continued in **Laos.** The process of democratization was started in **Liberia** through presidential and legislative elections in July 1997, but the country still remained below the threshold of democracy. The most successful warlord Charles Taylor won more than 70 percent of the votes cast in the presidential elections, and his National Patriotic Party got 76 percent of the seats in the legislative elections (Keesing's 1997, 41724; Chronicle 1997). **Malawi** succeeded to cross the threshold of democracy in May 1994 through presidential and legislative elections (see Banks et al. 1997; Chronicle 1993-1994). Since then it has remained a highly deviating democracy. Democratic institutions have been established in **Mali**, but the country is still below the threshold of democracy. President Konare was re-elected by 96 percent of the votes on May 11, 1997, and his party won 87 percent of the seats in the legislative elections in 1997 (Chronicle 1997; Keesing's 1997, 41626). Despite its low IPR value, **Mozambique** crossed the threshold of democracy in parliamentary and presidential elections in October 1994 (see Keesing's 1994, 40262) and has remained in the category of democracies since then. However, there have been political troubles, and the opposition boycotted the local elections (see Keesing's 1998, 42385). Democratic institutions function in **Namibia**, but the country is still in the category of nondemocracies because of the overwhelming dominance of President Nujoma and his party SWAPO (see Banks et al 1997). **Oman** is without any significant democratic institutions.

All attempts of democratization have until now failed in **Rwanda**, which was devastated by extreme ethnic violence in 1994. The Tutsi-dominated Rwandan Patriotic Front usurped power in July 1994. In **Sierra Leone**, a long period of military rule and civil wars ended in February 1996 when the country crossed the threshold of democracy in presidential and legislative elections (see Keesing's 1996, 40934). Sierra Leone became a new deviating democracy. However, a new military coup in May 1997 ended this experiment with democracy (Keesing's 1997, 41625). An intervention of Nigerian troops was needed to overthrow the military regime and to restore the civilian government (Keesing's 1998, 42048, 42113). **Somalia** has been without an effective national government since the overthrow of General Barre's government in January 1991. Civil war has continued in **Sudan**. No political parties were allowed to take part in presidential and parliamentary elections in March1996. Democratization has not yet succeeded in **Tajikistan**. Opposition boycotted both the presidential and parliamentary elections in 1994 and1995, and civil war continued. The first multiparty elections were held in **Tanzania** in October 1995, but the country remained slightly below the threshold of democracy. The ruling party's presidential cadidate Mkapa became elected by 61.8 percent of the valid votes, and the party (Revolutionary Party of Tanzania) garnered 80 percent of the elected seats of the National Assembly (see Banks et al. 1997; Chronicle 1995-1996). Politics has been violent in **Togo**, but the process of democratization started in1993 and 1994. President Eyadema became re-elected by 96 percent of the vote in August 1993, whereas his party won only 45 percent of the seats in the February 1994 parliamentary elections (Keesing's 1993, 39583; Chronicle 1993-1994). Togo remained slightly below the Competition threshold of democracy. Finally, in the June 1998 competitive presidential elections Togo crossed the threshold of democracy. President Eyadema won again, but his share of the votes decreased to 52 percent (Keesing's 1998, 42322). **Turkmenistan** is under a strong man government. President Niyazov's term was extended for an additional five years by referendum on January 15, 1994 (see Banks et al, 1997). The former military ruler, President Museveni, dominates politics in **Uganda**. He was popularly elected on May 9, 1996, by 74 percent of the votes. Political parties are not allowed to take part in elections. **Uzbekistan** is also below the threshold of democracy. President Karimov dominates politics, and the country has remained effectively a one-party state. **Vietnam** is still a one-party socialist country.

The review of the 43 countries of this category indicates that, from the perspective of democracy, most political systems in 1998 were basically the same as in 1993. Only one of the eight deviating democracies (Comoros) had ceased to be a democracy in 1998, although violent coups had interrupted the function of democratic institutions in two other countries, too. The other five countries contradicted the hypothesized decrease of the level of democratization throughout the period 1994-98. Of the 35 nondemocracies in 1993, 31 were nondemocracies in 1998, too. Their failures to cross the threshold of democracy support the hypothesis. However, four countries (Guinea, Malawi, Mosambique, and Togo) seem to have crossed the minimum criteria of democracy successfully. They became new deviating democracies. Thus 32 countries were nondemocracies as predicted in 1998 and 11 countries were, contrary to the hypothesis, democracies, although some of them were not deviating cases on the basis of their IPRI values.

3.2. Countries at the Transition Level of IPR

I did not predict democracy or nondemocracy for the 35 countries at the transition level of IPR. Because the level of resource distribution was high enough to support democratic politics, although not yet high enough to make democracy sure, both democracies and nondemocracies were expected to appear at this level of IPR. In fact, 17 of them were democracies and 18 nondemocracies in 1993. The even distribution of democracies and nondemocracies indicates that this transition level of IPR is indeed a watershed that separates democracies and nondemocracies from each other. It represents the level of resource distribution at which political systems usually become transformed from nondemocracies to democracies, or vice versa.

Let us see whether any significant changes in the nature of political systems have happened in the countries of this category since 1993. I shall focus on nondemocracies that crossed the threshold of democracy and on democracies that dropped to the category of nondemocracies.

Albania, Botswana, Bulgaria, Cameroon, Gabon, Honduras, India, Kenya, Madagascar, Papua New Guinea, Paraguay, Russia, Sao Tome and Principe, Ukraine, and Vanuatu (15) remained in the category of democracies, although several of them experienced serious political troubles and even temporary collapses of democratic institutions. **Albania** dropped temporarily below the threshold of democracy as a consequence of the irregular legislative elections in May and June 1996, in which the ruling Democratic Party of Albania won 87 percent of the seats (Chronicle 1995-1996). Violent demonstrations and a rebellion in the south followed (Keesing's 1997, 41451, 41504, 41556, 41596, 41653). Democratic institutions were re-established through new legislative elections in June and July 1997 (Keesing's 1997, 41703, 41747). Politics has been violent in **Cameroon**, **Gabon**, and **Kenya** in particular, but democratic institutions survived.

Brunei, Cape Verde, China, Côte d'Ivoire, Cuba, Guatemala, Haiti, Lesotho, Mauritania, Nigeria, Pakistan, Swaziland, United Arab Emirates, Yemen, Zaire, Zambia, and Zimbabwe (17) remained in the category of nondemocracies, although several of them approached the minimum thresholds of democracy. This concerns Cape Verde, Côte d'Ivoire, Guatemala, Haiti, Lesotho, Mauritania, Pakistan, Yemen, and Zambia in particular. **Guatemala** crossed the Competition threshold of democracy through competitive parliamentary elections in November 1995 and presidential elections in January 1996, but it still remained below the Participation threshold of democracy (15%) because of the extensive abstention rate (see Chronicle 1995-1996; Keesing's 1996, 40897). **Haiti** crossed the Participation threshold of democracy slightly in the parliamentary elections in September 1995 and in the presidential elections on December 17, 1995, but it remained below the Competition threshold (see Chronicle 1995-1996; Keesing's 1995, 40860). **Pakistan** was unable to cross the Participation threshold of democracy in the parliamentary elections on February 3, 1997 (see Chronicle 1997). **Yemen** slightly crossed the Competition threshold of democracy in the parliamentary elections on April 27, 1997, but because the House of Representatives had elected the president by a nearly unanimous vote in September 1994, Yemen remained in the category of nondemocracies. In **Zambia**, competitive presidential and legislative elections were held in November 1996, but the country was not able to cross either the Competition or Participation threshold of democracy (see Keesing's 1996, 41351).

In the **Central African Republic**, democratic institutions nearly collapsed as a consequence of an army rebellion in April 1996 and following fighting along regional-ethnic lines. French troops and a UN peacekeeping mission were needed to support the government (see Banks et al. 1997; Keesing's 1997, 41430, 41481; 1998: 42054, 42178). In **Congo**, democratic politics degenerated into ethnic civil war, too, and presidential elections were postponed. Finally, the former President Sassou-Nguesso, who was supported by rebel militiamen, usurped power on October 23,1997. Congo dropped below the threshold of democracy (see Banks etal. 1997; Keesing's 1997, 41723; 41800, 41848; 1998, 42054). **Moldova** crossed the threshold of democracy in the first multiparty parliamentary elections on February 27, 1994, and in the competitive presidential elections in 1996 (see Banks et al. 1997; Chronicle 1993-1994; Keesing's 1996, 41419).

Struggle for power has been intensive at the transition level of IPR, but drastic changes in the nature of political systems were few in the period 1994-98. The number of democracies decreased to 16 and the number of nondemocracies increased to 19.

3.3. Countries above the Transition Level of IPR

My general prediction for the countries above the transition level of IPR (6.3) was that they were expected to be or to become democracies. In fact, 76 of them were democracies as hypothesized and, contrary to the hypothesis, 18 of them were nondemocracies in 1993. I predicted democratization for the nondemocracies of this category because power resources seemed to be sufficiently widely distributed in those countries. Let us see what has happened in these 94 countries from the perspective of democracy.

All the 76 democracies of 1993 were still democracies in 1998. However, some of them are questionable cases. **Iran** is a questionable case for the reason that political parties are not allowed to take part in parliamentary elections, although both legislative elections in March and April 1996 and presidential elections in May 1997 were competitive (see Chronicle 1995-1996; Keesing's 1997, 41661). **Malaysia** is a questionable democracy for the reason that the ruling National Front won 84 percent of the seats in the May 1995 parliamentary elections, although its share of the votes was not more than 65 percent (Chronicle 1995-1996). The same concerns **Singapore**, in which the ruling People's Action Party won 97 percent of the seats in the January 1997 parliamentary elections, although its share of the votes was not more than 63.4 percent (Chronicle 1997). There are be grounds to regard these three countries as nondemocracies, although I have accepted them into the category of democracies.

Most of the 18 nondemocracies of 1993 remained nondemocracies throughout the period 1994-98, but some of them were able to cross the threshold of democracy, and there was popular pressure for democracy in nearly all of these countries. Let us examine each of them.

The struggle for democracy has been violent in **Algeria**, but in the competitive parliamentary elections of June 5, 1997, the country crossed the threshold of democracy clearly (Chronicle 1997). President Zeroual had been elected by competitive elections on November 16, 1995. He received 61 percent of the votes (Keesing's 1995, 40847). Democratization in Alegeria took place sooner than I had expected. I had stated in my book: "Algeria's IPR predicts democratization, but it may take a long time for competing groups to agree on a compromise" (Vanhanen 1997: 122). Competing groups have not yet agreed on a compromise, but democratic institutions were established. **Bahrain**, just like the other Arabic oil states — **Qatar** and **Saudi Arabia** — remained in the category of nondemocracies. I predicted democratization for these countries, but I assumed that democratization may be delayed by two or three decades because of the extreme concentration of economic resources in the hands of the ruling families. In the case of **Egypt**, I predicted that democratization will continue and that Egypt should cross the threshold of democracy very soon. The parliamentary elections in November and December 1995 were competitive, but the ruling party was able to capture 93 percent of the seats. President Mubarak had received 95 percent "yes" votes in the national referendum of October 4, 1993 (see Banks et al. 1997; Chronicle 1995-1996). The process of democratization has been slower than I expected. **Ghana** was another deviating nondemocracy to cross the threshold of democracy as predicted by its IPR value. In the presidential elections on December 7, 1996, Jerry Rawlings was elected by 57 percent of the votes, whereas his party, the National Democratic Congress, won 67 percent of the seats in the legislative elections at the same time (Chronicle 1995-1996; Keesing's 1996, 41400).

In **Indonesia**, the struggle for democracy has been violent. The country is still below the threshold of democracy, although President Suharto had to resign on May 29, 1998 (Keesing's 1998, 42274). I had predicted that "Indonesia will cross the threshold of democracy in the 1990s or in the first years of the next century" (Vanhanen 1997, 146). The presidential elections of November 1999 were an important step in this direction. **Iraq** is ruled autocratically by President Saddam Hussein. I noticed that a military regime has often been the last form of authoritarian rule before democratization and predicted that "the process of democratization will start in Iraq, too" (Vanhanen 1997, 122). Democratization has progressed slowly in **Jordan**. The supporters of King Hussein captured 85 percent of the seats in the legislative elections on September 1, 1997. According to my prediction, Jordan "will cross the threshold of democracy very soon" (Vanhanen 1997, 123). It has not yet happened. **Kuwait** crossed the Competition threshold of democracy in its parliamentary elections on October 7, 1996, but its extremely limited franchise and the concentration of executive power in the hands of the

Emir keeps it below the threshold of democracy (see Chronicle 1995-1996; Banks et al. 1997). Besides, the exceptional structure of Kuwait's population inhibits democratization. Non-Kuwaiti immigrants constitute a large majority of the population. **Libya** has been ruled by Colonel Qadhafi since the military coup d'etat in 1969. Because economic and coercive power resources are highly concentrated in the hands of the government, I hesitated to predict democratization, but I predicted that popular pressure for democracy will increase in Libya, too. **Maldives** is a problematic case for the reason that economic power resources may be much more highly concentrated than my indicators show. In other words, I am not sure whether Maldives belongs to this IPR category (see Vanhanen 1997, 142-43).

Morocco has approached the threshold of democracy, but it has not yet crossed it because of the dominant position of the king (concurrent powers). In the parliamentary elections of1997, Morocco crossed the Competition threshold but remained slightly below the Participation threshold (see Chronicle 1997). I predicted that "Morocco will cross the threshold of democracy soon" (Vanhanen 1997: 124). Morocco would need a transition to a truly parliamentary system. **Myanmar** (Burma) is a clearly deviating nondemocracy ruled by a military government. The popular pressure for democratization has continued several years in Burma. My prediction was that the struggle for democracy will continue and that attempts will be made to cross the threshold of democracy in the near future. **South Africa** crossed the threshold of democracy and ceased to be a deviating case in 1994 when the first non-racial parliamentary elections were held in April (see Chronicle 1993-1994). There have been partly competitive legislative elections in **Syria**, but because there has not been real competition in presidential elections, the country is still below the Competition threshold of democracy. I predicted that Syria "will be among the first Arab countries to democratize" (Vanhanen 1997: 124). It will be interesting to see whether it really happens. **Taiwan (ROC)** was the most highly deviating nondemocracy in 1993. On the basis of its very high IPR value, I predicted that "Taiwan will cross the threshold of democracy in the 1990s" (Vanhanen 1997, 148). It happened through the first direct presidential election on March 23, 1996 (see Keesing's 1996, 40996; Banks et al. 1997). I predicted democratization in **Tunisia** because the level of explanatory variables was sufficiently high, but until now only small steps toward democratization have been taken.

The review of deviating nondemocracies indicates that Algeria, Ghana, South Africa, and Taiwan were able to cross the threshold of democracy in the period 1994-98. So the number of deviating nondemocracies decreased from 18 to 14. Of these 14 countries, the status of Maldives as a deviating nondemocracy is questionable for the reason that its IPR value may be too high. Egypt, Indonesia, Jordan, Kuwait, Morocco, and Syria have some democratic institutions. Indonesia may be the next country to democratize. The seven other countries — Bahrain, Iraq, Libya, Myanmar (Burma), Qatar, Saudi Arabia, and Tunisia — constitute the group of the most entrenched deviating nondemocracies. It is remarkable that six of them are Arab countries. It may be that my explanatory variables do not take into account some regional factors that inhibit democratization in Islamic Arab countries.

3.4. Democracy in Former Socialist Countries

My comparison group includes 25 former socialist countries of East and East-Central Europe and Central Asia. Seven of them (Azerbaijan, Belarus, Kazakhstan, Kyrgyzstan,

Tajikistan, Turkmenistan, and Uzbekistan) are in the IPR category below 3.3 index points, five others (Albania, Bulgaria, Moldova, Russia, and Ukraine) at the transition level of IPR, and 13 (Armenia, Croatia, Czech Republic, Estonia, Georgia, Hungary, Latvia, Lithuania, Macedonia, Poland, Romania, Slovenia, and Yugoslavia) in the IPR category above 6.3 index points. These former socialist countries are not especially problematic from the perspective of my predictions. All seven countries below the transition level of IPR were nondemocracies as hypothesized and still are. Four of the five countries at the transition level of IPR were democracies and one nondemocracy (Moldova) in 1993. Now Moldova has also entered into the category of democracies. All 13 countries above the transition level of IPR were democracies as hypothesized.

According to my theoretical interpretation, the differences in IPR values explain why some of these countries are still nondemocracies and why most of them have successfully crossed the threshold of democracy. Low IPR values indicate that some crucial power resources are still highly concentrated. The values of the first four explanatory variables (Urban Population, Non-agricultural population, Literates, and Students) do not differ greatly from country to country, whereas there are significant differences in the estimated values of the last two variables indicating the distribution of economic resources (Family Farms and the degree of decentralization of non-agricultural economic resources). According to my estimations based on available information, agricultural and non-agricultural economic power resources are still much more highly concentrated in the hands of the governments in the new Central Asian states and in Azerbaijan and Belarus than in the other former socialist countries. Therefore the IPR values for these countries are low. The concentration of economic power resources supports the survival of authoritarian political systems.

A problem is that the level of democratization in 1993 was for many democratized countries much higher than expected on the basis of IPR. Large positive residuals indicate imbalance between the level of democratization and the degree of resource distribution. The highest positive residuals (over 15.0 index points) were for Bulgaria, Russia, Ukraine, Croatia, the Czech Republic, Hungary, Romania, and Slovenia). Large positive residuals predict decrease in the level of democratization. However, it may be that a better balance has been achieved in many of these countries since 1993 as a consequence of privatization programs, which have dismantled state monopolies and distributed agricultural and non-agricultural economic resources to private persons and companies as well as to local governments. It is reasonable to assume that the same trend of economic reforms continues in most of these countries. Therefore, I come to the conclusion that the established democratic systems have good chances to survive in former socialist countries.

4. Conclusion

This review of political developments since 1993 implies that I do not have any special reasons to change the predictions made on the basis of the situation in 1993. Most of the countries have remained democracies or nondemocracies as expected on the basis of their IPR values in the beginning of the 1990s. However, only some of the predictions concerning deviating cases have become confirmed until now. The number of deviating democracies has, in fact, increased by three to 11, whereas the number of deviating nondemocracies has decreased by four to 14. Some local factors affecting the degree of resource distribution that are not taken into account in my explanatory variables probably explain a part of the unexplained variation and of the appearance of deviating cases. The existence of persistent deviating cases indicates that my explanatory variables are not equally relevant for all countries. Their explanatory power seems to be, however, sufficient to produce approximately correct predictions on the chances of democracy in most countries across all cultural and other boundaries.

References

Arat, Zehra F. 1991. Democracy and Human Rights in Developing Countries. Boulder and London: Lynne Rienner Publishers.

Banks, Arthur S., Alan J. Day, and Thomas C. Muller, eds. 1997. Political Handbook of the World 1997. Binghamton, New York: CSA Publication.

Berg-Schlosser, Dirk, and Gisele DeMeur. 1994. "Conditions of Democracy in Interwar Europe: A Boolean Test of Major Hypotheses." Comparative Politics 26, 3: 253-79.

Chronicle of Parliamentary Elections. 1993-1997. Geneva: Inter-Parliamentary Union.

Dahl, Robert A. 1971. Polyarchy: Participation and Opposition. New Haven and London: Yale University Press.

Dahl, Robert A. 1989. Democracy and its Critics. New Haven and London: Yale University Press.

Diamond, Larry. 1992. "Economic Development and Democracy Reconsidered." In Reexamining Democracy: Essays in Honor of Seymour Martin Lipset, ed. Gary Marks and Larry Diamond. Newbury Park: Sage Publications.

Diamond, Larry, and Gary Marks. 1992. "Seymour Martin Lipset and the Study of Democracy." In Reexamining Democracy: Essays in Honor of Seymour Martin Lipset, ed. Gary Marks and Larry Diamond. Newbury Park: Sage Publications.

Diamond, Larry, Juan J. Linz, and Seymour Martin Lipset, eds. 1990. Politics in Developing Countries: Comparing Experiences with Democracy. Boulder, Colorado: Lynne Rienner Publishers.

Freedom House. 1991. Freedom in the world: Political rights and liberties 1990-91. New York: Freedom House.

Freedom House. 1992. Freedom in the World 1991-1992: Political Rights & Civil Liberties. New York: Freedom House.

Hadenius, Axel. 1992. Democracy and Development. Cambridge: Cambridge University Press.

Held, David, ed. 1993. Prospects for Democracy: North, South, East, West. Cambridge: Polity Press.

Huntington, Samuel P. 1991. The Third Wave: Democratization in the Late Twentieth Century. Norman and London: University of Oklahoma Press.

Huntington, Samuel P. 1996. "Democracy for the Long Haul." Journal of Democracy 7, 2: 3-13.

Huntington, Samuel P. 1997. "After Twenty Years: The Future of the Third Wave." Journal of Democracy 8, 4: 3-12.

Keesing's Record of World Events. 1994-1998.

Kornhauser, William. [1959]1965. The Politics of Mass Society. London: Routledge and Kegan Paul.

Lane, Jan-Erik, and Svante Ersson. 1994. Comparative Politics: An Introduction and New Approach. Cambridge: Polity Press.

Lerner, Daniel [1958]1964. The Passing of Traditional Society: Modernizing the Middle East. New York: The Free Press.

Lipset, S. M. 1959. "Some Social Requisites of Democracy: Economic Development and Political Legitimacy." American Political Science Review 53, 1: 69-105.

Lipset, S. M. 1983. Political Man: The Social Bases of Politics. Expanded Edition. London: Heineman.

Lipset, S. M. 1994. "The Social Requisites of Democracy Revisited." American Sociological Review 59, February: 1-22.

Lipset, S. M., Kyoung-Ryung Seong, and John Charles Torres. 1993. "A Comparative Analysis of the Social Requisites of Democracy." International Social Science Journal 136, May: 155-75.

Midlarsky, Manus I. 1997. Inequality, Democracy, and Economic Development. Cambridge: Cambridge University Press.

Olson, Mancur. 1993. "Dictatorship, Democracy, and Development." American Political Science Review 87, 3: 567-76.

Parry, Geraint, and Michael Moran, eds. 1994. Democracy and Democratization. London and New York: Routledge.

Pinkney, Robert. 1993. Democracy in the Third World. Buckingham: Open University Press.

Rueschemeyer, Dietrich, Evelyne Hubert Stephens, and John D. Stephens. 1992. Capitalist Development and Democracy. Cambridge: Polity Press.

Sorensen, Georg. 1993. Democracy and Democratization: Processes and Prospects in a Changing Western World. Boulder: Westview Press.
UNDP (United Nations Development Programme) 1991. Human Development Report 1991. New York: Oxford University Press.
UNDP 1993. Human Development Report 1993. New York: Oxford University Press.
Vanhanen, Tatu. 1990. The Process of Democratization: A Comparative Study of 147 States, 1980—88. New York: Crane Russak.
UNDP 1992. On the Evolutionary Roots of Politics. New Delhi: Sterling Publishers.
UNDP 1993. "Construction and Use of an Index of Democracy." In Monitoring Social Progress in the 1990s, ed. David G. Westendorff and Dharam Ghai. Aldershot: Avebury.
UNDP. 1997. Prospects of Democracy: A Study of 172 States. London and New York: Routledge.
Wittfogel, Karl A. [1957]1963. Oriental Despotism: A Comparative Study of Total Power. New Haven and London: Yale University Press.
World Bank. 1993. World Development Report 1993. New York: Oxford University Press.

II. CASE STUDIES

Prospects of Russian Democracy: A Cross-Regional Application of Vanhanen's Resource Distribution Theory of Democratization

CHRISTOPHER MARSH

1. Introduction

The subject of Russian democratic development is one of the most contentious issues in international affairs today. Some scholars are optimistic about the prospects of Russian democracy, and maintain that Russia is becoming more democratic or that there has been a "rebirth" of Russian democracy (Petro 1995). Others, however, contend that the prospects for democracy in Russia are dismal (Putnam 1993, 183) and even go so far as to conclude that "democratization in Russia will fail" (Eckstein, et al. 1998, 377). While these studies merit serious scholarly attention, the many differences in the theories used and the evidence presented leaves one wondering which assessment is most accurate and what in fact are the prospects for democracy in Russia.

One scholar who predicts "that a democratic system will survive in Russia" is Tatu Vanhanen (1997, 111). Vanhanen reaches this conclusion based on his resource distribution theory of democratization, which, briefly stated, posits that as resources within a society become more widely distributed power becomes dispersed as well, resulting in an increased likelihood that the society will develop and maintain a democratic political system. Analyzing a large number of countries over a period of centuries, Vanhanen has shown that his theory is both rigorous and has a great deal of explanatory power (see the previous chapter)

While Vanhanen's analysis focused on individual countries in order to determine their prospects for democracy, since his model is composed of simple and readily-available indicators, such an analysis can also be conducted using sub-state units. In the hope of generating a more in-depth account of the process of democratic development underway in the Russian Federation, I develop here an Index of Power Resources and an Index of Democratization modeled after the ones used by Vanhanen and analyze Russian democratic development from a cross-regional perspective. Such an analysis is useful in exploring and identifying regional variations in both levels of democracy and the distribution of power resources. Just as certain countries are better suited to develop democratic polities than others, I suspect that so too may regions within a single country be similarly situated. Indeed, if Putnam's (1993) cross-regional analysis of Italy has shown us anything it is that great variation can exist within a single country and that this can have significant implications for democratic development. A cross-regional analysis of Russian democratization should therefore alert us to important factors that national-level studies may overlook.

2. A Cross-Regional Application of Vanhanen's Resource Distribution Theory of Democratization

In his analysis Vanhanen reaches an optimistic conclusion regarding the propitious conditions for democracy in Russia. Although this study was published in 1997, the data Vanhanen employed are often from several years earlier. In the case of Russia, the 1990 and 1993 parliamentary and the 1991 presidential elections were used. Of course, we now have at our disposal more recent elections. For instance, the 1990 elections to the Congress of Peoples' Deputies can be discarded and replaced by the 1995 Duma elections. Likewise, the 1996 presidential election can be used in place of the Soviet-era election of 1991. In addition to simply applying the Vanhanen model in a cross-regional analysis, therefore, I also employ more current data sources, which should give us more confidence in the findings.

One of the most effective means of evaluating a country as large and diverse as the Russian Federation is by analyzing the variation among its constituent units. Russia proves a most suitable environment for such a cross-regional approach for several reasons. For one, it is the largest country in the world, and several of its regions are as large as countries themselves. Moreover, the number of political regions is large enough to provide reliable statistical findings. Secondly, the regions are quite diverse in several regards, such as language, ethnicity, culture, religion, geography, demography, and economic performance. Finally, despite the great diversity among Russia's regions, they are the primary political and administrative units of the Russian Federation, which means that the political behavior of the populace can be accurately gauged through voting statistics from national and regional elections.

The Russian Federation is comprised of eighty-nine political-administrative units, properly known as the "subjects of the Federation". They comprise twenty-one republics, six krais, forty-nine oblasts, two administratively-autonomous cities (Moscow and St. Petersburg), and eleven autonomous areas (ten autonomous okrugs and the Jewish Autonomous Oblast). Despite the significant differences between these units, they are generally referred to collectively as Russia's regions.

Although I am not here concerned with measuring the many correlates of democracy in Russia (see Marsh 1999 for such an analysis), I believe that Vanhanen's Resource Distribution Theory of Democratization can be useful in exploring the process of democratic development within a single country. In order to apply Vanhanen's model in a cross-regional analysis of Russian democratization, his Index of Power Resources and Index of Democratization must each be replicated on the regional level of analysis. Following that, the relationship between the distribution of power resources and the process of democratization can be explored by analyzing the quantitative association between the two indices.

2.1. Index of Power Resources

Following the method of creating the Index of Power Resources (IPR) developed by Vanhanen, I construct a similar index on the regional level of analysis using equivalent indicators. Not all statistics are available on the regional level, however, forcing me to select what I hope are comparable indicators for two of the variables. While this means that this study is not a precise replication of Vanhanen's model, the variables used do still permit us to conduct a meaningful analysis.

Below are the six indicators used by Vanhanen to measure the relative distribution of power resources. The first three (urban population, non-agricultural population, and students in higher education) can be replicated without any problem. While Vanhanen looked at literacy rates in each of the countries under study (indicator 4), since Russia has near universal literacy and there is no statistically significant variation among the regions on this measure, I have chosen to disregard this variable.

(1) The urban population as a percentage of the total population.

(2) The non-agricultural population as a percentage of the total population.

(3) The number of students in universities and equivalent degree-granting institutions per 100,000 inhabitants.

(4) The literate population as a percentage of the adult population.

(5) The area of family farms as a percentage of the total area of holdings.

(6) The degree of decentralization of non-agricultural economic resources.

The family farms variable presents us with a problem. Where Vanhanen considered the area of family farms as a percentage of the total area of holdings, there is no comparable statistic on the regional level of analysis. Information is available, however, on the number of farms in each region. By dividing the number of farms in each region by its population, I arrive at the per capita number of farms. This variable should be a good measure of the relative distribution of family farms, since the larger the number of farms per capita, the more widely distributed are power resources. While I use this variable in the analysis here, there are potential problems with using figures from Russian agricultural statistics, since there is no clear consensus on the degree to which agricultural land has been privatized. While one source declared back in 1994 that 90 percent of all agricultural land was no longer government owned (*Delovoy Mir*, April 2, 1994, 1), another source recently stated that over 90 percent of cultivated land is still in the hands of state and collective farms (Remington 1999, 141). If agricultural resources are still largely in state hands, it would be problematic to search for the distribution of such resources.

Finally, where Vanhanen used the degree of decentralization of non-agricultural economic resources, this variable can be rather closely replicated by considering the volume of non-governmental industrial production. This indicator taps into that segment of economic production which is relatively free from state intervention and thus serves as an alternative power resource.

Once these independent variables are calculated, they can be combined into an Index of Power Resources (IPR)[1] which measures the degree of dispersion of resources. Figure 1

Figure 1

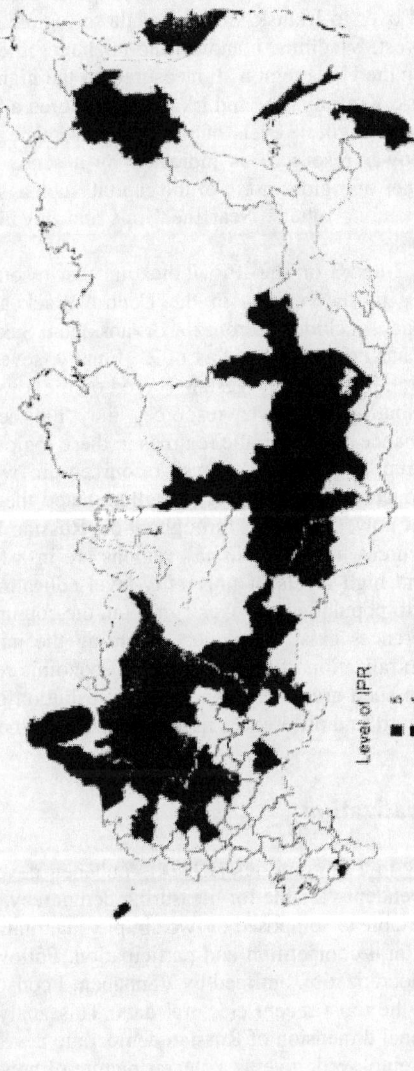

illustrates the levels of IPR in Russia's regions on a 5-point scale, with 5 representing the greatest dispersion of power resources and 1 representing its relative concentration. As the figure makes clear, there is great disparity in the distribution of power resources throughout the Russian Federation.

The regions in which power resources are most widely dispersed appear to be situated north of Moscow and, following an eastward path, across the Urals region through Krasnoyarsk and over to Irkutsk. Several of these regions, such as Murmansk and Karelia in the northwest, Vladimir, Ivanovo, and Nizhegorod east of Moscow, and Sverdlovsk and Tiumen in the Urals region all measured on the highest level of the IPR. In southern Siberia, Tomsk, Krasnoyarsk, and Irkutsk also scored a 5.

While not scoring on the highest levels of the IPR, several regions also appear to have widely dispersed power resources as indicated by a score of 4. This includes Moscow and a large number of regions north of the capital, such as Arkhangelsk, Komi, Vologda, and Kostroma, among others. Near the Urals and beyond, Chelyabinsk and Novosibirsk also scored a 4.

Regions which scored 2 and 3 on the IPR, indicating that resources are not widely dispersed, included many of the regions in the Central-Blackearth area, the north Caucasus, and Siberia. These included Voronezh, Bryansk, and Sakha with scores of 3, and Smolensk, Tambov, and Penza with scores of 2. Finally, several regions, such as the Altai Republic and Krai, Tyva, and Dagestan, scored on the lowest level of the IPR, indicating that the distribution of power resources may not be conducive to the establishment and maintenance of democratic regimes in these regions.

As Vanhanen discovered in his study, power resources are widely distributed in Russia. The analysis conducted here, however, has illuminated the great disparity that exists in the distribution of power resources throughout the Russian Federation. In terms of intellectual power resources, most of Russia's regions are in a favorable condition, with universal literacy and high levels of university-level education. While Russia is home to over ten cities with populations of over 1 million, the country as a whole is still largely rural. Great differences exist, moreover, regarding the number of farms per capita, the degree of decentralization of non-agricultural economic resources, and levels of industrialization. Given such great variation in the distribution of power resources, therefore, we would expect to find differences in the success of democracy to take root.

2.2. Index of Democratization

In his study of democracy in 172 countries (1997), Vanhanen develops an interesting and widely-applicable dependent variable for measuring democracy, called the Index of Democratization. This variable is composed of two simple quantitative indicators based on a polity's level of electoral competition and participation. Following the method of creating the Index of Democratization outlined by Vanhanen, I construct my own Index of Democratization using the most recent electoral data. This analysis should provide more insight into the regional dimension of Russian democratic development and, given the more current elections employed, give us a clearer picture of how Russia is faring in the process of democratic consolidation.

The first indicator used in the Index of Democratization is based on electoral participation. More specifically, this variable employs turnout rates for national elections such as presidential and parliamentary elections. These turnout rates, however, are taken as a percentage of the total population, not simply the registered voting population, as is commonly the case. Vanhanen explains that this figure is necessary to eliminate the possibility that countries with a small voter franchise but large turnout rates of those eligible will appear to be highly democratic (1997, 36). However, since I am here dealing with one country in which there is universal adult suffrage, such a device is not necessary. The elections used here are the 1996 presidential election, with the turnout rates for the first and second rounds of the election averaged together, and the 1995 Duma elections. The two components are averaged together to create the participation indicator.

The competition indicator is also composed of two components, one each for the degree of competition in presidential and parliamentary elections. To determine the level of presidential competition, the percent of votes for the winner of the 1996 Russian Presidential election (Boris N. Yeltsin) is subtracted from 100. To determine the level of parliamentary competition, the percent of votes for the party to win the most seats in the 1995 Duma elections is also subtracted from 100. Since the overwhelming majority of the 225 single-member district seats were contested by independents (*Tsentral'naya Izbiratel'naya Komissia Rossiiskoi Federatsii* [TsIK] 1996, 145), it made sense to simply disregard these seats and only consider the results from the contests for the 225 party-list seats.

Once these two components are calculated, they are then weighted and combined. Since the Russian Federation is a strong presidential system, the presidential competition component is weighted 75 percent while the parliamentary competition component is weighted 25 percent. This is done according to Vanhanen, who employed three different methods of weighting the components depending on the classification of the system (parliamentary dominance: 75 percent parliamentary competition and 25 percent presidential competition; presidential dominance: 75 percent presidential competition and 25 percent parliamentary competition; and 50/50 for concurrent powers). While Vanhanen classified Russia as a concurrent powers state in his study, the Russian Federation has clearly proven itself to be one of presidential dominance since that time (he used the 1991 presidential election and the 1990 and 1993 parliamentary elections), and therefore emphasis is placed here on the presidential component of the competition variable.

Vanhanen establishes minimum thresholds of democracy, above which states are likely to maintain democratic systems and below which the prospects of democracy are dim (Vanhanen 1997, 41). In terms of the level of competition, Vanhanen gives a minimum threshold of 30 percent. While Ingushetia just barely surpasses this minimum with 31.62 percent, most regions have no difficulty meeting this threshold, with an average of 54.05 and a maximum of 67.87 in the Chuvash Republic. Vanhanen sets the minimum threshold for participation at 15 percent of the total population. While the figure I use is the percentage of the eligible voting population, which would reduce this threshold to 11 percent, even the region with the lowest turnout, Khanty-Mansi, easily exceeds this threshold with a turnout of over 58 percent. When considering the levels of electoral competition and participation, therefore, all of Russia's regions seem to be in a reasonably good position, although some are more favorably endowed than others.

The participation and competition indicators are combined to create the Index of democratization by multiplying the two variables and dividing the product by 100. This equal weighting, of course, assumes that one variable is no more important an element of democracy than the other. This method of combining the two is also useful since the Index will result in "high values only if values of both basic indicators are high. If either of them is zero, the value of ID will also drop to zero"(Vanhanen 1997, 35). The result is an unbiased indicator of the level of democracy that can be used in any political unit for which there are the necessary electoral data.

Once created, the Index of Democratization can be applied to Russia's regions to determine the levels of democracy on the sub-national level.[2] As seen in Figure 2, many of Russia's regions score high on the Index of democratization. Regions which measured the highest on the 5-point scale, such as Voronezh, Belgorod, and Kursk, seem well poised to consolidate democratic rule. Many other regions also seem to be well situated, scoring on the 4th level. This includes Tver, Kaluga, and Tula, along with Amur and Chita in southern Siberia. Finally, regions such as Sakha, Pskov, and Yaroslavl, while not among the highest ranking regions, seem to have a substantial democratic base. Regions such as Yamalo-Nenets, Khanty-Mansi, and even the Leningrad and Moscow Oblasts, however, scored on the two lowest levels of democracy (1 and 2). Based on the Index of Democratization, these regions do not seem to be in a good position to consolidate democratic rule. Moreover, given that Russia's capital fell into this category, this could have negative repercussions for the rest of the country.

What is most surprising about these findings is that the regions which are typically referred to as the most democratic, such as Moscow, St. Petersburg, and Novgorod,[3] are among the lowest ranking regions, while regions such as Voronezh, Tambov, and Smolensk, which are bastions of local Communism, are ranked as the most democratic. How can this very counter-intuitive finding be reconciled with what we know about contemporary Russian politics? Perhaps what is typically thought of as 'democratic' is not what democracy in Russia means after all? These questions are of critical importance, but before we explore these issues, we must first examine the relationship between the Index of Power Resources and the Index of Democratization.

3. Distribution of Power Resources and Democratization in Russia's Regions

There are several ways we can examine the relationship between the distribution of power resources and democratization using the indices developed above. The first and simplest method is to correlate the indices and measure the strength of the relationship between the two. This will allow us to determine whether or not a statistically significant relationship exists, the strength of the relationship, and if the indices are positively or negatively correlated with each other.

The bivariate correlation between the Index of Democratization and the Index of Power Resources is strong and statistically significant (r = -.500, p = .000), albeit negative. This means that indicators which in other environments have been positively correlated with democracy are actually inversely related to the same measures of democracy in post-Communist Russia. This can be explained in two ways: 1) the theory does not hold for post-Communist Russia; and/or 2) the variables used here might not be good indicators of the theory under consideration. Before we explore the likelihood of each explanation, more in-depth analysis of this quantitative relationship is necessary.

Figure 2

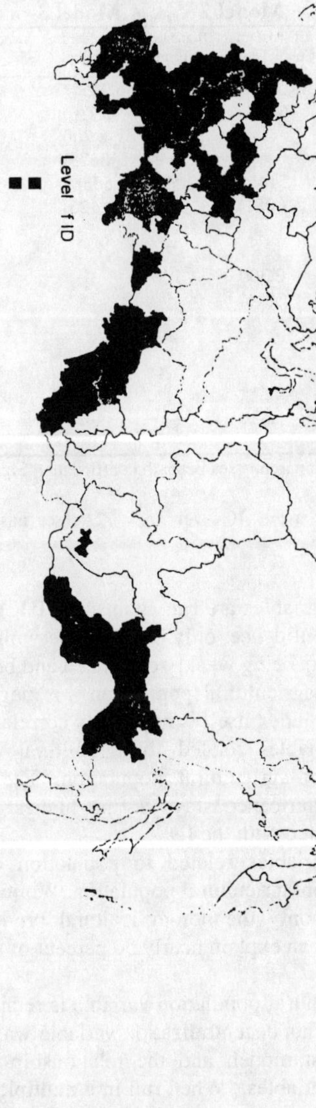

Since there are many indicators that compose the IPR, it may be useful to identify which sets of independent variables may be better predictors of the Index of Democratization. This is very important in this case, since not all of the independent variables are likely to be negatively correlated with the dependent variable.

Table 1. ***Regression Models of Power Resource Indicators Predicting the Index of Democratization***

	Model 1		Model 2		Model 3		Model 4	
Independent Predictors	Unstandard Coefficients	Standard Coefficients	Unstandard Coefficients	Standard Coefficients	Unstandard Coefficients	Standard Coefficients	Unstandard Coefficients	Standard Coefficients
Constant	74.198** (9.424)		85.509** (6.471)		86.945** (7.216)		79.560** (6.850)	
Urban Population	-3.900 (.079)	-.079			-8.200 (.073)	-.017		
Non-Agricult. Pop.	-.472** (.130)	-.558	-.514** (.081)	-.598	-.573** (.126)	-.672	-.589** (.070)	-.691
College Students	3.200 (.010)	.028						
Per Capita Farms	-2.000 (.016)	-.120	-2.300 (.016)	-.138				
Decentralization	.111 (.055)	.192					9.600* (.041)	.189
R-square	.455**		.436**		.470**		.505**	
R-square adj.	.414		.420		.455		.492	

Note: Standard errors are given in parentheses beneath coefficients. Significance levels are: * $p < .05$;
** $p < .01$; ^ moderately significant at the .10 level. $n = 72$ (cases missing data were excluded).

In model 1, all of the independent variables are run against the ID. While the model is significant at the highest levels of confidence, only one variable within the model itself is significant, with the other predictors being weakly correlated and beyond the .10 level of confidence. This variable - non-agricultural population - is negatively correlated, which goes far in explaining why the index itself is negatively correlated with the ID.

In model 2, only the two variables related to agricultural characteristics are considered - family farms and non-agricultural population. The model's strength decreases somewhat, while the significance stays at the highest level. These two variables are again negatively correlated with the ID.

In the third model, the two variables related to population characteristics are considered - urban population and non-agricultural population. While both variables are negatively correlated with the ID, only the non-agricultural production variable is significantly correlated. This model can explain nearly 50 percent of the variation in the dependent variable.

In the final model, the non-agricultural population variable is retained and run along with the decentralization variable. This decentralization variable was only weakly and insignificantly correlated in the first model, and the relationship was positive, not negative as with most of the other variables. When run in a multiple regression model along with non-agricultural population, however, this variable becomes significant on the .05 level of confidence and is again positively correlated with the dependent variable. Despite this positive relationship, as identified by the beta coefficient, these two independent variables together can explain over 50 percent of the variation in the level of democratization. This is the most robust multiple regression model identified here.

This decentralization variable is also probably the most reliable indicator of Vanhanen's theory of resource distribution used in this study. Given the nature of post-Communist privatization and economic liberalization, the volume of industrial production produced in the fledgling private sector is an important indicator of the creation of an independent sphere within the Russian economy. As it expands, the resource distribution theory of democratization would have us believe that the chances for democratic consolidation in Russia will improve.

While the multiple regression models analyzed above indicate that there exists a negative relationship between the IPR and the ID, the decentralization variable was the only variable that was significantly positively correlated with the ID within a model (model 4). When run in a simple bivariate correlation against the ID, the decentralization variable proves to be a powerful predictor of the levels of democratization in Russia's regions (r = .341, p = .001). What is most theoretically relevant, however, is that it is *positively* correlated with the ID. The positive correlation of this variable with the ID supports the resource distribution theory of democratization and, given the importance of this variable as discussed above, bodes well for the consolidation of Russian democracy.

Why is it that some of the independent variables used here are negatively correlated with the Index of Democratization, while other variables were not significantly correlated or, as with the decentralization variable, are positively correlated? The finding that several variables were not significantly correlated with the ID must not come as a surprise. This model was developed to measure the hypothetical distribution of power resources in a great variety of political and cultural environments. It can be expected, therefore, that different sets of independent variables will be the most powerful explanatory factors in different countries. Together, however, all of the variables get at the underlying concept of resource distribution.

The consistently negative relationship identified between the non-agricultural population variable and the ID is rather surprising. That this indicator, which proved to be the most powerful explanatory variable used here, was actually negatively correlated with the Index of Democratization, leads to suspect the validity of the theory under consideration. How is it that the most powerful independent variable in a model used to predict levels of democratization actually turns out to be a powerful predictor of a *lack* of democracy?

An answer to this question is perhaps found in the variable itself. The non-agricultural population variable, of course, measures Russia's industrialized areas. It is precisely these areas which have faced some of the most difficult times of the transition period. Many of these industrial areas are far from Moscow and St. Petersburg, where the positive aspects of the transition have largely remained. Instead, the industrial areas have experienced a drastic reduction in industrial output following the Soviet Union's collapse, a reduced standard of living, and have suffered from the failure of large industrial enterprises to pay wages. Given such circumstances, it is not surprising to find low levels of electoral participation or radicalized politics as represented by low levels of electoral competition. These facts go far in explaining low levels of the Index of Democratization found in these regions.

In contrast to the dim picture drawn by this segment of Russian society, the emerging private sector seems to provide a more optimistic future. As the strong correlation between the decentralization variable and the ID indicates, those areas in which economic power is more widely distributed tend to be more democratic. As Russia's transition to democracy and the free market continues, this relationship should provide a firm basis for political stability and the eventual consolidation of Russian democracy.

4. Conclusion

What can be concluded from this cross-regional application of Vanhanen's resource distribution theory of democratization? First, although power resources are widely distributed in Russia as a whole, there exists great disparity in the degree to which such resources are dispersed throughout Russia's regions. While Russia itself is favorably situated to maintain a democratic regime, therefore, the prospects for democratic rule in many of Russia's regions is still in question. Secondly, Vanhanen's Index of Democratization, although developed to measure democracy in cross-national studies, has proven useful in examining regional patterns of democratization within a single country. This helped us identify regions which are well positioned to consolidate democratic rule as well as those that may experience marked difficulties in making the transition to democracy.

The most surprising finding of this study, however, was the negative relationship identified between the Index of Power Resources and the Index of Democratization. This finding does not imply that the theory and model are invalid. It is simply attributable to the fact that the model was developed to test the distribution of power resources and levels of democratization in a great variety of political systems. When attempting to apply this model to a post-Communist environment, therefore, the impact that the country's history and individual characteristics might have on its utility and action must be taken into consideration. The negative relationship can thus be explained by the fact that Russia's industrial regions have been hard hit by the transition to the free market, and therefore behave quite differently from their counterparts in newly-industrializing countries, where such regions are breeding grounds for economic and political liberalism.

One key finding in this study does support Vanhanen's theory. In the regions which have been most successful in making the transition to the free market, as evidenced by the high levels of non-governmental industrial production, there is a positive relationship between the distribution of power resources and democratization. While many scholars have identified the pivotal role being played by the economy in Russian political development, the analysis conducted here has highlighted the dynamics involved in both the troubled industrial sector and the nascent private economy. This results in the theoretically-informed conclusion that, as the private economy expands and power resources in the private sphere become more widely distributed, the prospects for democracy in Russia will increase as well.

Notes

1 The scores for the Index of Power Resources ranged from -12 to 3.33. The scale developed is as follows: Level 1: -12.00 to -1.99; Level 2: -2.00 to -0.76; Level 3: -0.75 to 0.74; Level 4: 0.75 to 1.99; Level 5: 2.00 to 3.33.

2 The scores for the Index of Democratization ranged from 21.39 to 49.04. The scale developed is as follows: Level 1: 20 to 25.99; Level 2: 26 to 31.99; Level 3: 32 to 37.99; Level 4: 38 to 43.99; Level 5: 44 to 50.

3 For a study addressing the democratic attributes of Novgorod, see Nicolai Petro, *The Novgorod Region: A Russian Success Story* (Washington, D.C.: National Council for Eurasian and East European Research, 1999).

References

Berg-Schlosser, Dirk. 1993. "Democratization in Africa - Conditions and Prospects", paper presented at the ECPR Joint Sessions of Workshops, April 2-8, Leiden.

Bollen, Kenneth. 1980. "Issues in the Comparative Measurement of Political Democracy," *American Sociological Review,* 45:370-90.

Bollen, Kenneth. 1979. "Political Democracy and the Timing of Development," *American Sociological Review,* 44:572-87.

Coleman, James. 1960. "Conclusion: The Political Systems of the Developing Areas," in Gabriel Almond and James Coleman, eds., The Politics of the Developing Areas (Princeton, NJ: Princeton University Press).

Craumer, Peter. 1994. "Regional Patterns of Agricultural Reform In Russia," *Post-Soviet Geography,* 35:329-351.

Cutright, P. 1963. "National Political Development: Measurement and Analysis," *American Sociological Review,* 28:253-64.

Dahl, Robert. 1971. Polyarchy: Participation and Opposition. New Haven: Yale University Press.

Eckstein, Harry, Frederic Fleron, Jr., Erik Hoffmann, and William Reisinger. 1998. Can Democracy Take Root in Post-Soviet Russia? Explorations in State-Society Relations. Lanham, MD: Rowman and Littlefield.

Hadenius, A. 1992. Democracy and Development. Cambridge: Cambridge University Press.

Lerner, David. 1968 [1958]. The Passing of Traditional Society: Modernizing the Middle East. New York: The Free Press.

Lipset, Seymour. 1959. "Some Social Requisites of Democracy: Economic Development and Political Legitimacy," *American Political Science Review,* 53:69-105.

Marsh, Christopher. 1999. Making Russian Democracy Work: Social Capital, Economic Development, and Democratization. College Station, TX: Texas A & M University Press. Forthcoming.

Moroz, Oleg. 1995. *Literaturnaya Gazeta.* No. 46:10, quoted in Richard Sakwa, *Russian Politics and Society* (London: Routledge, 1996), 171.

Orlov, A. 1991. Interview with Vladimir Zhirinovsky. *Sovietskaya Rossiya,* October 2, quoted in Sakwa, 84.

Petro, Nicolai. 1995. The Rebirth of Russian Democracy. Cambridge, MA: Harvard University Press.

Putnam, Robert. 1993. Making Democracy Work: Civic Traditions in Modern Italy. Princeton, NJ: Princeton University Press.

Tsentral'naya Izbiratel'naya Komissia Rossiiskoi Federatsii [TsIK]. 1996. Vybory Deputatov Gosudarstvennoi Dumy 1995: Elektoral'naya Statistika. Moscow: 'Ves Mir' Izdatel'stvo.

Vanhanen, Tatu. 1997. Prospects of Democracy: A Study of 172 Countries. London: Routledge.

Warhola, James. 1999. "Is the Russian Federation Becoming More Democratic? Moscow-Regional Relations and the Development of the Post-Soviet Russian State." *Democratization.* Forthcoming.

Social Movements and Pluralist Theory: The Conundrum of Solidarity in Poland's' Democratization

JANE L. CURRY&IRENA PAÑKÓW

1. Introduction

As Polish society has gone through its transformation, so too should Solidarity have. In the process, Solidarity has both made and been made by the society and political structures that existed around it and against which it struggled in the communist era. In the entire elongated transformation period, the Solidarity social movement survived and dominated Polish politics with old goals and old institutional forms to which newer goals and forms of organization were tacked on as times changed. Even with the addition of divisions by industry on top of the communist era regional divisions, Solidarity's structures and goal do not really fit the new realities of postcommunist society. This has been the dominant piece of Polish politics even as Solidarity's name and segments of its membership and goals took on separate existences as organized pluralist groupings.

What has been unique about the process in Poland has been the permanency of this social movement throughout the last twenty years even when its initial goals were achieved and the political and economic system of Poland changed dramatically. As this happened, various formal interest groups and kinds of political parties formed out of and alongside this Solidarity movement. But, unlike social movements in the West such as the American civil rights movement or the 1968 student movements, Solidarity did not transmute into pluralist groups with more or less radical goals in response to the gains and losses of the movement. Nor did it lose its movement status as this happened and its „issues" were responded to through cooptation, enactment of legislation, or rejection and the emergence of opposition movements. Nor did repression, however much it appeared to be definitive and damaging, stop the „social movement" as it did in comparable situations earlier in Eastern Europe.

In the end, the continued existence of Solidarity as a social movement and its ties to the past deformed or, at least, partially determined the activities and demands as well as the organization of the various Solidarity based trade unions and parties. Poland, after all, was a state whose transformation began as a result of worker unrest over economic difficulties and where, now, workers' interests are not represented explicitly by any political party and, when they are partially acknowledged, they are underrepresented. Instead, after its initial victory against communist power, it seems to have been permanently stuck in a time warp: ever present and defining itself and its outgrowths as the opposition movement of „the whole society" even though it began to represent workers' economic interests; almost disappeared after Martial Law was declared, proving that government could impose sanctions for participation; and as it has become the governing power.

The permanency of Solidarity as a social movement and the impact of this on the associational groups the formed out of it are a reflection of the system and its transformation. They are also a reflection of the specific nature of Solidarity as a social movement. The organizational forms and demands that have been connected with the Solidarity social movement and symbol have been a reflection only in part of the opportunities various Polish political systems offered and the limits they imposed. In the case of the *social movement* and its spinoff associational groups, the central focus has always been on opposing the communist way. This was true even after communism was defeated. This has meant that, instead of taking on established institutional forms, Solidarity has deliberately attempted not to replicate, organizationally, its „communist opponents", whatever the cost. As a result, although from the start Solidarity consisted of autonomous units that worked on their own and it was an inchoate social movement that captured the national imagination and seemed to be „the" institution.

Ironically, this image of being a strong institution but being made up of vaguely regulated independent units and a general social movement worked in the communist era. It allowed Solidarity to both limit communism more and for a longer period than other movements and uprisings had been able to do. It also allowed Solidarity to shift into „underground mode" and survive. Finally, it allowed it to make the jump from illegal if unterrorized organization to the dominant negotiator with the communist rulers in the Roundtable search for a *modus vivendi* and finally, to being a victor in free elections within six weeks of the signing of the Roundtable Accords. What it has proved not to allow Solidarity to do is to adapt to pluralist standards that require groups to represent specific interests in the policy process and focus on resolvable issues.

As with any social movement, „Solidarity" began in opposition to the prevailing system, in its case the communist one, both in its organization and its values.[1] The ideology of communism posited that the society was a single entity, not divided by social classes. The impact of the „Gierek miracle's" failure hit all segments of the population equally.[2] „Solidarity", as a social movement, thus, was embraced or embraced the whole of Polish society. Its initial trade union demands[3] rapidly were replaced by a vague ethos to which almost everyone could subscribe and in which almost everyone could claim to be involved.[4] With this came a vague organizational structure that was all inclusive but which also left decisions - often made without any enforcement capability - to a small and identifiable cohort of individuals.[5]

Within this social movement, from the start, there were various associational groups. These had more structure and a focused concern with negotiating specific benefits for a specific group but they were never at the focus or the dominant actors. Nor, did the government dignify them as contact points for negotiations. So, like a variety of social movements elsewhere, „members" are defined by what they did and what they believed. Many movements also contain a number of associations, often in conflict with each other.[6]

Once its goals were achieved, though, its ideological *raison d'etre did not* metamorphose. Instead, it froze. „Solidarity" as a social movement continued to stress its opposition to the status quo even when it was the *status quo* and its leaders replaced the communist rulers.

True, once communism had ended Solidarity supported the general transformation to a democratic political system with a market economy. The problem for „Solidarity" is that it also had to maintain its original identity as a trade union to keep its supporters and organizational base. So, even as Solidarity took the lead in the government, in its „trade union incarnation", it opposed its own government's „shock therapy", privatization and salary policies because they brought hardship to the working class. Only between 1993 and 1998 when legacy parties from the communist era formed the ruling coalition, were pieces or positions of Solidarity not in conflict with each other. Then, although basic economic policies did not change, Solidarity (from outside the government) could coherently fight with „the sick system".

Solidarity-based associational groups' agenda formation has been influenced by the domination of this powerful and all encompassing „Solidarity" social movement and symbol that claimed to represent Polish society as a solid unit. In the legend of Solidarity, there were special interests but no real differences in the basic interests of the various members of society: what's good for one is good for all other „real Poles". That „good" was, after Solidarity's initial „self-limiting"[7] months and, particularly, after the declaration of Martial Law, the existence of the union as a legal organization and the abolition or transformation of communism. The result has been that the various organizations that have used the Solidarity name and claimed to be its representatives have not focused on, developed services for, and battled for their members.

For pluralist theory, the transformation of Solidarity may be analogous but it is no less significant. Pluralist theory has never in reality included social movements of any kind as effective modes of pluralist exchange in a society. Nor has it focused on the evolution of social groups into interest groups. Or, really at the engagement of groups as part of the government. Instead, it has assumed the naturalness of organized and focused interest articulations: that given the political freedoms, multiple specific groups naturally form to insert and push their specific interests into the policy process. Pluralism assumes that the society does not have a single set of interests or united front but, rather, that the peaceful negotiations and conflict among groups and between groups and the political elite that are aimed to achieve individual group interests. These are most often in conflict with each other or the achievement of one group's goals means losses by another group.

It also assumes that these groups are internally organized to use their particular resources to inform and press the political leadership. Finally, in the process of transformation, pluralist theory has been torn between democratization being a product of the development of nascent civil society under repression which would then turn into effective sets of pluralist institutions or its being the trigger for the development of civil society.

The experience of the „Solidarity" social movement and its group outgrowth defies all of these assumptions. Solidarity began as a social movement that managed simultaneously to resist becoming „normalized" as a party or interest group and to force its way on the authoritarian political establishment. Only the imposition of Martial law halted the open power of Solidarity. But, even from the underground Solidarity was able to impact the government and to create the impression of a united society against communist rule. As a result, even as there were opportunities for open negotiations and multiple group voices, Solidarity remained dominant. As a special case, Solidarity then is evidence of the potential of social movements, of the ability of a group to maintain simultaneous but conflicting identities, and maintain a privileged position in politics.

2. „Solidarity” as a Legal Movement

From its inception through the fifteen months of 80/81 when it was a legal organization, Solidarity was a social movement opposing the existing system and involving a wide membership of self-designated members. It was also a series of autonomous associational groups, each involved in negotiating for specific gains for their groups under the titular umbrella of „Solidarity” and with the explicit or implicit claim that each was a national issue and the explicit or implicit threat of support from national Solidarity. In most cases, this was encouraged by Solidarity's inchoate national leadership; „intellectual issues” like censorship were given off to intellectuals to negotiate and local units were left essentially unrelated and free to act as they wished as „Solidarity”.

As a whole „Solidarity” was forced by the political system's options to focus on systemic issues rather than specific group needs because the system was so impoverished it could not provide real material gains for any large group of the population. Solidarity's self-appointed organizational leadership, coming largely from the Gdañsk shipyard group and those they linked in, was the result of the political elites' regularly calling on „names” in the organization to serve as negotiating partners. There were, after all, no elections until the late spring, 1981, when elections for representatives to the National Council were held.

The governance decisions made by Solidarity prior to its summer National Congress, nearly a year after Solidarity had emerged, only amplified this formation of a broad „social movement” with autonomous segments acting independently and often as associational groups. The nomination and election of representatives was done in open assemblies that anyone could attend and speak as a candidate. The assemblies were representative of regions. Their length and results were determined by how many people decided to speak and who was the most fiery speaker.

In the end, this meant that the National Congress was in no way a coherent whole nor were coherent options expressed and debated. Individuals were elected as distinct individuals by voice vote based, most often, on oral appeal rather than program. There were no established units to which they adhered. Issues appeared with no logic or control on the agenda.

The governance structure went further in making Solidarity unstructured: the National Council elected at the National Congress had no authority over individual units. Instead, any decision in the name of Solidarity had to be agreed to by all 40 members of the National Council and regional units retained the right to go their own ways. Communist ways of governance clearly had been rejected so totally that the normal requisites for associational interest groups to deal in pluralist societies were rejected with them.

At the same time, the governing elite and the general social situations changed in relation to the social movement and, in doing so, forced some redefinition of Solidarity as a social movement and associational group. In trying to control the radicalization of the Party itself, the original encouragement of communist party members to join „Solidarity” (the social movement) was shifted in the spring, 1981, to a prohibition on joint membership. This negated the inclusionary nature of „Solidarity” and forced a defined boundary line on it for its membership. At the same time, it did not give „Solidarity” a „group” to represent since both the Party and „Solidarity” had and sought membership from all classes and championed interests and demands across the spectrum from economic to purely political and cultural.

In fact, the economic situation was so bad that „Solidarity", as a trade union, could promise no real gains. It was more likely that it could force the government to give in on political issues than to open the state's empty coffers and produce nonexistent meat or other food and consumer goods. This meant that the trade union, the associational outgrowth of „Solidarity", was virtually guaranteed failure in any demand but purely local and almost personal battles and demands.

The result of the internal dynamics of the „Solidarity" movement, „Solidarity" associational groups, and the external environment was that Solidarity, by the middle of 1981, was really a broad social movement with a powerful if undefined social identity and sense of popular membership. Its evolution was blocked. The other layer and reality of „Solidarity" was an uncoordinated gaggle of small localized associational groupings within which there was much social interaction. In this process, there was little real associational group activity as we know it in a pluralist society. Solidarity actions tended to be localized, personalized, and focused on highlighting or resolving a particular local issue or pressuring the larger „social movement" to hear and enforce local group concerns and disaffection by taking or threatening dramatic public action that could force a response from the ruling elite and the „Solidarity" leadership.

In the end, „Solidarity" as a social movement and as a group of associational groups seemed to the governmental and Party elite as too much of a threat to tolerate. This sense came, ironically, at the very point when Solidarity leaders felt that the movement had lost its social support and was grinding down rather than being able to draw mass support. As a result, „Martial Law" was declared. It involved the internment of activists of Solidarity and other ancillary organizations as well as a handful of former Party officials; government takeover of Solidarity buildings and equipment; the suspension of most social and political organizations not only from the solidarity era but from the earlier communist era; and the closing of the media as well as the deployment of thousands of troops around the country and a cutoff of virtually all communications channels within Poland and with the outside world. „Solidarity" was caught unprepared. Popular reaction to Martial Law was negative but restrained.

3. Solidarity in a Pluralist System

The hopes for a rapid and smooth pluralization of Polish politics lay, from the start, in the Solidarity experience. After all, „Solidarity" as a social movement was able to withstand the powerlessness and defeats of its associational formations, both trade unions and professional organizations, in the early eighties and to transform itself into a variety of forms, depending on that the system allowed, that kept it alive and maintained the image of unity and national solidarity.

The realities of Polish politics have been far different. Although Poland is not one of the least successful democratizers, it has not been as successful as many imagined. Politicians coming out of the Solidarity movement turned on each other early on it the process. The parties they have formed have not been able to build strong bonds and have not generated clear platforms nor have they survived successive elections. Polish politics have been marked by a real disconnect between the „image issues" that politicians use such as past history and the more material concerns of the population. Ironically, workers' interests have been openly and explicitly unrepresented even though Solidarity and its communist era trade union equivalent, OPZZ, have been part of every government since 1989.

Effectively, the strength of „Solidarity" as a social movement and the legacy of its origins forced the Polish communist elite to give up its control over power in favor of a pluralist system. Now, the legend and continued presence of Solidarity as a social movement blocks the formation of a truly pluralist or even corporatist state. The apparently associational groups that have spun off from the social movement have, ultimately, been unable to represent specific groups and have also been unable to unite for something as opposed to against. In fact, they remain tied to their now fulfilled goal of defecting communism, however defeated it already is, through the achievement of systemic transformation as it was begun in 1989, no matter who gets hurt.

The initial moves by the government to negotiate with Solidarity and develop some sort of *modus vivendi* with it were not unlike those the government made in 1980-81. To begin the negotiations, it pinpointed and sought out „leaders" of Solidarity with whom to negotiate. Most of these individuals were known from their work and visibility in citizens' committees, the underground press, academics, and the old liberal media. The other source were the men around Lech Wałęsa. In doing so, the communist rulers played a major role in establishing the leaders for the solidarity movement and „trade union" after they had kept it illegal for almost eight years. Beyond this, in setting the agenda, the political elite essentially assumed Solidarity leaders from the early eighties were viable as representative of the „other", the society. In this way, the communist rulers established the leadership with which it would fight.

The sense the Polish population had of the governing elite as united and in control of all the levers of power meant as well, that the leaders who entered into the negotiations did so with a conscious sense that they needed to be united under one leadership. The government and „Solidarity" leadership's decision to enter into Roundtable negotiations was a preemptory attempt to bloc what both sides saw as possible uncontrollable mass unrest. As a result of this and the sense Solidarity leaders had that they were working against a strong monolith, Solidarity negotiators committed themselves to work as an elitist organization in coordinated bargaining so that the goal of Solidarity's relegalization would be paramount. What Solidarity's wanted was a pact between the „society" and the communists. As partners in negotiations, one side would represent the whole society based on Solidarity and the other, the government. In fact, even Solidarity leader Bronislaw Gieremek saw that the government never „stood against us [Solidarity] but rather against impatient workers and the possibility of a deadly social upheaval".[8]

In the subsequent election, the image of „Solidarity" as the only institution against the communist monolith was key. Candidates who were trusted as *not* having been associated with the „Solidarity" movement, however marginally, were signified by posters in which they appeared with Lech Wałęsa, the human symbol of the movement. Beyond that, though, no questions were asked by the Solidarity sponsors as to what individuals stood for. There was no common line. In the end, both its campaign and the election results made it clear that „Solidarity" represented the society against the communist minority.

After their election victory, the „Solidarity" that was swept into government was still a vague social movement, led from the top with mass activity occurring in the form of spontaneous electoral work.[9] What dominated the thinking of those who had taken on the task of organizing the electoral campaign was that Solidarity had to be united to defeat the communists, its only real goal.

Once it had won the election, its leaders were catapulted into the top leadership of the system. They began to move, to remove or transform the institutions that had held communist rule in place and made pluralism impossible in the past. As this happened,

"Solidarity" seemed to fragment in what was played out as the „war on the top". The split was between those who had entered into politics to „represent the society" and those who ostensibly claimed to focus on union work and eschew politics. The initial fight was to get control of the symbols and name of the social movement. This initial split was played out underneath the rhetoric over control of the movement or the direction into which the movement should evolve. What it was focused on were the personal interests of Lech Wałęsa, who had opted out of institutional governmental power initially and, by 1990, was fighting to return as president of the country.

The identity of the social movement „Solidarity" with the society as a whole and general social needs made it impossible for „Solidarity" to transform effectively into a normal trade union or political party that represented specific group interests. This, even though „Solidarity", after the elections of 1989, was suddenly able to create and did create the institutional base for pluralism and it had a history that began with a specific, working class constituency.

The dilemma left the representation of group interests and the possibility for real pluralist representation and balancing of interest in an awkward position in postcommunist Poland. On the one hand, there was a trade union tied with the old traditions of Solidarity. That union, in all of its national and regional meetings, wrestled inconclusively with the question of what it should represent and how it should act since the possibility opened for it to dominate the government. At the same time, it was engaged in providing traditional union services and representation in various negotiating forums.

Ironically, although Solidarity had deliberately rejected any element of interest group organization that had any parallel in the organization of communist party rule, after 1989 it found itself having to fill many of the voids left by the dismantling of the communist party system. This was particularly true at the factory level. There, in the early nineties, Solidarity committees took over the guidance and coordinating functions of the factory level party organization of the communist era and also its role in attempting to mobilize workers support of the party's national leadership. This time, though, the goal was support of the Solidarity governments not the communist rulers.

On the other hand, the public's view of Solidarity and its political view of itself have regularly emphasized that it does not represent any specific constituency or protect anyone's interests. In fact, when asked if any organization existed in Poland to represent their group's interests, 53% said there was no institution at all to represent their interests, 12% said the trade unions represented their interests and 21% said it was „hard to say".[10] That said, most also see leaders of the union along with owners and directors of private and state firms and priests as the beneficiaries of the economic reforms that have hurt the rest of the society.[11]

What the public seems to have concluded from the Solidarity experience about the potential of pluralism in Poland is relatively negative. Public opinion polls show the sense of over half the population (54%) is that there is a need for a new organization to represent group interests.[12] They also show that individuals who saw Solidarity as the leading force for „hope, the fight with communism, protecting workers, and aiding the poorest" in the early eighties saw it, in 1993, as doing all of these things negatively and worsening the situation in the country.[13] In effect, the mixing of political and trade union roles and Solidarity's leadership in the making of political and economic changes in Poland have convinced people that there is little hope for their situation to right themselves: the resulting perception is that the elite control and popular interests are not represented. The formation of the Solidarity Electoral Coalition from a loose grouping of rightist parties who had lost in the 1993 election and the Solidarity based trade unions was seen by the public not as either a mistake or a possibility for any real gains. It was, in the public's mind, simply a necessary vehicle in the right's political battles.[14]

Since the first Solidarity congress after 1989, the problem of how Solidarity should participate in politics, its relationship to various political parties, and whether it should function as its own political party have been major topics of debate among the activists within Solidarity. The two options, from the beginning, were to form a catch-all party aimed at dominating parliament and taking responsibility for national policy or working as a union connected with a political party with specific responsibilities and concerns. Given both international pressures and the sense in Polish circles of the necessary dichotomy between capitalism and communism, this party was bound to be a promarket one.[15] Effectively, Solidarity union representative always appeared as candidates to parliament either as parts of the union ticket or as parts of party, *qua* electoral coalitions that support a liberal market economy.

Initially, there was no clear distinction between Solidarity union representatives and the rest of the noncommunist grouping „sponsored by Lech Wałęsa". Those union representatives voted for the Balcerowicz Plan even though it went against many of the guarantees of the Roundtable Agreements that had been designed to protect workers' interests and that, ultimately, brought down workers' standards of living as they opened up the possibilities for bankruptcy and unemployment. In later elections and parliaments, „Solidarity" the trade union always had deputies in parliament. They voted for free market reforms. Most often „Solidarity" leaders and representatives then walked out of parliament and participated in strikes against the stringency measures for which they had voted. Solidarity went further in 1993 and joined in a vote of no confidence against the coalition in which it was a member.

After Solidarity and right wing parties lost the 1993 elections which had the „vote of no confidence" triggered, their response was not to reformulate their approaches or platforms or to focus on union issues. Instead, it was to harden their traditional lines against the communists and „fight for control". To do this, Solidarity eschewed any sense of being nonpolitical and focused on serving as the motor for „Solidarity Election Coalition". Solidarity, the trade union *qua* social movement, served as the motor for the movement, providing not only candidates but a support base and infrastructure as well as the leadership for the new coalition. Once the Coalition had won the election, it fell to the post 1989 Solidarity leadership with over half of the parliamentary seats of the Coalition, to form a new government.

Does this portend or indicate the institutionalization of the social movement? No. The program of the Solidarity coalition is one of a „social movement": the system is sick, its recovery requires the removal of the communist government and a moral renewal.[16] The process continues: with victory in the elections, there has been some elite level talk of movement toward reforming the coalition into a political party and Solidarity. The party has yet to establish itself formally. So, the head of the trade union has been both the head of the coalition and its parliamentary club. But, the reality of that is more as stated by the press attache of Solidarity: „we do not represent workers, we represent Poland".[17]

4. Conclusion

Solidarity is clearly not the same social movement as it was in 1980 and 1981. It, or groups using its legend, clearly responded to the changing dynamics and dimensions of the various political and economic systems that emerged as a result of its actions and other pressures. But, in the process, the social movement has never died out nor has the transformation of Solidarity in the democratization process followed what would have been a logical course, comparable to social movements of groups left out of „normal" pluralist polities in the West and Third World. Instead, the initial form and path of Solidarity had had such a hold that it has determined and deformed the evolution of Solidarity.

For pluralist theory, social movements have always been problematical. They do not enter into the political „battlefield" in normal „formations". Instead, their goals and formations are broad and open, attacking the system, generally from outside, to advocate for their goals. In the process, they create their own social system. The result is that social movements tend to be internally elitist not pluralist even as they press for their position in a pluralist system. In the end, these were not the groups of pluralist theory. Instead, the assumption or observation of reality was that social movements evolve naturally into more politically effective and membership based interest groups that work normally within pluralist political systems.

Solidarity has not done this. True, along the way, it was a segmented group in which units claimed its mantle and made specific claims. But, these groups have never evolved from demanding and opposing to advocating. Nor have they been stable. In fact, Solidarity, by all standards, has not even tried to be representative of any specific group. Nor has there been a demise of the „social movement" formation in which top leaders speak for and provide direction for the „movement". Instead, Solidarity had been mired in the past, opposing the communist system and communist control long after it was over and claiming to represent the society long after there is no way to claim „society" has common interests or claims. Indeed, the very dissension within the movement has been over pluralist versus elitist policies within the movement itself.

Why then has „Solidarity the social movement" not whithered away and interest groups typical of pluralist society emerged from its carcass? Why too has it been so difficult to build a pluralist political process in Poland, the one country in Eastern Europe where independent and communal political activity did happen?

„Solidarity" initially survived and was able to adapt because of its *ad hoc* segmentalized structures and its general social power. After this structure allowed it to move from at least a partially underground social movement to an electoral powerhouse, it did not adapt to the needs of traditional representation in the new society. Instead, its structure makes it possible for individuals to lay claim to the name and legend from its fight against communism in the early eighties. This fits with the coming and going of „Solidarity" organizations.

Ironically, the social image and the social base it claimed reflected the ideology of communism (which, in turn, reflected historical traditions in Poland when „the society" was separate from the foreign rulers) in its denial of the reality or viability of group interests. This refusal to see honor in defending particular groups continues to block the establishment of Solidarity as a representative group today. Political dynamics being what they are, if one movement historically dominates the landscape and claims to represent the society, development of real interest representation is impeded.

Since the nature of „communism" always was vague and the results of the initial transformation were not what people expected, Solidarity could picture communism as it wished and its old opposition to communism to defend itself and give itself a *modus vivendi*. After all, in the initial rush to democracy and capitalism, Solidarity deputies were a major force in bringing the new system in.

Beyond this, the nature of the birth of Solidarity and the unbelievability of its original successes against the communist monolith made it appear to be invincible. This legend has so overwhelmed the political landscape that it became a symbol all claimed and that overrode all later organizations.

If these are, indeed, valid explanations for Solidarity's immutability, what they suggest for pluralist theory is that the legacy of systems and organizations/movements is at lest as important if not more important than the nature of the freedoms or needs it has or the rules of the system in which it exists. „Path dependency" or inertia rather than practical politics can be the crucial and determining factor. In fact, in the Polish case, the experience with Solidarity as a more pluralist/civil society organization than any other in Eastern Europe in the communist period probably did not, as we originally assumed, ease the transition to a democracy or the emergence of functioning groups. Instead, its history created a legacy that was strong enough to rein in and deform this potential.

For Polish politics in general, Solidarity's power is also a conundrum. In the other countries of Eastern Europe, there were not large scale organizations with a history of both independence from the communist polity and popular action. Solidarity should have been that for Poland. People had participated. They had been heard and made decisions outside the direction of the communist party.

The presence of Solidarity and its old leaders' battles with each other over control have not been positives for Polish politics. Since Solidarity had no real plan for what after communism, the leaders responded to its almost instantaneous movement into power reactively. Their initial decisions left them tried to liberal capitalism and market dominance. As a result, it was hard for them to represent the working class, the prime losers from the transformation, without saying they had made a major miscalculation. In addition, since the initial decisions were made without any early plans for taking over and staffing the government, the leadership rapidly divided and turned on itself. Positions tended to be platforms rather than vehicles for establishing policy.

The commitment of Solidarity to represent „the society" against communism tied it to supporting all that was not communist. In doing this, it has made it impossible for any noncapitalist model to be considered, although the right does make gestures toward greater social welfare. This fixation on the market, partially, insures the system can not go back toward what it was before 1989, no matter what the social disaffection. More importantly, though, the power of Solidarity to set the public agenda since 1980 and the agenda it has set for itself to represent the society as a whole and not recognize the natural divisions in capitalist society have alienated the population. They have created a population that, instead of pressing for its rights violently or through establishment channels, has come to assume that it will not be heard and protected, that everyone is a sure loser in the political system. In the end, this bodes for popular silence, allows the elites to fight battles over historical issues of „communist-not communist" when the population cares about getting economic relief, and leaves the policy spectrum sterile - lacking in ways to move beyond the „them or us" mentality that defined Polish politics in the communist era.

Notes

1 *Social Movements and Social Change*, ed. by Robert H. Lauer (Carbondale: Souther Illinois Unversity Press, 1976), p. xiii.

2 *Poland's Permanent Revolution*.

3 Julian Pańków, *Negocjacje jako sposób rozwiązywania konfliktów społecznych*, COM SNP, Warszawa 1988. „Poles 80", Results of Survey Research, Sisyphus, Sociological Studies vol. III,

Crises and Conflicts, The Case of Poland 1980-81, PWN 1982. Władysław Adamski, *Structural and Generational Aspects of a Social Conflict,* Sisyphus, ibid.

4 Rudolf Herberle, *Social Movements* (New York: Appleton-Century Crofts, 1951), p. 439 as quoted in J.A. Banks, *The Sociology of Social Movements* (London: Macmillan, 1972), p. 8.

5 Georges Mink, *Siła czy rozpadek. Historia społeczna i polityczna Polski (1980-81),* wyd. SPACJA - zakład Fundacji Logos, Warszawa 1992.

6 „Introduction", *Protest, Reform, And Revolt,* ed. by Joseph R. Gusfield (New York: John Wiley and Sons, 1970), p. 6.

7 Jadwiga Staniszkis, *The Self-Limiting Revolution.*

8 Bronisław Gieremek, *Gieremek opowiada, Żakowski pyta. Rok 1989* (Warsaw: Plejada, 1990), p. 80.

9 Paweł Śpiewak, *Narodziny polskiej demokracji,* in *Bitwa o Belweder,* ed. by M. Grabowska and I. Krzemiński (Drakow: Wydawnictwo Literackie, 1991), p. 200.

10 Biuletyn CBOS, Potrzeba reprezentacji interesów i poczucie jej zaspokojenia, Warszawa, lipiec 1992.

11 „Konflikty 'stare' czy 'nowe', Biuletyn CBOS (May, 1994).

12 Biuletyn CBOS jak w przypisie 11.

13 „NSZZ 'S': wczoraj i dziś", Biuletyn CBOS (July, 1993).

14 „AW 'S': wspólny program czy pragmatyzm?" Biuletyn CBOS (November, 1998).

15 Josef Orzel, *Zjazd musi wybrać przewodniczącego I formule,* Tygodnik Solidarność no. 7 (February 15, 1991).

16 Irena Pańków. A less polite statement of purpose is that of Jaroslaw Kaczyński who said „now damn it wu".

17 Interview with the Solidarity National Commission Press Spokesman on July 13, 1988.

Consolidation of Hungarian Democracy

GABRIELLA ILONSZKI

1. Introduction

The main argument of this chapter is that Hungary has become a consolidated democracy. This can be demonstrated by broad institutional developments as well as by procedural and personnel details. I chose to apply both approaches, however, briefly. First, I will argue for the 'consolidation' thesis in the context of institutional developments; and second I will discuss in a more detailed manner how the elements of consolidation can be grasped in the framework of the Hungarian parliamentary political elite.

2. Broad dimensions of consolidation

After the `transition literature' more recent academic publications focus on the stabilization of new democracies (see particularly Linz and Stepan, 1996) not to mention here those writings which inevitably raise questions concerning 'defective' democracies, that is the experiences of countries that could not fully pursue their democratization process. Parallel to this, 'qualification of democracy' has been on the agenda, meaning that both country experts and comparativists seek to characterize the nature or the quality of the new democracies. This interest and high profile of the topic is not incidental because a growing number of countries has joined the democratic group both in the context of the third wave developments and also independently. Nevertheless, their political reality and performance have become more and more diverse. When seeking to identify the 'quality' of the Hungarian democracy I will argue for its liberal and consolidated character. As to the first, the conceptual framework of Diamond (1996, 1997) can be instructive. According to that a growing dichotomy prevails between electoral democracies (where the only and exclusive democratic domain is that of elections) and liberal democracies where individual and group liberties are protected and ensured for example by alternative channels for expressing interests and values and alternative sources of information.

The process of democratic consolidation is much more dependent on actors and behavior. To identify whether a political system belongs to the consolidated group Linz and Stepan established three requirements: an institutional-procedural, that is the existence of liberal-democratic institutions; a behavioral, namely that elites accept the existing framework and there are no challenger groups among them; and finally an attitudinal, meaning that the public attitude is responsive to democratic values and considers the system as legitimate. Diamond is even more straightforward in this respect by saying: "In essence, consolidation is the process of achieving broad and deep legitimation, such that all significant political actors, at both the elite ad mass levels, believe that the democratic regime is the most right and appropriate for their society, better than any other realistic alternative they can imagine." (1997:37)

In the first part of the chapter I will argue that the evolving Hungarian political system can be regarded a liberal and consolidated democracy according to the above mentioned criteria and I will put forward diverse indicators and features to prove that.

However, a further qualification of the Hungarian democracy is appropriate. The way in which the economic deficit of late communism and the transition was transformed into a cultural and social deficit and how the elite scenario of the Hungarian transition determined the quality of the new liberal democracy is often left out of the analysis. More concretely, as to the first point, it can be proven by hard data that the wide public paid for the economic failure of the previous regime and the subsequent marketization. Just to mention a revealing figure: the real wage per person was 80% in 1997 of the 1989 level, while the price index in 1997 was 584 percent of the 1989 level (Ferge, 1999). As to the second point, it is widely known that the elites played an important role in the Hungarian transition. This fits well the Hungarian political tradition in which a non-participatory political culture and different elite compromises tended to prevail. These two characteristics are largely intertwined: the formation of a new political elite, its stabilization and consolidation occurred in parallel with the growth of the cultural and social deficit: impoverishment of large social groups and the educational, healthcare, and cultural systems which, despite the fact that they were not highly developed in the communist period, were able to ensure a safety minimum and service for all. Under these conditions it is particularly important how the evolving elite-framework can further qualify Hungarian democracy, probably providing a third qualitative remark, being a consolidated, liberal, and elite democracy. Thus in the second part of the chapter I will briefly examine some aspects of elite stabilization and professionalization.

3. Elements of consolidation

3.1. Electoral dimension

Hungary has shown a stable electoral pattern from the beginning of the democratization period. The original electoral law of transition has not been substantially changed, and elections followed each other in a straightforward pattern. After the founding elections of 1990 - which were often considered as a protest election against the communist regime - the second and third elections brought about a peaceful alternation of government with different political tendencies getting into government positions. That is, after the conservative center-right government coalition of 1990 (consisting of the Hungarian Democratic Forum (MDF), the Christian Democratic People's Party (KDNP) and the Smallholders' Party (FKGP)), in 1994 a center- left coalition was formed (with the Socialist Party (MSZP) and the Alliance of Free Democrats (SZDSZ) being the members) and in 1998 again a conservative - although a more modern and less traditional conservative coalition was formed with the Alliance of Young Democrats-Hungarian Civic Party (Fidesz-MPP) as the senior member and the FKGP and the MDF as junior members of the coalition. The three peaceful alternations of governments constitute an impressive record and clearly indicate the extent of consolidation in this respect.

Table 1. ***Division of Seats in the First, Second and Third Democratic Parliaments, 1990-1998*** *(no. and % of mandates)*

party	1990		1994		1998	
	number	%	number	%	number	%
MDF	164	42.5	38	9.8	17	4.7
SZDSZ	92	23.8	69	17.8	24	6.2
FKGP	44	11.4	26	6.7	48	12.4
MSZP	33	8.5	209	54.1	134	34.7
Fidesz-MPP	21	5.4	20	5.1	147	38.1
KDNP	21	5.4	22	5.7	-	-
MIÉP	-	-	-	-	14	3.6
other	10	2.8	2	0.5	1	0.2
total	386	100.0	386	100.0	386	100.0

Naturally, however, the three abrupt changes in the electoral arithmetic should also be interpreted from another dimension, that is the lack of stability in voting behavior. In each election the majority of voters changed their party support, and the elections are often seen as protest votes - either against the previous regime in the case of the first elections, or the previous government in the latter two cases. The paradox between party system stability and electoral volatility can be connected to the principal argument of the chapter: stability on the level of high politics in the party system does not necessarily go together with stable political sympathies among the electorate. In fact this leads us back again to the differences in the elite and mass dimension of politics in Hungary.

3.2. Party dimension

Some of the parties had been formed as large umbrella organizations in the process of the transition. Nevertheless, these umbrella parties belong to past memories only. All the parties on the political scene have become well structured, and institutionally refined political entities by now - although the process of party consolidation was not unproblematic. There were occasional party splits, for example, but the overall picture is that a stable multi-party system has been formed with a strong tendency - particularly in the last two to three years - towards bipolarization, that is with two big parties and a couple of smaller parties around them. More concretely, on the left the big Socialist Party dominates the scene (indeed, the clearance of the party's communist record also belongs to the consolidation process) while on the right the Fidesz-MPP, the current governing party is the dominant force with the inclination to absorb the small MDF and other potential actors to form a German type CDU/CSU combination in the future. Minor parties include the MDF, the Smallholders, the liberal SZDSZ and the 1998 newcomer in the parliamentary arena, that is the nationalist MIEP, the Party of Hungarian Justice and Life. In all three parliamentary terms there were 6 parties in parliament, in the first and second terms even the same six parties (Socialists, Smnallholders, Free Democrats, Young Democrats, Hungarian Democratic Forum, and Christian Democrats), the only difference in the third term being that the Christian

Democrats (partially absorbed by the Young Democrats by now) were replaced by the MIEP nationalists.

Although you can always except the unexpected in politics, on the basis of the past ten years one can conclude that in Hungary the early formation of parties contributed to their success and with the possible exception of the first and largest system-transformer, the Hungarian Democratic Forum's early birth cemented them in politics. New parties do not seem to have many opportunities to get established.

It must be emphasized again, however, that party system stability dominates over electoral volatility. Thus, recent studies could argue (Tóka, 1998) that inspite of common expectations (based mainly on previous Latin-American examples) volatility is not detrimental to democratic consolidation in Hungary (and in other Central European countries). Tóka sees the main reasons - at least partially - in elite behavior: "social actors do not confront one another without the mediation of political representatives.... electoral volatility....and uncertainty fail to undermine politicians' commitment to the democratic rules of the game" (Toka, 1998).

The consolidation of parties can also be proved by the coalition scenarios which the parties followed. While the first coalition was somewhat haphazard (understandably so due to the lack of time to establish party programs and coalition policies) the second coalition lumped together the successor of the communist party (MSZP, socialists) and their previously most vehement critics and opponents (SzDSz, the liberals) and in the third coalition a once radical neo-liberal party (Fidesz-MPP) dominates the socially sensitive national conservative MDF and the national radical Smallholders (FKGP). Coalition politics thus was handled very pragmatically among elite groups. They often lost their original color and atmosphere for the sake of stable power structures.

3.3. Political Dimension

As the previous elements might already suggest the Hungarian system is also consolidated politically. On the elite level, we cannot find any substantial groups that can be considered as an anti-system force. Extremism of any kind is not a feature of Hungarian democracy. The only potentially debated issue in this respect is the position and the evaluation of the MIEP, the Party of Hungarian Justice and Life. With their nationalist slogans they embody an unacceptable political alternative for many, but they certainly accept the rules of the democratic game and support the government in many economic and social (welfare) areas.

The MIEP is a small group, having only 14 MPs in the 386 member Hungarian parliament. Moreover, these 14 seats were exclusively gained in single member districts, and the party could not gain any mandates on the party list (the Hungarian electoral system is a mixed system, which combines single member constituencies with a double ballot majority system, and party lists in addition to a national compensation list which promotes proportionality).

Political stability can be demonstrated on the mass level as well. Social unrest or mass demonstrations, strikes of any significant scale have been virtually unknown in Hungary. It has happened only twice, first in 1990 and second in 1997 that an organized and relatively large social group (the taxi-drivers and agricultural producers respectively) protested against some government policies. Radical political subcultures have not been formed either (Szabó, 1998) The level of political involvement and political participation reveal the image of a non-participatory political society. Grey is beautiful for many political commentators and social groups alike.

3.4. Constitutional dimension

Somewhat paradoxically: although Hungary is the only country in East Central Europe where a new constitution was not installed, the constitutional framework is working well. Indeed, the constitution as a power map which outlines the interconnection of different major political institutions has been performing without failure. While the previous government (1994-98) sought to establish a new constitution on a consensual basis and eventually failed to do so, the current government does not seem to be interested at all in the constitutional issue, probably on the grounds that if the constitution is working it does not make sense to change it.

Already the first constitutional choice that evolved in the process of transition was a good one in the sense that it fits the Hungarian constitutional tradition and provided stability (Lijphart, 1993). That is, a parliamentary system of government was formed, despite the initial attempts of the Communist party to ensure more continuity by a stronger and directly elected, possibly communist president.

Although the constitutional framework seems to enjoy acceptance among all major political groups occasional controversies occur - mainly concerning the strong prime ministerial role (often compared to a chancellor-type democracy). This is rooted first of all in the constructive confidence vote and also in some majoritarian elements of Hungarian democracy. Nevertheless the opposition is not interested in changing this setup either because it has some guarantees for its influence. For example, the policy areas that require a qualified majority legislation are precisely and clearly identified. The only substantial change in this old-new constitution has been the growing dominance of representative institutions and the decreasing importance of direct democracy.

3.5. International dimension

Although it is most often argued that post-communist countries, including Hungary, have been in a much less favorable position internationally than their Southern European counterparts because they received less political and economic-financial support in the democratization process, Hungary is in a relatively better position. For example, up to 1995 34.2 percent of international investment in all post-communist countries went to Hungary, and within Central Europe (in the classical sense, that is including the Baltic countries as well) Hungary attracted the most international investments - more than Poland and the Czech Republic.

The international consolidation of the Hungarian system does inevitably depend on other actors to a large extent. Recently, Hungary has been in a favorable position in this respect as well. After the elections in Romania in 1995 and in Slovakia in 1998 cooperation with the new governments in these two countries has become easier and two potential conflict areas (due to the position of ethnic Hungarians in the two states), even if they have not disappeared entirely, been reduced.

From a broader perspective, Hungary has become a full NATO member in 1999 and negotiations are in well advanced stage regarding entry to the EU. Although the latter will certainly be a longer process than many politicians both in Hungary and in the EU tend to admit, the sheer possibility itself demonstrates that Hungary is accepted as a potential partner.

4. A concrete case for consolidation: professionalization of the parliamentary political elite*

In the following I argue that elites directly contributed to the consolidation process and that their activities, their social and political background, and the functions they play mark an elite version of consolidation.

The importance of elites can be understood in two respects. First, it implies that - as a result of the way in which systemic change took place, that is arguing from the transplacement scenario, employing Huntington's terminology (1991) - the new political elite groups quickly merged with what was left of the old political elite and the cooperation of the two elites became part of everyday political practice. Although the past records of some politicians are occasionally mentioned and debated, these issues do not represent a salient political issue. More recent analyses also emphasize (Higley et al. 1996, 1998) that not elite settlement but elite accommodation and accommodative behavior among elites have prevailed in the transition and since then.

The other implication of the consolidation of the political personnel is the professionalization of the political elite. The political elite (either new or old) showed a very quick adaptation to Western practices (norms, behavior etc.) while they also became more professional both in terms of living in politics and doing politics in a more expert-oriented way. I will introduce some elements of this professionalization process in the second part of the chapter mainly in the parliamentary context. The focus will be 1) the characteristics of the parliamentary elite, 2) professional background of MPs 3) professionalization trends in the entire parliament and 4) how these are reflected in committees as potentially expertise-oriented parliamentary bodies.

1) Although we cannot include here a more detailed analysis of the social background of MPs (see Ilonszki, 1998) Table 2 reveals some interesting tendencies. It demonstrates that the parliamentary elite of different parties has become more similar to each other. Initial differences, for example in terms of age, have gradually diminished. The radical very young or young parties of the transition (Fidesz-MPP and SzDSz) grew older while both the post-communists and the conservative parties' representatives grew younger. The Hungarian parliamentary elite has become ever more educated in the past three elections, and although the increase is not substantial (from 88.5 percent to 91.7 percent) the figures certainly place the Hungarian MPs among the most educated parliamentarians in Europe. More importantly, however, the direction of change in the type of degrees and education reveals that without any exception, in each party, persons with a humanities background decreased and were replaced either with lawyers or with experts in natural sciences or engineering. More refined studies clearly prove that parties seek very similar candidates. The MPs' similar profile is an indication that a certain group with particular characteristics is being formed.

2) This development is even more obvious when we look at Table 3.

*The empirical analysis and the data that are used in this part of the article originate from two international research projects in which the author was working on the Hungarian case. Comprehensive results will be subsequently published in a) Olson. D. - Crowther, W. eds. Committees in Post-Communist Parliaments and Cotta, M. - Best, H. eds. Long-term Transformation of Parliamentary Elites.

Table 2. ***Age and education of MPs 1990-1994-1998*** *(in %)*

	MDF			SZDSZ			FKGP			MSZP			Fidesz-MPP			KDNP			MIÉP			Total		
	1990	1994	1998	1990	1994	1998	1990	1994	1998	1990	1994	1998	1990	1994	1998	1990	1994	1998	1990	1994	1998	1990	1994	1998
Average age in years	44.7	49.6	46.8	42.4	45.4	47.5	58.6	56.4	50.8	52.0	45.3	48.5	27.8	35.2	41.3	54.7	54.1	-	-	-	52.9	46.0	46.5	46.1
Education																								
elementary	0	0.6	0	0	0	0	4.9	7.7	2.1	6.1	0.5	0	0	0	0	4.8	0	-	-	-	0	1.6	0.8	0.3
Middle ed.	4.8	0	6.7	10.6	8.6	4.2	19.5	34.6	19.1	9.1	8.1	7.5	27.3	0	5.4	14.3	9.1	-	-	-	7.1	9.9	8.8	8.0
Higher ed.	94.5	100	93.3	89.4	91.4	95.8	75.6	57.7	78.1	84.8	91.4	92.5	72.7	100	94.3	81.6	91.0	-	-	-	92.9	88.5	90.4	91.7
Type of degree																								
Law	14.7	28.9	21.4	26.2	28.1	39.1	25.8	46.7	36.1	7.1	10.7	15.4	37.5	35.0	26.3	58.8	40.0	-	-	-	0	20.9	20.4	23.8
Humanities	41.9	42.1	21.4	46.4	46.9	39.1	29.0	26.7	19.4	67.9	41.4	40.7	56.3	45.0	30.5	23.5	15.0	-	-	-	61.5	43.1	40.5	34.6
Engin., natural sciences	14.9	28.9	57.1	27.4	25.0	21.7	45.2	26.7	44.4	25.0	48.4	43.9	6.3	20.0	41.2	17.6	45.0	-	-	-	38.5	36.0	39.1	41.6

Table 3. ***Typical Professional Background of MPs 1990-1994- 1998*** *(in %)*

	MDF			SZDSZ			FKGP			MSZP			Fidesz-MPP			KDNP			MIÉP			Total		
	1990	1994	1998	1990	1994	1998	1990	1994	1998	1990	1994	1998	1990	1994	1998	1990	1994	1998	1990	1994	1998	1990	1994	1998
Teachers, professors	21.8	18.4	0	16.0	14.3	4.2	2.0	4.0	9.3	12.1	13.5	8.5	18.2	15.0	11.0	4.8	18.2	-	-	-	21.4	16.1	13.8	9.4
Writers, journalists	3.6	0	0	1.1	1.4	0	1	0	0	6.1	1.9	0.8	4.5	5.0	0	9.5	4.5	-	-	-	0	3.6	1.8	0.3
Lawyers	7.3	13.2	14.3	12.7	12.9	12.5	3.0	12.0	9.3	0	4.3	3.1	0	0	7.4	14.3	13.6	-	-	-	7.1	7.5	7.4	6.6
Managers, businessmen	10.9	10.9	0	14.9	18.6	4.2	8.0	4.0	16.3	6.1	24.0	21.7	9.0	15.0	16.9	9.5	9.1	-	-	-	0	11.4	18.8	16.6
Politicians	0	5.3	42.9	0	4.3	70.8	1	12.0	23.3	21.2	16.3	35.7	4.5	35.0	27.9	0	9.1	-	-	-	21.4	2.3	13.3	33.2

Here the most typical professions are indicated. We can again witness how the 'humanity' professions lost their importance, but two other elements deserve attention as well. First, a relatively large proportion of MPs (16.6 percent as of 1998) are in business although with some interesting party-differences: the post-communist MSZP and the governing Fidesz having the largest number of managers and entrepreneurs among their ranks, and second, a growing number of 'politicians' have taken root in the parliamentary elite. Politicians are those who work in the party hierarchy, or clearly have some other political positions (for example as mayors). One-third of the parliamentary elite can be regarded as professional politicians. 3) How do these professional politicians become further professionalized will need a more in-depth analysis. Although professionalization is often interpreted differently, here I chose the length of practice and the nature of political experience or the lack of it as possible indicators to decide how far each party and the entire parliament have gone in establishing a core professional group of politicians.

Table 4 shows that the number of new MPs has constantly decreased (from 93.1 percent through 61.1 percent to 47.9 percent) and on the other side of the equation those with parliamentary experience increased. The number of MPs embedded in local politics has come close to 30 percent; the number of those with a government or party position has stabilized. (The initially large proportion of MPs with a party position - 77.5 percent in 1990 - is misleading because it contains all the newcomer opposition politicians whose career was tied to and meant a function in a newly formed party. This figure also reveals the importance of early party formation and the role the new party political elite has played in the transition).

4) Since committees represent the most expertise oriented institution within the parliamentary framework I pursued the analysis of the membership of parliamentary committees further to examine patterns of professionalization with respect (1) to the entire parliament, (2) to the parties and (3) regarding the differences between committees. My hypothesis was that a) membership continuity and consequently professionalization patterns will be more pronounced in committees than in the entire parliament, b) parties will show different professionalization patterns, c) the comparative importance of committees can also be detected by membership continuity figures.

4.1. The overall parliamentary level

As to the parliamentary arena, we must note that large turnover rates in new democracies are a feature of the party-political scene and do not result from parliamentary performance. Thus it is important to test how the efforts to establish stability and professionalize parliamentary work can be detected in parliament and in committees. Table 5 describes different numerical aspects of committee positions.

First of all, the number of committee positions has constantly increased: at the starting point, that is in May 1990, the number of positions was 300 (standing and special committees together) while at the end of 1997 it was 415. Even if we exclude the seats in temporary committees, positions in standing committees alone outnumber the number of seats in the entire House (387 versus 386) at the end of the second legislative term. Widening was often due to functional needs, functional clarification and committee initiatives. Also, important committee positions can bring bring visibility.

Table 4. ***Some Dimensions od professionalization of MPs 1990 - 1994 – 1998*** *(in %)*

	MDF			SZDSZ			FKGP			MSZP			Fidesz-MPP			KDNP			MIÉP			Total		
	1990	1994	1998	1990	1994	1998	1990	1994	1998	1990	1994	1998	1990	1994	1998	1990	1994	1998	1990	1994	1998	1990	1994	1998
(%) of new MPs*	95.2	31.6	52.9	97.9	22.9	12.5	100	73.1	64.6	818	81.8	15.7	100	30.0	77.0	100	50.0	-	-	-	64.3	93.5	61.1	47.9
Local politics background	10.5	7.9	41.2	5.6	11.4	8.3	5.6	23.1	25.0	0	35.3	9.7	0	10.0	50.7	0	27.3	-	-	-	14.3	4.6	27.5	29.0
Party position	68.4	39.5	29.4	88.9	32.9	45.8	94.4	42.3	18.8	58.6	15.3	9.7	100	35.0	18.9	100	42.5	-	-	-	42.9	77.5	27.5	18.7
Government position	0	36.8	0	0	0	41.7	0	0	0	20.7	0	11.2	0	0	0	0	2.7	-	-	-	0	4.6	6.4	6.5
Parliamentary experience*	4.8	68.4	35.3	2.1	75.7	83.3	0	26.9	33.3	20.7	15.3	83.6	0	70.0	18.9	0	36.4	-	-	-	7.1	5.2	36.3	47.4
No political position	78.7	7.9	23.5	62.8	14.3	0	61.4	26.9	39.6	36.4	43.5	12.7	40.9	20.0	28.4	42.9	13.6	-	-	-	35.7	64.4	30.6	22.5

* new MPs are those who did not have a mandate at the end of the previous parliamentary term while those with parliamentary experience are incumbents. The two figures do not necessarily end up in 100 percent because there is a growing number of 'returners', that is MPs who return to parliamentary benches after a shorter or longer pause. Sometimes the interval is long indeed, for example one returned in 1998 who was a sitting MP in 1945-1947. The share of returners in totals is 1.3% in 1990, 2.6% in 1994 and 4.7% in 1998.

Table 5. ***The number and distribution of committee positions 1990-1997***

	1990 May	1993 May	1994 June	1995 November	1996 December	1997 December
number of MPs in parliament	386	386	386	386	386	382
number of positions in standing committees	249	287	291	375	387	387
number of positions in special/temporary committees*	51	82	43	16	41	28
number of positions altogether	300	369	334	391	428	415
number of MPs without committee position	115	83	89	73	62	63

* A new Standing Order in1994 autumn eliminated special committees and the role of temporary committees (comprising investigation committees and case committees) has increased

The demand to ensure proportional representation for the parties also increased membership to some extent. Thus we can assume that not exclusively functional needs but also personal and political interests made committee positions more numerous. Nevertheless, there are many MPs who do not have a committee seat while others occupy more than one. As the table shows, although the number of MPs without a committee position has decreased almost continuously, the number of MPs without a committee position was still relatively high near the end of the second term (63 MPs that is ca. 16 per cent). By contrast, as of July 1997, 101 MPs, or if we exclude the positions in the less important temporary committees 66 MPs (17 per cent) had two or more committee positions (see Table 6), which means the number of those without a committee position and those having more than one position is almost identical.

Table 6. ***Some characteristics of MPs with multiple posts as of July 1997.***

parliamentary party group	member of two or more committees	member of two or more committees (temporary committees excluded)	incumbent MPs among them (number and % of the first group)	electoral incumbency of the party	has leadership position in the parliamentary party group
MSZP	22	9	3 (13%)	15%	0
SZDSZ	23	16	19 (82%)	75%	2
Fidesz-MPP	14	11	11 (78%)	70%	1
KDNP	12	9	5 (40%)	36%	1
FKGP	11	7	6 (54%)	27%	2
MDF	9	8	7 (7%)	68%	3
MDNP	11	6	9 (81%)	-	3
Total	101	66	60 (60%)	-	12

MSZP Hungarian Socialist Party; senior member in the coalition government between 1994-98
SZDSZ Alliance of Free Democrats; junior member in the coalition government between 1994-98
Fidesz-MPP Alliance of Young Democrats-Hungarian Civic Party
KDNP Christian Democratic People's Party
FKGP Independent Smallholders Party
MDF Hungarian Democratic Forum
MDNP Hungarian Democratic People's Party, a splinter group of the MDF, formed in 1996

Thus, there is a group of MPs that is more embedded and another that is less embedded in parliamentary work than the average. We can assume that the former group constitutes a more *professional segment* of the parliamentarians.

It is important to examine the background of those who have multiple committee positions. According to the hypothesis incumbency is more pronounced among committee members than in the House as a whole. Indeed, while the incumbency rate was 36 percent in the entire parliament in 1994 (137 MPs from a total of 386), it is close to 60 percent among those with several committee seats: 60 MPs of the 101 that have two or more committee positions, and it is more than 90 percent if we exclude the less important investigation committee positions (that is 60 MPs are incumbents of those 66 that have 2 or more standing committee positions). More experienced MPs obviously acquire more positions than newcomers do.

4.2. The parties

The second assumption is that professionalization patterns are different in different parties. The origins and roots of parties are different in this respect at least on two grounds: first, the Socialists had a comparative advantage in contrast to all the other new parties because they were able to 'learn' political skills in the communist period; second, the Free Democrat and Young Democrat parliamentary elites are more embedded in different professional areas than the MPs of Smallholders, Democratic Forum or Christian democracy who have a smaller professional network capacity. In order to clarify the background of this more professional group and demonstrate how committees act as possible agents of parliamentary institutionalization in this respect, it is essential to include the dimensions of the general parliamentary incumbency as well as the position of incumbent MPs in each parliamentary party. Table 6 shows some interesting facts. The number of MPs with multiple committee positions was the highest among the two governing parliamentary parties (MSZP - socialists, and SZDSZ- free democrats). Since these parliamentary party groups are larger than the opposition parliamentary groups larger numbers do not mean higher proportions, however. In fact, members in smaller parliamentary party groups more often serve in two committees, otherwise their party could not fill the committee posts available to them.

In a more detailed analysis, incumbency rates in the individual parties were diverse, ranging from the lowest 15 per cent of the socialists (MSZP) to the highest 75 per cent of the free democrats (SZDSZ). There were apparently different continuity patterns in each party. In the two highly stable parliamentary party groups, the Free Democrats and the Young Democrats (Fidesz-MPP), incumbents have multiple committee positions in a larger proportion than the otherwise also high incumbency rate of these parties had been: 82 per cent versus 75 per cent and 78 per cent versus 70 per cent. Thus, while incumbents generally tend to have more committee positions than non-incumbents, this trend is even more explicit in parties that show high stability anyway. We can conclude that the performance of the entire party *helps professionalization trends* considerably. Even in the Smallholders (FGKP) and the Christian democrats (KDNP), the share of 'multi-functionaries' is higher among the incumbents than the party's general incumbency pattern: 54 per cent versus 27 per cent and 40 per cent versus 36 per cent respectively.

The large governing socialist parliamentary party group seems to be the exception to the rule - for several reasons. First, the general incumbency rate of the party was very low due to their landslide victory in 1994, and second the party does not provide the incumbents with multiple committee positions - they rather serve in the government. Thus, it seems that there are at least two ways to reward incumbents: *government hierarchy* and *committee positions.* As for the former the socialists are a good example, while in all the other parties parliamentary incumbents serve in high proportion in committees (or in several committees). Virtually all the 137 parliamentary incumbents have a committee (or several) position or a government post with a handful (mainly temporary) exceptions.

4.3. Differences between committees

The third hypothesis is that in more important committees personal continuity will be even higher than on the average committee level. To test this hypothesis *personal continuity* within the *same committee* will be examined. This comparison will be made first between the first and the second legislative terms (inter-term comparison) and second within the second legislative term (intra-term comparison). The *inter-term* comparison might be still relatively early because overall parliamentary incumbency is low and two parties in particular (the MSZP and the MDF) performed very differently in the two national elections. Thus, I will leave out from the analysis of the inter-term personal committee continuity both the MSZP (socialists) (because the size of their parliamentary party group changed from a mere 31 to 209, and as we have seen socialist incumbents are rewarded by government - or party - positions), and the Forum (MDF), the leading force of the first democratic coalition (due to their electoral failure in 1994 and subsequent party split).

I found that in the second term among the remaining four parliamentary parties 80 committee members were incumbents, and 34 of them served in the same committee both in the first and the second term. Not surprisingly, this group almost exclusively consisted of Free Democrats and Young Democrats, the two parties that demonstrated professionalization trends in other respects as well. Although these figures are lower than in established legislatures with a long democratic tradition, considering the low level of general parliamentary incumbency they are obvious signs of continuity.

The number and share of committee members as compared to the size of committees ranges from 110 percent (altogether only 21 served in the Education committee while the committee size was 19) to 165 percent (in the Human Rights Committee 33 served for shorter or longer periods while the committee size was 20). These figures do not necessarily indicate consistency, however, because it might well happen that several MPs enter a committee for a short period and occupy the 'same' seat while in the meantime a large majority of committee members remain the same. Differences range from 30 percent (Immunity Committee) to 81 percent (Foreign Affairs). Some important committees perform relatively badly (for example the Interior Committee with 50 percent consistency). On the other extreme, in addition to Foreign Affairs, Education, Agriculture, Cultural Affairs, Defense, Economic and Cultural Affairs are above the two-third-consistency level. It can be assumed that parties tend to select the members to these committees more carefully. It will require further and deeper analysis in the third legislative term whether these patterns will prevail or not. As of now it is sufficient to conclude that a remarkable degree of consistency exists in some cases while committee differences are also obvious.

The professionalization of parliament within the committee framework becomes evident if we examine the professional background of committee members. The analysis clearly shows the patterns of specialization in committees. Table 7 indicates the percentage share of the most frequent degrees in all the committees. These shares do not necessarily correspond to the share of members because several members have more than one degree, thus their answer will appear in two (or rarely in three) places.

Table 7. ***Dominant degree in commitees (in % of responses) as of 1996***

Committee	Humanities	Agriculture	Medical	Engineering	Law	Economy
Constitutional	19	7	0	3	63	3
Interior	13	16	10	13	16	16
Foreign Aff.	29	3	6	9	12	18
Defence	25	15	0	16	0	16
Budgeting	10	17	0	10	10	47
Economic	3	9	0	31	3	44
Social	16	4	40	0	12	26
Environmental	5	5	16	37	11	11
Cultural	45	0	0	5	10	10
Human Rights	36	5	5	9	14	5
Education	62	4	0	12	0	12
Agricultural	0	63	13	3	0	3
Immunity	27	0	0	0	46	0
Nat. Security	27	9	0	9	27	18
European Int.	0	7	0	14	7	71
Auditing	12	12	8	20	20	20
Employment	21	0	5	5	5	16
Social Org.	18	12	6	12	6	0
Const. Prep.	8	0	4	4	77	0
Entire parliament*	9%	9%	7%	10%	21%	9%

*Another 7% had other degrees (like theology or military academy). Altogether cc. 72% of MPs have an MA degree, the above list in the given categories adds up to 65%

Different committees show different professional degree patterns. For example, in the Constitutional Committee, the Committee on Constitutional Preparation and the Immunity Committee the share of law degrees is much above the parliamentary average; economy degrees dominate in the Budgeting, Economic and European Integration Committees and, just to give a final example, humanities degrees in the Education committee.

Thus, the three hypotheses about membership patterns were confirmed: committee positions could be tied to a well-outlined membership group (that is incumbents) despite a high parliamentary turnover rate; there were significant differences between the parties in this respect (that is in some parties professional politicians are more numerous than in others); and both the inter-term and intra-term committee continuity tend to indicate that committees began to work as agents of parliamentary institutionalization. As a further point we also found that the consolidation of membership went further than that: specific professional background requirements began to appear in certain committees. Indeed, it seems that it is justified to talk about consolidation patterns in terms of political personnel and professionalization.

5. Concluding remark

This case study about parliamentary political elites sought to demonstrate that they form a clearly distinguishable group which shows a growing degree of stability and professionalization. The parliamentary political elite proved to be a fast learner in Hungary not only in stabilizing itself but also in finding the means and ways (as the above committee section has illustrated) to employ institutions for further strengthening its positions. The first elite groups in the transition had a major role - they were sitting at the chess table. This gave a special flavor - elite dominance - to the transition. It seems that a large group among them has remained in politics in the last ten years and is largely embedded in its elite positions. Not only the political system but the political elite has also become largely consolidated. It will remain the task of the next ten years to assure that consolidation takes the form of further societal integration as well.

References

Diamond, Larry (1996) 'Is the Third Wave Over?' Journal of Democracy 1996 (7) no. 3 July

Diamond, Larry (1997) The End of the Third Wave and the Global Future of Democracy. Reihe Politikwissenschaft, Vienna, Political Science Series no. 45 1997 July

Ferge, Zsuzsa (1998), Szociálpolitika 1989-1997 (Social Policy 1989-1997) in: Magyarország évtizedkönyve (Political Decade Book of Hungary), Budapest: Demokrácia Kutatások Magyar Központja

Lijphart, Arend (1992), 'Democratization and Constitutional Choices in Czecho-Slovakia, Hungary and Poland 1989-1991' Journal of Theoretical Politics, no. 4

Higley, John - Jan Pakulski - Wlodzimierz Wesolowski (1998) 'Introduction: Elite Change and Democratic Regimes in Eastern Europe) in: John Higley and Jan Pakulski eds. Elite Change and Democratic Regimes in Eastern Europe. Routledge, 1998.

Huntington, Samuel P (1991), The Third Wave: Democratization in the Late Twentieth Century. Norman: University of Oklahoma Press

Ilonszki, Gabriella (1998) 'Representation Deficit in a New Democracy: Theoretical Considerations and the Hungarian Case' Communist and Post-Communist Studies no. 2

John Higley - Judith Kullberg - Jan Pakulski (1996) 'The Persistence of Post-communist Elites) Journal of Democracy no. 2

Linz, Juan J. - Alfred Stepan (1996), Problems of Democratic Transition and Consolidation. Baltimore: Johns Hopkins University Press

Szabó, Máté (1998) A tüntetések szerepe a magyar demokratizálódásban (The Role of Demonstrations in Democratization in Hungary) in: Magyarország évtizedkönyve (Political Decade Book of Hungary), Budapest: Demokrácia Kutatások Magyar Központja

Tóka, Gábor (1998), Political Parties in East Central Europe' in: L. Diamond - Marc F. Plattner - Yun-han Chu - Hung - mao Tien eds. Consolidating Third Wave Democracies. The Johns Hopkins University Press: Baltimore and London

Post-Soviet Geopolitics and the Politics of Identity in Democratic Consolidation: The Case of Estonia

PAMI AALTO

1. Introduction

In this chapter, I examine the connections between post-Soviet geopolitics, the politics of identity and democratisation. I argue that these three concepts and the processes they connote are interrelated. Specifically, I examine the case of Estonia. I invoke a heuristic model, which enables us to examine the construction of geopolitical discourses in Estonia. I argue that these discourses derive from subjective experiences and perceptions through the mediating function of identity politics. Effectively, I use the model to analyse how developments both at the discourse and subjective levels are influenced by competing modes of identity politics. Finally, I argue that this analysis gives us grounds to claim that the early 1990s enclosure of political space in Estonia is turning into an opening up of political space. I also argue that this shift has created better prospects of democratic consolidation in Estonia.

2. Post-Soviet Geopolitics: Focus on the Construction of Discourses

The initial connotation of the term "post-Soviet geopolitics" can be related to the territorial changes brought about by the collapse of the Soviet Union - the emergence of fifteen more or less new states and some twenty new boundaries (cf. Paasi, 1999). The territory of these states is, almost as a rule, subject to either manifest or latent controversy. There is, therefore, ample room for geopolitical imagination. For example, Russia tries to accommodate secessionist tendencies in Chechnya and Tatarstan. Georgia, Ukraine, and Moldova struggle with irredentist movements in, respectively, Abkhazia, Crimea, and the Trans-Dniestr region. Estonia and Latvia, for their part, still lack border treaties with Russia in spite of years of negotiation.[1]

Territorial changes aside, post-Soviet geopolitics refers to the re-structuring of military and political allegiances in the "East" and "West" of Europe, i.e., to the enlargement processes of the EU and NATO, and to Russia's efforts of acquiring a peace-keeping role and promoting closer integration within the Commonwealth of Independent States (CIS). Furthermore, post-Soviet geopolitics connotes the struggle of governments and large multinational companies for access to new markets and natural resources. The specific aspects of post-Soviet geopolitics that I wish to examine in this chapter are, however, discursive. Put simply, I focus on the *construction of discourses* within a single case, Estonia.[2] I argue that whether we are examining geopolitical discourses that touch upon territorial, political, military, or economic issues, more often than not, we confront the question of *identity politics*. That is to say, geopolitical discourses do not exist in a vacuum (Häkli 1998, 335-338). Rather, they spring up from subjectively perceived and experienced social contexts that are coloured by different modes of identity politics.

In short, post-Soviet geopolitics has different faces in different discourses, but the point is that these discourses are often coloured by peoples' conceptions of issues like "the place one does belong to" and its symbolic boundaries, specific conceptions of who may legitimately exert influence there, and by more general accounts of the "Self" and "Other". These conceptions account for variation between enclosure and opening up of political space -- therefore, they also account for issues that are of crucial importance in democratic consolidation.

The first question is, accordingly: how does one best examine the construction of geopolitical discourses? In International Relations (IR), the notion of construction is most conventionally understood as the interplay between state agency and the social structure of the international anarchy. This kind of a "mainstream IR constructionism" holds that state-agents continuously engage with practices like self-help and power politics, and consequently, make and re-make international anarchy (e.g. Wendt 1987; 1992). In the same fashion, states engage with identity practices like "democracy", which they externalise into the international level. Subsequently, in their international agency, states can become constrained by these very same identity practices, like the norm to behave "democratically" (Katzenstein 1996; Checkel 1998). In short, in focusing on the interplay between state agency and international structure, "mainstream IR constructionism" neglects the intra-state *processes* in which identity practices are constituted (Aalto, forthcoming). In other words, "mainstream IR constructionism" ignores intra-state construction processes, and thus, cannot account for intra-state shifts in identity politics. This approach, I argue, is not very well applicable in post-Soviet space. This is because post-Soviet identities are not constant but mostly in a flux. The key argument I wish to advance is, consequently, that shifts in identity politics may have profound effects on discourses. In order to summarise this argument, I invoke a heuristic model (Fig. 1).[3]

I assert that geopolitical *discourses* derive from *subjectivity* through the mediating function of *identity politics*. Furthermore, employing the framework of the Copenhagen School of Security Studies (Buzan 1997; Buzan et al. 1998; Wæver 1995),[4] I allow two possible discourse level modalities. By advancing *securitising discourses*, agents move issues into a specific "security realm" defined by a sense of emergency. Through securitising issues, agents claim that they concern the survival of a highly valued referent object. In advancing *de-securitising discourses*, for their part, agents move issues back into the realm of "normal" bargaining politics. In addition, I allow two possible subjective level modalities, *conflictual everyday life* and *ambivalent everyday life*. I use the model in the two following sections to analyse developments both at the discourse and subjective levels.[5] I argue that conflictual everyday life, and securitising moves and discourses, accounted for the early 1990s tendency towards an enclosure in Estonia's political space. I also argue that a subsequent return to ambivalent everyday life and the emergence of de-securitising discourses account for the current opening up of political space, thus creating better prospects for democratic consolidation.

Figure 1. ***A Heuristic Model: the Construction of Geopolitical Discourses***

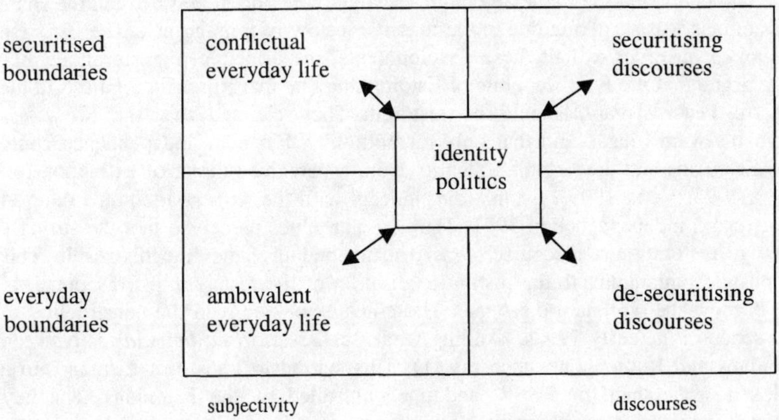

3. Conflictual Everyday Life and Securitising Discourses: Enclosure of Political Space

The 1970s and 1980s witnessed a gradual transition to conflictual everyday life in the then Estonian Soviet Socialist Republic (ESSR) (Kukk 1993, 365-382). The ever increasing pace and extent of Russification and Sovietisation of Estonia conditioned this transition. The bulk of Estonians experienced very negatively developments like the introduction of new "forbidden zones" and "no-go cities" connected with the Soviet military establishment, the launching of new russification campaigns in schools and kindergartens, and the building of new blocks of flats for the inflowing Russophone immigrants -- at a time when the Estonians' own accommodation needs were mostly neglected. Estonians started gradually to perceive their space as shrinking. They started to identify themselves more clearly with the fellow Estonians, whom they conceived to be equivalent with themselves in terms of their common differentiation from the "colonising other", the immigrant Russophones. This kind of a subjective juxtaposition of Estonian and Russophone/Soviet identity was a necessary precondition for the emergence of the Estonian Independence Movement in the late 1980s. At certain tense moments, in the extreme, the "colonising other" lost all of its positive dispositions and became depicted as a negation of the Estonian identity. These moments represented the operation of a form of identity politics that Laclau and Mouffe (1985) term the *logic of equivalence*:

> "Through equivalence something is expressed which the object is not. Thus, a relation of equivalence absorbing *all* the positive determinations of the colonizer in opposition to the colonized, does not create a system of positive differential positions between the two, simply because it dissolves all positivity: the colonizer is discursively constructed as the anti-colonized. In other words, the identity has become purely negative" (p. 128)

These subjective perceptions and experiences of the "Other" contributed to the emergence of tensions and occasional conflicts between the Estonians and immigrant Russophones. Societal conditions turned, consequently, favourable for constructing securitising discourses. By and large, Estonian elites started to argue that the survival of the Estonian identity is at stake, as opportunities for using publicly the Estonian language and endorsing the Estonian culture became more and more rare, and the share of the Estonians was shrinking due to the massive inflow of immigrants.[6] The Estonian elites invoked, in order to halt these developments, the principle of restoration; they started to argue that the First Republic of Estonia, the one that Russia recognised in the 1920 Tartu Peace Treaty, should be restored. They claimed that the Soviet-era developments were illegal, and that only restoration of Estonia's independence could save the Estonians and the Estonian identity from a perceived threat of extinction (cf. Taagepera 1993; Vetik 1999). Estonia did, indeed, with the August attempted coup in Moscow, regain independence in 1991. The Estonian elites perceived that the strongly securitising "restorationist discourse" was instrumental in achieving this result. This perception was tantamount to the institutionalisation of the restorationist discourse. In short, it became the dominant discourse. The elites employed it in the construction of political space in the early 1990s, building what I call *securitised boundaries* between the Estonians and Russophones (see Fig. 1). This started to transform Estonia into a more closed space than the ESSR, and one controlled by the Estonians. The key objectives of the restorationist discourse can be summarised as follows:

The project of "Estonisation" of Estonia. The 1938 Law on Citizenship was restored, in order to, at least symbolically, restore the demographic situation of the First Republic. The law restricts the body of citizens to citizens of the First Republic, and to their descendants. According to the amended 1995 version, non-citizens - in practice, the bulk of the Russophone immigrants - must pass a test of Estonian language, culture, and constitution, and apply for citizenship through naturalisation.[7] An amendment to the Law on Civil Service, for its part, states that all Civil Servants must be citizens, or must have submitted an application for citizenship, whilst the 1989 and 1995 Laws on Language define Estonian as the only state language.[8] Moreover, a parliamentary decision was adopted stipulating that all secondary education should be in the Estonian language by 2007. In parliamentary elections, only citizens can participate. People who have been resident for more than five years in one place can vote in municipal elections; also, they can stand as candidates if they can display a sufficient command of the Estonian language.

Demarcation of the Estonian state. Estonia started to demand the restitution of the Narva and Pechory (Petserimaa) territories that Russia ceded to Estonia in the 1920 Tartu Peace Treaty. These demands were partly motivated by identity concerns. The territories are small in size, and they do not possess any particular economic or geo-strategic value. But, in the 1920 Treaty, Russia recognised the independence and sovereignty of Estonia "forever", with these territories included. Because the Estonian elites perceived the 1920 Treaty as the "birth certificate of Estonia", they demanded that Russia should recognise it, with all of its territorial clauses included. During 19941997, however, Estonia dropped the territorial claims. This move was designed to finally reach a border treaty and a well-controllable border with Russia.

Escape from Russia's sphere of influence and a "return to Europe". Despite having launched the project of "Estonisation", Estonian elites perceived Estonia as handicapped by the large Russophone population of which Russia proclaimed to be the legitimate protector - if necessary by force. To escape this geopolitical burden, Estonia consistently resisted all pledges by Russia to join the CIS organisation or to enter into any bilateral security arrangements. The desire of the Estonian elites was, by contrast, to consolidate Estonia's independence from Russia by seeking membership in the EU and NATO. They conceived of membership in these two "Western" organisations as guaranteeing an escape from Russia's sphere of influence and a "return" into Estonia's "natural" location, "Europe". However, factions among Estonian elites have come to resist any efforts by these organisations to ask Estonia to re-consider the project of "Estonisation".

4. A Return to Ambivalent Everyday Life and the Emergence of De-Securitising Discourses: An Opening up of Political Space

Everyday life returned to calmer forms after the occasionally tense times of the Independence Movement. The conflictual tendencies had, as Smith (1998, 14) notes, largely disappeared by 1995-6. The reasons are obvious: Estonians viewed the withdrawal of the Russian/Soviet troops in 1994 in a very positive light, interpreting it as a sure sign of consolidation of Estonia's independence. The Estonians also have, each one individually, just like the Russophones, to put questions of ethnic survival away from one's immediate everyday agenda, since harsh post-Soviet reality forces everyone soon to focus on personal survival. Moreover, the Russophones do not have very strong incentives to engage with any kind of a serious protest movement. Quite simply, they perceive that to stay in Estonia is their best bet, especially when compared to the persisting turmoil and insecurity in Russia.[9] There are several factors assuring the Russophones that they can live peacefully in Estonia: the presence of the Organisation for Security and Co-operation in Europe (OSCE) High Commissioner for National Minorities, and the rather pragmatic policies adopted by the Estonian Government in residence permits questions and toward the about 10,000 Russian/Soviet military pensioners in Estonia. Also, recently, Estonia partially eased the naturalisation procedures.[10]

Everyday life has, then, came back into certain settled paths and routine activities characteristic of people's general way of conducting day-to-day existence (cf. Heller 1984, 166-182). The "Other" is again habitually and in an unreflective way identified as simply different. The "Other" is, just as in the Soviet era, before the gradual transition to a conflictual everyday life, described as having certain dispositions differentiating him or her from the "Self". Some of these dispositions are approved and some others disapproved. Ambivalence between approval and disapproval signifies the prevalence of what I call *everyday boundaries* between the "Self" and "Other"; the Estonians and Russophones live in their own circles, mainly separated from each other, but respecting and sometimes even praising the difference. This is, in Laclau and Mouffe's (1985, 130) terms, the operation of the *logic of difference*: "the logic of equivalence is a logic of the simplification of the political space, while the logic of difference is a logic of its expansion and increasing complexity". Thus, a return to ambivalent everyday life means that the formerly dominant mode of identity politics - the logic of equivalence - is now clearly subdued in spite of the fact that echoes of it can still be found. This situation allows for the emergence of de-securitising discourses.[11] These discourses resist the restorationist discourse and its aim at an enclosure of political space. The key ideas in these de-securitising discourses can be summarised in the following way:

De-securitising the inter-ethnic situation. As far as Estonians are concerned, notwithstanding the fact that they almost unequivocally praise the historical significance of the project of "Estonisation", groups among them display a genuine willingness to assist the immigrant Russophones in engaging with the Estonian society. Recently, the Estonian authorities also joined in these discourses, in the form of Estonia's new integration strategy adopted in 1998. The document argues that the understanding of the immigrant Russophones as a problem should be replaced by an attitude of taking them as a resource and equal participants in state building. The message is that with the success in implementing the project of "Estonisation", the Estonian identity is no longer *that much* threatened by the presence of a large bulk of Russophones in Estonia.[12] This is something that the Russophones themselves are very keen to point out.

Estonia as a bridge between the "East" and "West". Having appeared occasionally during Estonia's Independence Movement, this idea is now experiencing a renaissance. The more appealing version of this story operates with an economic argument: Estonia should normalise relations with Russia in order to promote transit trade and other economic opportunities. The Russophones, especially those living in the Russian-dominated Ida-Virumaa county, North-Eastern Estonia, often advocate, too, state-assisted co-operation with the Pskov and Leningrad oblasts. The more radical version of this story, by contrast, focuses on culture. The Estonians are often inclined, at least privately, to accept that Estonia is located between the "East" and "West". But only small groups among them, in opposition to the Russophones, are willing to embrace wide-ranging political multiculturalism.

De-mystifying the "return to Europe". That groups among Estonians dispute the view of the Russophones as a potential "fifth column" with dangerously close links with Russia, persuades them to dispute, too, the image of a "prowling giant of Russia". Therefore, if there is no outstanding Russian threat, there is no overriding need to join the EU and NATO either. Quite simply, these Estonians argue that Estonia needs not to forget, as it has mainly done so far, social and regional development programmes in a rush for an early EU entry and for all of the competitiveness it presupposes. Estonia should not, furthermore, increase military spending either in a quest to join NATO, an organisation that might potentially drag Estonia into conflicts in which Estonia has no stake at all. The Russophones, in particular, are eager to insist on, as they put it, the meaninglessness of Estonia's NATO bid.

5. Implications for Democratic Consolidation

I argue that my analysis of developments both at the subjective and discourse levels gives us grounds to speak of an opening up of political space in Estonia. What is more, I argue that this opening up has created better prospects of democratic consolidation. At the subjective level, with a return to a more ambivalent modality of everyday life, people feel more secure than during the turbulent times of the Independence Movement and the first years after Estonia's regaining of independence. Now people can, in relative terms, to think, move, purchase, and invest freely. This is a necessary precondition for any democracy to function properly. When this basic condition is met, there is more room for all other expressions of democracy. People need to feel secure, otherwise, there is a big risk of a democratic failure (Miles 1995, 58).

In a country like Estonia, which has a large Russophone population and which is prone to be handicapped by Russia's great power ambitions, it is significant that the Estonians and Russophones begin to feel, at least to a certain extent, that they can trust members of the other group (cf. Weibull & Holmberg 1997, 214). This relative calmness and emerging trust in inter-ethnic relations allows for a smooth functioning of day-to-day political processes and the orderly organisation of free elections, without any big worries of unrest or violent election campaigns. Therefore, it is misleading to assert that electoral competition and opportunities for participation alone are a *sufficient* condition of democracy. It should be mentioned, too, that they are conditioned by general societal processes (cf. Linz & Stepan 1996, 4). True, in Estonia, there are "everyday boundaries" between the Estonians and Russophones, but equally true is that one can travel across these boundaries. Though perhaps not socially encouraged, it is not specifically sanctioned either. Contacts with members of the other group make people aware of differences, but at the same time, these contacts may help them to accept that the "Other" has a human face.

It is important to bear in mind, however, that the developments in the 1990s, on the whole, have increased the Estonians' sense of security in the first place. Vihalemm and Lauristin (1997, 280-282) imply that this was in order to prevent the Estonians from developing a permanent sense of insecurity, which might hamper any prospective accommodation efforts. In any case, the recent subjective and discourse level developments help the Russophones to feel more at ease in Estonia. At first, in an "Estonised" Estonia, many of them felt slightly puzzled and unwelcome. This feeling seems considerably subdued by now, as reflected by a Russophone politician who immigrated into Estonia during the Soviet period:

> "In Russia, I don't feel at ease, but rather, slightly tense. I don't feel I can walk freely, so to say. By contrast, in Narva [Russian-dominated town in North-Eastern Estonia -- *P.A.*], and Estonia at large, I feel comfortable. It's my country and my government. I feel protected by the law. I am assured that I can turn, if necessary, towards our institutions and get legal advice. I feel myself at home here. Many Russians feel much more secure here in Narva than in, I'm afraid to say, Russia today. It is a very insecure place to work and live in...we already have a certain degree of stability" (Male, 49).[13]

There is evidence that the Russophones are increasingly adapting and integrating into life in independent Estonia. First, in a survey study conducted in 1995, 69% of Russian respondents claimed that the Russophone population is loyal to Estonia. Second, the Russophones are gradually loosing their business and personal ties in Russia. Third, the young Russophones are adopting the same individualist and competitive values as young Estonians. Fourth, the Russophones use the Estonian language more often than they used to when speaking with the Estonians (Vihalemm & Lauristin 1997; cf. Kirch 1997). It is perhaps fair to accentuate, this evidence notwithstanding, that what is at issue, is essentially the Russophones' integration into the Estonian society. This integration is starting to take place on terms that are defined by the Estonians on the basis of their security and geopolitical concerns. Thus, at issue is not a genuine process of mutual integration. The odds are, however, that the Russophones' integration process *may*, through time, gain even more momentum and draw with it those, too, who currently resist.[14] Estonia's relative economic success may add to this.

These developments are perhaps more in evidence for the Russophone elites than for the grassroots. To put it roughly, the current Russophone elites are the ones who opted to stay in independent Estonia. The majority of the more Moscow-minded ones immigrated to Russia in the early 1990s. The remaining elites are, moreover, often proficient in Estonian, often possess Estonian citizenship, and are more capable of adapting into life in post-Soviet Estonia than the bulk of the Russophone population of which many are industrial workers. Therefore, the Russophone elites' *subject positions* (Doty 1997, 384-386) persuade them to get engaged with the Estonian society. For example, the Russophones have, from 1995 onwards, six MPs elected into the Estonian Parliament. These MPs and other Russophone elites are often critical of the Estonians' geopolitical discourses, but at the same time, they have no particular incentives of trying to mobilise the broader Russophone population into a confrontation with the Estonians. Nor do they have the means of doing so because of the internal factions among the

Russophone population.[15] For them, a much more attractive option is to concur with some of the arguments advanced in the emerging de-securitising discourses. The resulting common reference points for Estonian and Russophone elites, consequently, provide important building blocks for democratic development in Estonia.

In conclusion, I wish to accentuate, alongside which Vanhanen (1998), and Linz & Stepan (1996), that Estonia has definitely passed the stage of *democratic transition*. The subjective and discourse level developments that I have outlined in this chapter put the rather well-functioning political procedures more firmly in place. These procedures have proved capable of producing elected governments that can formulate new policies, rule without a need to share power with any undue bodies, and deliver certain goods that respond relatively satisfactorily to at least some of the expectations of the Estonian and Russophone publics. This is in stark contrast with the CIS states, in which disorder and promises of democracy have so far, more often than not, turned into an incomplete order accompanied by a more or less authoritarian rule. Of course, the recent tendencies in Estonia do not rule out the possibility of opposite developments.[16] Thus, perhaps it is fair to say that for Estonia, controversy continues to prevail over the direction that *democratic consolidation* is going to take. This is a question of whether we will be witnessing a further opening up of political space - whether an "ethnic democracy" or a "liberal democracy" will become the dominant model (cf. ibid., 433; Gillespie & Vetik 1999, 141-142). In this chapter, I have demonstrated that factors like geopolitical discourses and identity politics affect the prospects of these possible outcomes. At the same time I remain convinced that I have not exhausted the complex web of issues that one might take into account in assessing the problems in building a viable democracy.

Notes

1. On the basis of the 1920 Tartu and Riga Treaties, in the early 1990s, both Estonia and Latvia posed territorial claims to Russia, but subsequently dropped them. All parties have accepted the present de facto borders. Russia has, however, resorted to stalling tactics and refused to sign the practically finalised border treaties.
2. I exclude from my analysis "external" discourses in other states - most prominently, Russia. These "external" discourses are of course noted and interpreted in Estonia, and ,therefore, have an impact on Estonian discourses as well. For an analysis of Russia as the "external" factor, see e.g. Aalto (1997), Brubaker (1996), and Haabsaar & Kirch (1997).
3. The model derives especially from Bloom's (1990) work on the "national identity dynamic" and from Burton's (1972) work on the subjective roots of conflict. For an analysis of the concepts that I employ, see Aalto (forthcoming).
4. The Copenhagen School framework focuses on agents' discursive security constructions. It refuses to postulate any objective definitions of security situations, but argues that agents' discursive security constructions have important social consequences.
5. This is based on my fieldwork experiences and the material I compiled in Estonia during January-February 1996, and February-May and October-December 1998. For a more detailed analysis, see Aalto (forthcoming); see also Aalto (1997).
6. In 1934, the share of the Estonians was 89.6 %, whereas in 1989, it was a mere 61.5%.
7. Due to the emigration of about 100,000 people from Estonia after 1989, the Russophones currently number about 500,000. About 250,000 of them do not have any citizenship. An estimated 80,000 are Estonian citizens by descent, whilst about 100,000 have opted for Russian citizenship (see Vetik 1999). Only about 70,000 have been naturalised. What is more, about one third of these people have been naturalised by following a simplified procedure. This means that the number of those who have actually passed the tests on language, culture, and constitution is rather small. The Russophones often consider the language test too demanding as it presupposes that a successful candidate commands a vocabulary of about 2,500 words (Juvakka 1997, 21-23).
8. The use of Russian is, however, allowed in Russian-dominated regions during a transition period (Juvakka 1997, 19).

9. Survey studies have consistently indicated that only a very small faction among Estonia's current Russophone population plans to leave.
10. The new Amendment to the Law on Citizenship adopted in December 1998 entitles parents without citizenship to apply for a simplified naturalisation of their children born after 26 February 1992. The simplified naturalisation scheme does not require passing the tests on the Estonian language, culture and constitution. It is estimated that this amendment concerns about 6,500 children (*Postimees* 9 December 1998). The recommendations of the EU and various other organisations such as OSCE were instrumental in implementing this change in citizenship legislation.
11. I exclude from my analysis, here, too, "external" discourses (see note 2). Russia's recent "softer" rhetoric and policy toward Estonia, and the pressure applied by international organisations like OSCE and the EU, has certainly, too, contributed to the emergence of de-securitising discourses (see e.g. Smith 1998, 15; 1999, 317).
12. The estimated share of Russophones was roughly one third of Estonia's population in 1996. This includes 28% of ethnic Russians, 3% of Ukrainians, and 2% of Byelorussians (Lauristin et al. 1997, 305).
13. This is a quote from an interview that I conducted in Narva, Estonia, December 1998.
14. We may think of those Russophones whose social and economic well-being was connected to the Soviet structures, and who now find themselves made redundant and incapable of coping well - e.g. pensioners and groups of factory workers, and disillusioned young Russophones who do not find themselves willing and fit enough to compete in the Estonian society.
15. For example Smith (1998) points out that there is considerable cultural, political, and social diversity among the Russophone population, which makes references to a unified diaspora problematic.
16. For example Aleksei Semjonov (1998: 267-268), the director of the Legal Information Centre for Human Rights in Tallinn argues that due to a hostile and demonstratively arrogant attitudes both on the part of the Estonian state and the Estonians after 1991, the Russophone population has gradually started to display signs of alienation. According to him, the Estonians' emerging pro-integrationist attitudes have failed to translate into political practices, which may be leading to a manifest conflict.

References

Aalto, Pami (1997) 'Post-Soviet Ethnic Conflicts and the Level of Everyday Life', *The Finnish Review of East European Studies* 4(3), 8-27.

Aalto, Pami (forthcoming in 2000) *Constructing Post-Soviet Geopolitics in Estonia. A Study in Security, Identity, and Subjectivity*. PhD Thesis, University of Bradford.

Bloom, William (1990) *Personal Identity, National Identity and International Relations*. Cambridge: University Press.

Brubaker, Rogers (1996) *Nationalism Reframed. Nationhood and the National Question in the New Europe*. Cambridge: University Press.

Burton, John (1972). *World Society*. Cambridge: University Press.

Buzan, Barry (1997) 'Rethinking Security After the Cold War', *Cooperation and Conflict* 32(1), pp. 5-28.

Buzan, Barry & O. Wæver & J. de Wilde (1998) *Security: A New Framework for Analysis*. Boulder: Lynne Rienner.

Checkel, Jeffrey T. (1998) 'The Constructivist Turn in International Relations Theory', *World Politics* 50(January), pp. 324-348.

Doty, Roxanne Lynn (1997) 'Aporia: A Critical Examination of the Agent-Structure Problematique in International Relations Theory', *European Journal of International Relations* 3(3), pp. 363-392.

Gillespie, David J. & R. Vetik (1999) 'Perspectives of Students at Estonian Universities on Estonia's Independence and Democracy', in R. Vetik, *Inter-Ethnic Relations in Estonia 1988-1998*, pp. 132-150. Tampere: University of Tampere.

Haabsaar, Enn & A. Kirch (1997) 'Influence of Russia on the Integration of Russians in Estonia: Historical Retrospection and the Current Trends', in A. Kirch (ed.) *The Integration of Non-Estonians into Estonian Society: History, Problems and Trends*, pp. 74-93. Tallinn: Estonian Academy Publishers.

Heller, Agnes (1984) *Everyday Life*. London: Routledge & Kegan Paul.

Häkli, Jouni (1998) 'Discourse in the Production of Political Space: Decolonizing the Symbolism of Provinces in Finland', *Political Geography* 17(3), pp. 331-363.

Juvakka, Kai (1997) 'Kielikysymys Viron kansalaisuuspolitiikassa', *The Finnish Review of East European Studies* 4(1), pp. 17-33.

Katzenstein, Peter J. (ed.) (1996) *The Culture of National Security: Norms and Identity in World Politics.* New York: Columbia University Press.
Kirch, Aksel (ed) (1997) *The Integration of Non-Estonians into Estonian Society: History, Problems and Trends.* Tallinn: Estonian Academy Publishers.
Kukk, Mare (1993), 'Political Opposition in Soviet Estonia 1940-1987', *Journal of Baltic Studies* XXIV(4)(Winter), pp. 360-384.
Laclau, Ernesto & C. Mouffe (1985) *Hegemony & Socialist Strategy. Towards a Radical Democratic Politics.* London: Verso.
Lauristin, Marju & P. Vihalemm, with K. E. Rosengren & L. Weibull (eds) (1997) *Return to the Western World. Cultural and Political Perspectives on the Estonian Post-Communist Transition.* Tartu: Tartu University Press.
Linz, Juan J. & A. Stepan (1996) *Problems of Democratic Transition and Consolidation. Southern Europe, South America, and Post-Communist Europe.* Baltimore and London: The John Hopkins University Press.
Miles, William F. (1995) 'Tragic Tradeoffs: Democracy and Security in Chad', *The Journal of Modern African Studies* 33(1), pp. 53-65.
Paasi, Anssi (1999) 'The Political Geography of Boundaries at the End of the Millennium: Challenges of the De-Territorializing World', in H. Eskelinen & I. Liikanen & J. Oksa (eds) *Curtains of Iron and Gold. Reconstructing Borders and Scales of Interaction*, pp. 9-24. Aldershot etc.: Ashgate.
Postimees 1998 [Estonian daily].
Semjonov, Aleksei (1998) 'Vene küsimus: kelle stsenaariumi järgi?', in M. Heidmets (ed.) *Vene küsimus ja Eesti valikud*, pp. 263-268. Tallinn: TPÜ Kirjastus.
Smith, David J. (1998) 'Russia, Estonia and the Search for a Stable Ethno-Politics', *Journal of Baltic Studies* 29(1), pp. 3-18.
Smith, David J. (1999) 'The Restorationist Principle in Post Communist Estonia', in C. Williams & T. D. Sfikas (eds) *Ethnicity and Nationalism in Russia, the CIS and the Baltic States*, pp. 287-323. Aldershot, UK: Ashgate.
Taagepera, Rein (1993) *Estonia: Return to Independence.* Boulder, CO: Westview Press.
Vanhanen, Tatu (1998) 'Predictions of Democracy Revisited', paper presented at the IPSA Research Committee 13 Regional Conference "Perspectives of Democratic Consolidation in Central and Eastern Europe", Tallinn, Estonia, November 19--22.
Vihalemm, Triin & M. Lauristin (1997) 'Cultural Adjustment to the Changing Societal Environment: The Case of Russians in Estonia', in M. Lauristin & P. Vihalemm, with K. E. Rosengren & L. Weibull (eds) (1997) *Return to the Western World. Cultural and Political Perspectives on the Estonian Post-Communist Transition*, pp. 279-298. Tartu: Tartu University Press.
Vetik, Raivo (1999) *Inter-Ethnic Relations in Estonia 1988-1998.* Tampere: University of Tampere.
Weibull, Lennart & S. Holmberg (1997) 'Two Young Democracies and an Old One', in M. Lauristin & P. Vihalemm, with K. E. Rosengren & L. Weibull (eds) (1997) *Return to the Western World. Cultural and Political Perspectives on the Estonian Post-Communist Transition*, pp. 211-226. Tartu: Tartu University Press.
Wendt, Alexander (1987) 'The Agent-Structure Problem in International Relations Theory', *International Organization* 41(Summer), pp. 335-370.
Wendt, Alexander (1992) 'Anarchy Is What States Make of It: The Social Construction of Power Politics', *International Organization* 46(Spring), pp. 391-425.
Wæver, Ole (1995) 'Securitization and Desecuritization', in R.D. Lipschutz (ed.) *On Security*, pp. 46-86. New York: Columbia University Press.

Communist Continuity among Estonian Elites: Myth or Reality?

JÜRI RUUS

1. Introduction

The Communist Party was the ruling power in Estonia for more than 50 years representing the " territorial organization" of the Communist Party of the Soviet Union. The current transition towards democratic form of government started from the crisis of legitimacy that the old regime could not resolve. The manner in which the new regime was inaugurated has had a significant effect on its subsequent evolution. Fair opportunities, freedom of choice, incorporation of new actors, renewal of political identities and many other characteristics of the politics of transition stand in sharp contrast with the mode and tone of the previous regime.

The questions to be asked in this chapter about transition from authoritarian rule are: Do the old regime's political figures retain important positions of power? How are the former communists represented in political bodies (parliament and cabinet) during different stages of transition? History often has demonstrated that even a radical change of power does not push the previous elite out of power. The concept of 'elite change' becomes increasingly ambiguous during revolutionary transitions, because a number of competing power centers and leaders emerge, who all claim to be more legitimate than others. Revolutionary transitions are usually connected with changes of leadership. The French and Russian Revolutions and Germany in 1933 are examples of this. "Pacted transitions" are based on compromises between old and new elites (O'Donnell and Ph. Scmitter, 1986). When alternative elites are absent, as was the case in the totalitarian states founded on Leninist principles of organization (Zhang, 1994), one may assume that the position of former regime supporters will remain strong also after the change of the regime.

The term 'elite' can be defined in several ways. If only top political figures are considered then it is clear that they cannot survive a regime change. If elite refers to the members of Communist Party, then they are strongly over-represented in the current Estonian parliament. The basic question is whether the transition has been carried out to a large extent on the basis of continuity involving many former communists (including rank and file members) into the new regime or whether the power door has been closed in front of them. My assumption is that the role of the former communists was and still is substantial. Whether and to which degree the new elites include rank and file members or nomenclature people is an empirical question.

The research design of this chapter is relatively simple. I use data from different stages of the transition towards democracy in Estonia. The analysis is based on cohorts of members of the Central Committees of the Estonian Communist Party, who have been elected to the last three republican Communist Congresses and were part of the Soviet nomenclature. Data includes investigations of party archives, interviews, questionnaires and other written material.

2. The Old Soviet Nomenclature

To understand how the elite has changed after the Post-Soviet authoritarian period, one should remember what it represented in the past. The Soviet nomenclature elite had distinct characteristics defined by its institutional character. Lists of key State positions were compiled at the CPSU Central Committee. One could not be appointed to these key positions without agreement from the leading party organs. The top level Nomenclature comprised persons, who occupied positions subject to approval by the Politburo or Secretariat of the CPSU Central Committee.

Despite the differing character of the positions included in the top nomenclature, the Soviet elite was monolithic in its nature. As a whole, it may be called party and state elite. It was monolithic in the sense that all its members were communists who had been approved by the top level of the party. They were obliged to profess Marxist-Leninist ideology. Since the Tenth Party Congress in 1921 any dissent and different factions within the party were prohibited.

One may get some idea of the structure of the Soviet elite by analyzing the members of the republican CP Central Committee. The following groups were always represented: the republic's leadership - the Bureau and the Secretariat of the Central Committee embodying the legislative power, the heads of the apparatus of the Estonian Communist Party (ECP) Central Committee (the actual executive power), the heads of the regional committees of ECP, the ministers, the leaders of the armed forces, the leaders of the Soviet youth groups, trade unions, artistic and literary societies. Formally the ECP Central Committee and the Supreme Soviet included also workers, collective farmers, engineers, and scientists.

A vast and elaborated system of privileges existed for members of the nomenclature. The existence of the system was conditioned by the deficit character of the Soviet economy. Members of the nomenclature were not rich in the "Western" sense of the term, but their living standards differed strikingly from those of the ordinary people. One can mention special shops, hospitals, living conditions with all modern conveniences. Also rank and file party members were seen as a more advanced, politically more conscious section of the population, members of the highest form of socio-political organization, and characterized by ideological and organizational unity, monolithic cohesion and a high degree of conscious discipline. These attributes together with the image of the party as the "tried and tested militant vanguard" already implied a distinction between party members and the masses. And although there were around 19 million party members and probationary members, they nevertheless constituted less than one tenth of the adult population of the former Soviet Union. Hence, one could classify also the majority of rank and file members of the CPSU as belonging to some kind of Soviet elite. Party membership was a basic condition for making a career.

3. The Estonian Communist Party and the Popular Front

Until at least Summer 1988 the real top leadership of Estonia was not in Tallinn but in Moscow and more specifically in the CPSU Politburo. Then the old hard-liner First

Secretary, Karl Vaino, was replaced by a pro-Gorbachev reform communist, Vaino Väljas. A wide range of changes among social positions took place in the Communist Party Central Committee, and in both central and local government.

It is interesting to note that of the seven members of the executive committee of the Popular Front founded in April 1988, five were members of ECP. This means that the Popular Front was essentially founded by the liberal wing of the communist establishment.[1] The struggle of the hard-liners and reform communists lasted for a couple of years. By the spring of 1990 the authority of the Estonian Communist party had been eroded, and it quickly disappeared from the center stage of Estonian political life.

At the 20th Congress in 1990, the ECP declared for the first time its support for full independence, and at the same time announced its own breakaway from the CPSU. In the past, the ECP stated, it had underestimated and denied the importance of independent statehood because the ECP had not been an independent political force, but a regional branch of the CPSU. Of the 441 Estonian delegates at the crucial 20th ECP Congress (March 25, 1990) 432 voted for leaving the CPSU. The Non-Estonian delegates refused to vote and split in turn into two factions. It was stated that party members should decide themselves if they want to belong to CPSU or not. The Congress elected a 55- member Coalition Party Central Committee, comprising of 32 ethnic Estonians, 20 Russians and 3 from other nationalities. Earlier at least half of the ECP Central Committee staff was comprised of non-natives.

Most PFE (Popular Front of Estonia) members who had belonged to the ECP left it in early 1990. Despite its declared pro-independence stand, in 1991 the Communist Party of Estonia attracted only one percent support under its own label. However, under the lofty label of "Free Estonia" the communists netted another 10 percent. "Free Estonia", chaired by the former Prime Minister and top communist Indrek Toome, was a grouping that avoided becoming a party. It included CPE members as well as those whose status was publicly unknown. Its program was equally unclear. The approach was to suggest that they had more managerial expertise than the PFE and could thus obtain a better deal for Estonia from the Kremlin. However, the electoral coalition "Free Estonia" secured only 13 mandates out of 105 in the elections of the Supreme Soviet in 1990.[2]

After the August 1991 putsch the Moscow oriented branch of ECP was declared illegal in Estonia on grounds of being part of another country's political system. The whole traditional communist power system collapsed as well. However, the pro-independence ECP continued to operate. It held its 21st Party Congress on January 26, 1991. With its two thousand members, ECP was one of the largest parties in Estonia at the beginning of transition. The main strategic goal stated at the Congress was to achieve full independence of Estonia from the Soviet Union, thus joining the mainstream of Estonian politics. The last Communist Congress elected 92 new members to the Central Committee, comprising 72 Estonians, 15 ethnic Russians and 5 from other nationalities. [3]

In 1992 the party transformed itself into Estonian Democratic Labor Party - a leftist party completely abandoning communism as an ideology. The new name was favored by 90% of the party members.[4] In November 1992 the Congress declared the new party a legal successor of the Estonian Communist party, the pro-independence wing of the CPSU in Estonia. The program statement of EDLP saw Estonia's future as a civilized, democratic and stable society. The EDLP supported a multi-ethnic rather than a mono-ethnic state, and also integration into the European structures. Many former top communists continued in this party under the new label. However, the party's bid for power was unsuccessful. Both in 1992 and 1995 parliamentary elections the "Left Opportunity Electoral Coalition" failed to pass the five per cent national electoral threshold necessary to win representation in Parliament.

4. The role of communists in Estonian politics in 1990-1996

The first period of transition towards democracy in Estonia led to a "quasi-parliamentary" system. The electoral process in 1990 was not free in the classical liberal democratic sense. It was considerably constrained by the communist institutions and practices. The Estonian Supreme Soviet elections in March 1990 took place against the background of the continuing presence of KGB, a communist controlled Soviet army, centralized system of command economy, not entirely free press and limited freedom of international travelling. The same factors overshadowed the elections to the Estonian Congress in February 1990. The Estonian Congress was a kind of alternative parliament elected by the citizens of the pre-World War II Estonian citizens and their descendants, excluding the Soviet era immigrants.

However, the situation in 1990 was very different from that of the previous elections, as the Soviet empire was publicly challenged and socialism as a system openly questioned. The Estonian Popular Front won the Supreme Soviet elections, but fell short of gaining absolute majority (42 out of a total of 101 seats). The reform-communist "Free Estonia" and it rural allies got 25-29 seats. Among the105 members of the elected Supreme Council, 69 (or 66%) were former members of the Communist Party, 5 of them had previously belonged to the Soviet Communist Nomenclature. A top member of the ECP Politburo, Arnold Rüütel remained chairman of the Supreme Soviet and one of the leaders of the Popular Front. The post of the Chairman of the Presidium was quite powerless in the beginning of Perestroika, but became increasingly important after 1988. Following the March 1990 elections, the Chairman of the Supreme Council clearly emerged as the highest and the most important state official in Estonia. In 1992, in the first round of the presidential elections, which ran simultaneously with the parliamentary elections, Rüütel gathered 41 per cent of the votes against Lennart Meri's 29,5 per cent, Rein Taagepera's 23,3 per cent and Lagle Parek's 4,2 per cent. However, the new Estonian Parliament elected Lennart Meri in the second round.[5] In the parliamentary elections of 1995 Rüütel received the largest amount of votes again. He ran as the leader of Rural People's Party in an electoral alliance with Coalition Party and together they won the March 1995 elections, receiving 32,1% of the votes.

Edgar Savisaar's cabinet, formed after the Supreme Council elections in April 1990, contained no representatives of the radical nationalists. The Savisaar's cabinet comprised 23 ministers, from whom 13 were former rank and file members of the Communist Party. Three of Savisaar's ministers were still Communist party members, when the government was formed. Savisaar himself resigned from the party a short while before.

The Second Cabinet, to succeed Savisaar's government was appointed to hold office until the introduction of the new constitution and new elections. The new Prime Minister was the former Minister of Transportation, Tiit Vähi, a former state manager from Southern Estonia, who previously also belonged to the ranks of communists. Vähi's middle-aged cabinet (21 ministers) included 14 former members of CPSU, none of whom belonged to the Soviet nomenclature.

The Third Cabinet was formed after the September 1992 nationwide elections. The previous nomenclature was practically not represented there. It had a strongly intellectual cast, and was seen by many observers as a honest, capable, and relatively free from links with communist bureaucracy. Four of the 15 Cabinet members were expatriate Estonians, who had returned only recently.

Table 1. ***Former members of the communist party in Estonian cabinets***

Year	Prime minister	Number of former CP members/ Cabinet size	Percent former CP members
1990	Savisaar	13 of 23	56%
1992	Vähi I	14 of 21	67%
1992	Laar	1 of 15	7%
1995	Vähi II	10 of 16	62%
1997	Siimann	7 of 15	47%

5. Estonian former communist nomenclature - what are they doing now?

Are most of former communists retired or are they still seeking higher positions under the new regime?

Table 2. ***The Central Committee elected by the 19th Congress of the Communist party of Estonia, according to their position in 1986 and 1996***

	Social position in 1986		Social position today	
1.Business	-		46	(34%)
2.Pensioners	-		39	(29%)
3.Jobs in state and collective farms	10	(7%)	-	
4.Science and teaching	3	(2%)	9	(7%)
5.State enterprises previously and now	12	(9%)	6	(4%)
6.Full-time position in Central Committee	45	(33%)	1(EDLP)	(1%)
7.Military	1	(1%)	-	
8.Mass media	2	(2%)	1	(1%)
9.State bureaucracy	62	(46%)	16	(12%)
10. Dead			10	(7%)
11.Those ,who have left Estonia			7	(5%)
Total	135		100%	

Sources: Eesti kommunist, 1986, N.2, Tallinn, lk.34-35 and calculation by the author (private farmers are included in business).

As can be seen in the table, quite a few former political elites are already pensioners. Seven Russian nomenclature persons left the country and are living in Moscow and in St. Petersburg. However, most of the former communist nomenclature persons are engaged in business (34%), working as heads or managerial directors of private firms, stock companies, etc. They could easily use previous connections and recourses, especially in the first accumulative phase of development of market economy. Business activity helped them to rehabilitate their communist past, since it coincides with entrepreneurship orientations and mentalities of the Estonian society as a whole.

Table 3. ***Age categories by 1996 of the 135 elected members (1986) ECP Central Committee today***

Age 35-40	-	
Age 41-45	3	(2%)
Age 46-50	9	(7%)
Age 51-55	14	(10%)
Age 56-60	28	(21%)
Age 61-65	29	(21%)
Age 66 and more	42	(31%)
Dead	10	(8%)
Total	135	100%

As can be seen in the table 3, ninty percent of former Estonian communist nomenclatura are older than 50 years, 59% continue to work. Many of them are in state bureaucracy and state enterprises, working as directors, Chairmen of County Councils, key persons in local municipalities and trade unions. For instance Valeri Tsetvergov (an ethnic Russian), who worked in 1986 as the First Secretary of CPE Narva Town Committee is now the director of Baltijets factory, or Eduard Tserevasko, who worked as the manager of Central Committee Party Organizational Work Department is now holding the position of Manager of the Secretariat in the Estonian parliament.

How does the social mobility look for the next two cohorts of the former Estonian nomenclature? In the last table, 55 new members elected to the 1990 Communist Congress are represented. Again, as in table 2, most of the people found new jobs in private business, working as heads or managers of private firms. An interesting facts to notice from the table is that, there is nobody unemployed among former nomenclature. One could in fact distinguish between two broad categories – people in private business and those, who are employed in public sector like science, education, mass media. An interesting facts to notice from the table is that there is nobody unemployed among former nomenclature.

Table 4. ***New Central Committee members elected by the 20th Congress of the Communist Party of Estonia, according to their positions in 1990 and 1996.***

Fields of activities	Social position in 1990		Social position today	
1. Business	1	(2%)	30	(55%)
2, Pensioners	-		-	
3.Jobs in State and collective farms	1	(2%)	-	
4.Science and teaching	4	(7%)	4	(7%)
5.Full- time position in Central Committee	23	(42%)	-	
6.State enterprises	20	(36%)	4	(7%)
7.Military	2	(4%)		
8.mass Media	3	(5%)	3	(5%)
9.State Bureaucracy	1	(2%)	5	(9%)
10.Dead			2	(4%)
11.Those ,who have left the country			7	(13%)
Total	55	100%		100%

Source: Eestimaa kommunistliku Partei XX kongressi materjalid, Tallinn, 1990, p.72-73
Note: Seven former members of CC CPE had left Estonia.

Notes

1. Lieven, A. (1993) "The Baltic Revolution. Estonia, Latvia and Lithuania and Path to Independence, p. 227. Yale University Press, New Haven and London.
2. Taagepera, R. (1993) "Estonia, Return to Independence," p.193, Westview Press.
3. Eestimaa Kommunistliku Partei XXI Kongressi materjalid, II part p. 65-69. Tallinn 1991
4 The Baltic Independent, Nov 27 – Dec 4 1992.
5. Park, A. (1995)" The Political Leadership, p. 152, Estonian Academy of Sciences, Tallinn.

References

Hill, R.J. and Frank, P. (1983): The Soviet Communist Party, Allen and Unvin, London.

Lieven, A. (1993): The Baltic Revolution. Estonia Latvia and Lithuania and the Path to Independence. Yale University Press, New Haven and London.

O'Donnell, G., Scmitter, P. C. (1986): Transitions from Authoritarian Rule. Tentative Conclusions about Uncertain Democracies. John Hopkins University Press, Baltimore.

Park, A. (1995): The Political Leadership. Estonian Academy of Sciences.

Steen, A. (1996): Elites, Democracy and Policy Development in Post Communist States. A Comparative Study of Estonia, Latvia and Lithuania. Research report 2/96 Department of Political Science. University of Oslo.

Steen, A. (1997): The New Elites of the Baltic States: Circulation and Change. Scandinavian Political Studies Vol. 2O. No 1.

Taagepera, R. (1993): Estonia, Return to Independence. Westview Press

Zhang, A. (1994): Corporation, Totalitarianism and Transition to Democracy. Comparative Political Studies vol. 27. No 1.

The European Union as an External Factor of the Democratization Process in the Czech Republic

LENKA ROVNA

1. Introduction

Using criteria established by Jean Blondel the Czech Republic can be characterized as a relatively stable multiparty political system based on parliamentary democracy.[1] There are free elections held on a regular basis and there has been a peaceful alteration of governments of different colors without any political disturbances. When talking about transition towards democracy we can also employ Dankwart Rustow's[2] notion of "habituation" referring to the last stage of the consolidation of democracy, when democracy becomes the way of life of society. For instance, in the German case, too, as Rustow suggests, it took one generation to 'finalize' the transition towards democracy.[3]

"The overall picture at the level of the population as a whole is therefore one of attitudinal support for liberal democracy, but of support which has more the characteristics of a gesture than of a way of life; while many appreciate the freedoms which they have gained, they are not truly engaged in the democratic process, perhaps not surprisingly given the history of the countries concerned."[4] M.Potůček in his work "Not Only the Market" points out that: "... not only Czech society, but also Czech political representation in many ways did not cross the shadows of the past. Political slogans stating, that our country finished the transition towards market economy and a standard European democracy have to be filed in the archive of the quotations which are more generated by the propagandist needs of the moment than the realistic evaluation of the actual situation".[5] The author points out that the role of the state was weakened which had a negative impact on many fields of the life of society such as: the growth of criminality, the weakness of legislature vis-a-vis privatization, corruption, conflict between public and private interests. The unfinished reform of health care, social care and the alarming situation in education were also considered as topics on this agenda.[6]

It is also necessary not to underestimate the other danger in new democracies: "... a number of scandals have affected the political elite and the government: this has happened most recently in the Czech Republic, Slovenia and Estonia. This does not of course render these countries unique, given what occurs in many parts of Western Europe and elsewhere in the world. However, repeated scandals may well erode the already rather passive popular support for democracy characterizing these countries."[7] These relatively stable, but still fragile democracies, with many "left-overs" from the Communist past are still in danger that the model of democracy as a plural multiparty parliamentary system can be deformed by corruption, non-effective civil service, divided society etc.[8]

There are several factors playing an important role in forming and promoting democracy such as economic prosperity, the constitutional and legislative framework, the development of civil society, as well as a non-profit and non-governmental sector, 'normally' functioning and well structured political parties, stabilized and relatively consolidated political elites with no influential anti-system forces etc.[9] All these aspects relate to internal factors.

Referring to the Czech case we have to stop at a very important internal factor - economic performance. After being considered to be a success story the Czech Republic slid down with its negative growth and unfinished economic reform, which did not result in establishing a prosperous modern economy.[10] Unemployment, which used to be less than 4% is growing dramatically and the Minister of Labor and Social Affairs Vladimír Špidla expected an unemployment rate of 11% before the end of 1999. Faster implementation of modern technologies which seem to be necessary for the economic reform will lay off more employees. The Czech Republic will follow other European countries with its unemployment rate reaching 10%. How the society is going to cope with this unprecedented situation is not clear yet.[11]

Jean Blondel also emphasized the role of external factors which may play a quite positive and stabilizing role.[12] The most important and stabilizing factor for the development of democracy and a prosperous economy seems to be the identification with Western values which are expressed institutionally by the joining of NATO and EU. The day for joining NATO was March 12, 1999. "Central Europe's long-term destination is not in doubt, even if its time of arrival is. Its closeness to the EU has already helped it to weather the recent financial storms. But it could become a worry if the EU economy takes a further turn for the worse. Poles, Hungarians and Czechs alike are looking west, anxiously".[13] It is more than obvious that the EU plays a very important role in the fourth stage [using Rustow's theory] of the development of democracy in Central European countries, the stage when democracy becomes the way of life, not only a "gesture".[14]

2. The road towards EU membership

Official diplomatic relations between Czechoslovakia and the European Community were established in September 1988, in December the "Trade Agreement" on industrial products was signed. After the fall of the communist regime in May 1990 "A Trade and Cooperation Agreement" was concluded. An Association Agreement known as "Europe Agreement" was signed on December 15,1991. After the division of Czechoslovakia a new European Agreement was ratified with the Czech Republic on October 4, 1993 including liberalization of trade,[15] intensive political dialogue, economic and technical cooperation, cultural contacts and support for newly established industrial branches.[16]

A very important decision was taken at the European Council in Copenhagen in June 1993 when a discussion concerning the further "widening" or "deepening" of the EU was held. The EU concluded that the associated countries in Central and Eastern Europe which so desire should become members of the Union. The accession could take place when the states will be able to assume the obligations of membership by satisfying the economic and political conditions.[17] At the Essen Summit in 1994 the EU suggested the strategy for associated countries called "the pre-accession strategy". The main instruments are European Agreements which offer to the associated countries trade concessions and other advantages, the Structured Dialogue which helps the associated countries to become familiar with the institutions and decision making processes in EU, and Program Phare providing them with grants targeting the reform process.[18]

The White Paper approved at the session of the European Council in Cannes in summer 1995 set out the legislation which candidate countries would have to implement to meet the acquis communautaire.[19] The European Council in Madrid in December 1995 referred to the need, the context of the pre-accession strategy, "to create the conditions for the gradual, harmonious integration of the applicant countries..."

To meet the criteria of the EU the Czech government established in November 1994 the Government Committee for European Integration headed by Prime Minister Václav Klaus, the other members were the Ministers of Finance, Industry and Trade, Agriculture and Foreign Affairs. The Working Committee is chaired by the Deputy Minister of Foreign Affairs. A year later the Czech government approved and published the timetable for the accession: "Priorities for the Implementation of the White Paper in the Czech Republic". The need to change the administrative structure, the administration of the environment, direct and indirect taxation, personal data protection and social policy was expressed.[20]

During the last five years great progress in the development of relations between the Czech Republic and the European Union has taken place. The exports from the Czech Republic to the EU countries grew from 4.9 to 11.7 billion ECU and imports from 6.1 to 15.8 billion ECU. The Czech Republic improved its trade relationship with the EU which represents 60% of its foreign trade.[21]

The change in the relationship, and a new quality of relations were also expressed in the participation of the Czech Republic in the programs of the EU such as SOKRATES, LEONARDO, KALEIDOSKOP, MATTHAUS, and the implementation of the programs ISPA and SAPARD which are intended to be a structural help in the pre-accession period. In 1990-1997, the Czech Republic received a contribution of 493 million ECU from PHARE for the support of the system transformation in all sectors: protection of the environment, support of enterprises, harmonization of law, social policy, cross border cooperation etc.[22]

In January 1996 the Czech Republic submitted its application to join the EU and was invited by the Luxemburg Summit of the European Council in December 1997 to be one of the first six countries to start negotiations.[23] Screening started in April 1998 with the first six countries.[24] "Screening is the first phase of talk on accession to the Union, prior to the negotiation itself. The European Communities' legislation has been divided into 31 chapters; during the screening, the individual legal norms are being examined in multilateral and bilateral discussions. Legal analyses are carried out and Czech legislation is scrutinized regarding its compatibility with EU norms.[25] So far, 17 out of 31 chapters have been analyzed... We expect it to be completed in the summer of 1999."[26]

"The Regular Report from the Commission on the Czech Republic's Progress Towards Accession" was published in November 1998.[27] The Report shows how the Czech Republic is progressing in the light of the Copenhagen criteria and especially the rate at which it is adopting the Union acquis.[28] The EU as an external factor influencing the transition towards democracy thus plays a crucial role. It was a kind of cold shower for Czech politicians and Czech society to learn about the Political Criteria: "The Accession Partnership with the Czech Republic mentions as medium term priorities further work on the integration of the Roma; strengthening of laws which guarantee press freedom; further attention to ensuring equal access to public services".[29] The evaluation of the Commission states that: "The change in Government has not resulted in any major shift in the country's policy towards the European Union".[30]

The critical tone of the Report continues: "There has been virtually no progress in public administration reform since July 1997".[31] It is not only to please the Commission to adopt the acquis. A functioning civil service is considered to be a major feature of a functioning democracy, a factor guaranteeing the functioning of the market economy [for instance the control of capital markets, economic competition, functioning of financial offices etc.], a factor of institutional cooperation at all levels of the internal market, and a key condition for the adoption of the acquis communautaire.[32]

As a very serious warning we have to consider the critique of the Czech Republic in handling the problem of human rights. The General Evaluation states that: " Developments in the Czech Republic confirm the Opinion that the Czech Republic fulfils the Copenhagen political criteria. Nonetheless the Czech Republic needs to devote continuing attention to the reform of the judiciary, to fighting corruption more effectively and to improving the situation of the Roma".[33]

Regular reports and comments of the EU addressing the Czech government and society help the country in the process of further democratization during its transition period until democracy will be "the way of life". To make the process truly democratic citizens have to make their decision with the full knowledge of such a process. The other important feature influencing the attitude of Czech citizens and political elites towards EU is the level of support for the enhanced accession of the Czech Republic joining into the EU.[34]

3. Conclusions

The positive development of the attitude of Czech citizens towards the EU can be encouraged by a more open approach of the government itself which was not always the case in the past and with an increase in the amount of information available to the people.[35] The result is a growing support for the membership in the EU.[36] The slogan "back to Europe" is finding its real shape and structure.

The Ministry of Foreign Affairs "has specified the aims, principles and tools of the Communication Strategy and defined target groups... We carry out some projects, with for example, Czech TV, regional dailies and specialized magazines. We issue various publications. At the end of 1998, we plan to launch the operation of specialized Internet sites." This has been pointed out by the main negotiator for the accession Pavel Telička.[37]

All these activities are supposed to prepare the citizens for the referendum and to give them knowledge necessary to make their choice freely and democratically.

The EU as an external factor is thus playing a crucial role in the further democratization and modernization of the Czech Republic. Following the pre-accession strategy the Czech Republic is getting closer to become a functioning and stable democracy with a prosperous market economy and a modern effective state serving its citizens. This, of course, cannot only be a process involving exclusively officials from Brussels and narrow strata of Czech political elites. The Czech society has the rare historical chance to manage its own life and to steer the country "back to Europe". This process is not going to be easy. Czech citizens with full knowledge have to make their own choices.

Notes

1 "..in the five countries [Czech Republic, Hungary, Poland, Estonia, Slovenia - L.R.] and in most of Eastern Europe, political developments in the 1990s can be regarded as having been broadly satisfactory, especially given the economic and social difficulties which these countries underwent... Support for democracy is widespread, although not overwhelming." Paper given by J.Blondel, Democracy in the five candidate countries, Seminar "The New European Borders", Trieste, 27-28 November, 1998

2 Dankwart A.Rustow, Transitions to Democracy, Toward a Dynamic Model, in: Comparative Politics, Number 3, April 1970, pp.337-364

3 V.Dvořáková, J.Kunc, O přechodech k demokracii [About transitions toward democracy], SLON, Praha 1994

4 Jean Blondel, ibid.

5 Martin Potůček, Nejen trh, Role trhu, státu a občanského sektoru v proměnách české společnosti, (Not Only the Market, The Role of the Market, State and Civil Sector in the Changes of Czech Society), SLON, Praha, 1997, s.167

6 M.Potůček, ibid, p.167

7 Jean Blondel, ibid, p.4

8 see Demokracie a ústavnost [Democracy and Constitutionalism), Ed. by Jiří Kunc, Universita Karlova, Praha, 1996

9 see: V.Dvořáková, A.Gerloch, Krystalizace struktury politických stran v České republice po roce 1989, Česká společnost pro politické vědy, Praha, 1996

10 "The Czech economy is already doing badly; GDP fell by 2,9% in the 12 months to the third quarter of last year. It has yet to recover from its currency crisis in 1997, when interest rates were raised sharply to defend the koruna. The Czechs are also paying the price for half-baked economic reforms. Their privatization scheme put a premium on speed rather than rational restructuring. The banks, still state-owned, have been repeatedly bailed out. Perhaps because they do not have a large foreign debt to service, the Czechs appear complacent about the need to shake up their economy further." The Economist, February 13th, 1999, p.84.

11 The Interview with the Minister of Labor and Social Affairs Vladimír Špidla, Mlada Fronta Dnes, 13.2.1999, p.1,15

12 "Almost certainly, one important factor influences these polities in the direction of a stable democratic path, namely the fact that they have wished to join the European Union as soon as possible: such a development occurred earlier in the case of Spain, Portugal and Greece. It is therefore critical that the Union should not delay the admission of the five countries to the point where they might show less goodwill." Jean Blondel, ibid.,p.4

13 The Economist, February 13th, 1999, p.84

14 see Jean Blondel

15 Czech Republic can export 70% of all Czech products without customs and restrictions, on the other hand ^)% of European export is influenced by these restrictions. Due to the fact that the rate of agricultural products is 6%, in fact the Czech Republic has the most advantageous agreement among the Central/Eastern European countries. (Gerhard Sabathil, Česká snaha o přijetí do západních institucí a odpověď z Essenu, Mezinárodní politika, 1, 1995, s.6)

16 Gerhard Sabathil, Česká snaha o přijetí do západních institucí a odpověď z Essenu (Czech Effort to be Accepted to Western Institutions and an Answer from Essen), Mezinárodní politika, 1, 1995, p.7

17 Membership requires:
- that the candidate country has achieved stability of institutions guaranteeing democracy, the rule of law, human rights and respect for and protection of minorities;
- the existence of a functioning market economy, as well as the capacity to cope with competitive pressure and market forces within the Union;
-the ability to take on the obligations of membership, including adherence to the aims of political, economic and monetary union. [Agenda 2 000, p.1]

18 Předvstupní strategie Evropské Unie pro přidružené země střední Evropy, (The Pre-Accession Strategy of EU for Associated Countries of Central Europe),European Commission, DG IA,p.5

19 ibid

20 Agenda 2000, Commission Opinion on the Czech Republic's Application for membership of the European Union, Brussels July 15, 1997

21 Gerhard Sabathil, Příprava České republiky pro vstup do EU,(The Preparation of the Czech Republic to EU), Mezinárodní politika, 1, 1999. p.10

22 Gerhard Sabathil, ibid, p.10,11

23 Barbara Lippertová, Strategické otázky rozšiřování Evropské unie na východ po lucemburském summitu, (The Strategic Questions of the Enlargement of European Union to the East after Luxembourg Summit), Mezinárodní vztahy, 2, 1998, pp.17-27

24 Pavel Telička, Tempo jednání o přistoupení závisí na dořešení vnitřních problémů EU, (The Speed of Negotiations about Joining Depends on Solving Internal Problems of EU), Mezinárodní politika, 1, 1999, p. 4,5

25 Petr Greger, K vybranným právním aspektěm a souvislostem Amsterodamské smlouvy, (To Selected Judicial Aspects and Connections of Amsterdam Treaty), Mezinárodní vztahy, 2, 1998, pp.5-16

26 EU Membership Talks Launched, An Interview with Pavel Telička, Deputy Czech Minister of Foreign Affairs and the chief negotiator for accession of the Czech Republic to the European Union, November-December 1998, p.1-6

27 Petr Greger, Český právní stát v bruselském prizmatu (Czech Rule of Law in Brussels Perspective], Mezinárodní politika, 1,1999, pp. 8,9

28 "In accordance with the guidance provided by these Council Conclusions, the progress report on the Czech Republic follows the same structure as the Opinion. It
-describes the relations between the Czech Republic and the Union, particulary in the framework of the European Agreement;
- analyses the situation in respect of the political conditions set by the European Council [democracy, rule of law, human rights, protection of minorities];
- assesses the Czech Republic's situation and prospects in respect of the economic conditions mentioned by the European Council [functioning market economy, capacity to cope with competitive pressure and market forces within the Union];
-addresses the question of the Czech Republic's capacity to adopt the obligations of membership, that is, the acquis of the Union as expressed in the Treaty, the secondary legislation and the policies of the Union. Regular Report from the Commission on Czech Republic's Progress Towards Accession, Brussels, November 1998

29 ibid

30 ibid

31 ibid

32 Petr Greger, Český právní stát v bruselském prizmatu, Mezinárodní politika, 1, 1999, p. 9

33 Regular Report from the Commission on Czech Republic's Progress Towards Accession, Brussels, November 1998

34 "... although the level of knowledge of these issues still remains rather low among the public. This, of course, is not a fault of the public; rather it is a result of the current state of our relationship with the EU. There is mostly a lack of information about the most important matters, about the actual impacts of approximation to the EU on individual areas of people lives." [An Interview with Pavel Telička, Deputy Czech Minister of Foreign Affairs and the Chief Negotiator for accession of the Czech Republic to the European Union, EuroInfo, November-December 1998, pp. 4,5]

35 Peter Bugge, České vnímání perspektivy členství v EU, Havel vs. Klaus (Czech Perceptions of the Perspective of Eu Membership), Politologická revue, 2, 1998, pp. 76-110

36 odpora vstupu České republiky do EU [%]

	V.93	III.96	XI.96	I.97	IX.97	II.98
YES	66	42	51	58	58	61
NO	12	21	26	23	22	15
DOES NOT KNOW	22	37	23	19	20	24

Pramen: IVVM
Zpráva o vývoji České společnosti, 1989-1998, (The Report about the Development of Czech Society, 1989-1998), Editor Jiří Večerník, vedoucí týmu Petr Matějů, p. 319

37 An Interview with Pavel Telička, p.5

III. PATTERNS OF PERFORMANCE AND CONSOLIDATION

The Media in Democratization

JANE L. CURRY

1. Introduction

The relationship of the role of free media in the processes of democratization and democratic consolidation is neither unilinear nor simple. Free media and the free access to information as well as the right to express the entire range of opinion is an absolutely necessary if not sufficient part of every democracy. Democratization, whether done from the top or from the mass level, often has been triggered by and certainly has involved a freeing and expansion of the media, information, and expression of opinion in general. But, just as no democracy allows all of its media complete freedom, free media can also be problematic for a new democracy's consolidation.

That said, the tragedy in this - from a scholarly perspective - is that the media and the need for "free media" have been "givens" in the democratization process. Democratization theorists have regularly listed media freedom as a necessary part of democracy. They have not studied in any serious fashion either how the media come to be freed or how free media affect the processes of democratization and consolidation. After the fact, some limited research has been done on what journalists think and do. Some anecdotal evidence has been collected on how the media pushed the limits. We know that the opening up of the media, even marginally, has stimulated elite and mass action in countries all over the world.

There are some studies of various roles the media seem to play in democracy. We know, logically, you cannot have free discussion and free voting without voters/citizens having sources and forums to express their views, learn about issues, and be challenged by what others think. But, we do not know how this can be made to happen even though Western governments have spent millions of dollars restructuring, retraining and retooling journalists and the media systems in the democratizing countries of Eastern Europe and the Soviet Union. Nor are we clear as to whether "too much" or "too sudden" freedom of the media can be counterproductive in societies where the new governments have not yet established their legitimacy, ability to distribute goods and services, penetrate the society, and channel full participation. Even less are we clear how the media help or hurt in the development of new national identities, particularly in countries where there are ethnic, regional and class divisions that have the potential of exploding the democratization process and reversing it. To do this, we need to know far more about the ways in which audiences unaccustomed to a free press take in the new messages and criticism, the dynamics and rationales behind the decisions newly freed journalists make, and the ways elites come to see and deal with the media in different democratization processes.

Therefore, this chapter is a call for research, not assuming that the media are simply a given of the democratization and consolidation processes or of democracy itself. What we do know is that a free press is an important part of any stable democracy when it plays the role of informer, watchdog and gatekeeper. We also know that the press has an important function of integration both of elites with the population and of different groups in the population. At the same time, no press or media is entirely free. Even societies that proclaim press freedom as a primary point in their constitutions have clear limits on what the media can say and do and sanctions if those limits are overstepped.

2. Three Worlds of Media

Perhaps in dealing with questions of the mass media and communication in general in the process of democratization, the distinctions between societies undergoing democratization are more important than in any other area of democratization. At a minimum, it would seem, we need to look at three different "worlds" of democratization.

(1) The "first" world of what are now Western democratic societies went through the development of the media space with the overall process of democratization and industrialization. Printing and distribution were "invented" gradually as the church, the dominant ideological force, sought to spread and standardize its reach. Literacy then spread slowly in response to both the first moves of industrialization and "civilization". The print media developed initially out of commercial needs to announce ship arrivals and commercial or legal transactions. Only later were the print media addressed to other audiences. That was a product of the development of political parties and their need to reach out to potential publics.

Messages were, until the mid-nineteenth century, directed to the upper classes. Only as democratization and full literacy reached down to the working classes did the print media and their messages also reach out to them with the advent of what some called the "penny press". By this time, on the whole, traditions of processing messages and democracy were established both on the part of the elite and the masses.

Beyond this, the limited nature of communication processes in the print era was both slow and basically nationally limited. This meant that few messages came in any meaningful time frame to the peoples of other states. In fact, the "free media" was controlled in both its audience and its ability to stimulate action. News simply did not travel fast enough to bring the masses to the barricades. Instead, the messages that travelled were usually about issues that were already resolved by the time the print media went out or were over. These technological limitations thus limited the ability of the media to truly mobilize its readers.

In the case of western Europe, then, when the media did expand into broadcasting and then into the myriads of other forms that have come with the computer revolution, democracies were established, national identities were firm, and journalists, readers, and elites had developed patterns of interaction and understanding that made the media an important element in maintaining democracy as the "fourth branch of government", the information gatekeepers, and the community builders.

(2) In the "second world of development", the communist world and the "late" democratizers of Western Europe (Spain, Portugal and Greece) the media infrastructure was well developed technically and the population highly literate by the time the democratization process began. But, the media had been closely controlled and, in the cases of the communist world, directed. In most cases, as well, there were two other important media influences: foreign broadcasts and informal or "underground" communication channels. These provided the population with alternate views of events

as well as criticism of their systems. In the end, they also challenged the regime controlled or limited media.

With this, the democratization began with at least two if not three cadres of journalists: those that had worked within the regime controlled media, those that had worked outside of it, and those that had worked abroad broadcasting into their own countries. They were able and did start media democratization as soon as it was possible. They also came to their new freedoms with very different goals and perceptions. Ironically, the establishment journalists have been some of the main leaders in the free media - with or without retraining - not only technically but also professionally. Former underground journalists were leaders in the dissident movement. Some moved into political positions and others into legal journalism but many carried with them the sense that the media was not to inform or to be a gatekeeper but to lead and be a spokesperson for "the cause".

These states also had populations that were trained to read the media not for what they said but for what was "between the lines" and why information was given. They were also not accustomed to the deluge of options and negative information that they received in the free media. In the same way, both the old and the new elites had learned about the media in the communist or authoritarian eras. They each, from their different experiences, had come to see it as something to be possessed and used to define a ruler or a group.

The initial explosion of media freedom came without a functioning legal system to regulate what the media did and did not do. In most cases, there was little preparation for most of the population for the appearance of "free media". With the explosion of the free media came, as well, a commercial explosion that resulted in the media serving as an engine to increase demand and to demonstrate to the population the levels of the problems, their insolubility, and the resulting inequities in the system. All of this has made the free media both a necessary part of "freedom" in these countries and a problematic element that may have increased the existing tensions between ethnic and class groups as well as the alienation of the population from their new leaders.

(3) The "third world" of the media is one in which there is a real division between the politically active and literate population and the inactive and illiterate or non-media oriented segments of the population. In these countries, development, prosperity and democracy are not universal. Rather, they are reflected only in a small segment of the population, one from which journalists and most political elites come and for whom they write.

In these societies, the media have played two distinct functions. Domestic and foreign aid media are agents of the spread of development and mobility. This is a political and democratizing role to the extent that these media are creating a new and more potentially politically active population. The elite media, to the extent that they are able financially and politically, serve as watchdogs and reporters of elite activities and a base for elite discussion. Their reach, though, is not far out of the urban centers.

Essentially, democratization, when it has happened in these countries, has not happened through the media. Rather, in Latin America and a few countries in Asia and Africa, it has happened as a result of negotiations between the opposition and the authoritarian establishment. These have been called either in response to a sense on both sides that both would lose control or an external or internal sense that authoritarian rule was no longer legitimate and effective. If it played a role, the media served as reporters of the riots or demonstrations that underlay some of this fear. In most cases, it seems, these discussions were not the result of media discussions but closed Roundtable sessions from which the media got information.

The media, then, in these "third world" democratizations are much smaller players in the democratization process. Where they have a reach outside of the major cities, they do, though, have two potentially destabilizing roles that make democratic consolidation difficult if not impossible: 1) the developmental media and, to the extent that the poor can either read or afford it, the political media inform from one group to another and may create senses of relative deprivation and of ethnic conflicts even with benign stories and 2) because many cannot afford to generate their own programming, they broadcast Western serials and news that raise expectations and break cultural taboos, thus weakening the elite's legitimacy and increasing demands in a situation where the regime does not have the resources to fulfill them.

3. Issues, Actors and Questions

3.1. The What Dilemma

The democratization process, wherever it occurs, by definition results in freedom for the press. Indeed, it is often stretching and unrest in the media which spurs the democratization process on by raising questions about the elite, its policies, and the repression that the elite has to respond to. Journalists may first be martyrs and heroes but they gradually become political actors for change - often being involved in negotiating rather than reporting the transformation.

Once it occurs, freedom involves opportunities for journalists to write what they want and new publications to emerge with commercial and political interests. How this occurs depends on both the conditions of the democratization process and the nature of the economic conditions of the democratization process and the nature of the economic conditions and transformation. In slow, negotiated democratization in Eastern Europe and the former Soviet states, control simply collapses and there is no fit in the laws. When the economic situation opens up, the search for markets and readers is much more intense as the media is a low investment, quick turnaround enterprise. Competition and the resulting search for a saleable story then mobilizes the media.

In all cases, though, this freedom for the media is necessary for new parties to emerge and be known and the electorate to be both mobilized and educated. It is essentially the first and most ongoing visible sign that the system really has changed for the population it touches.

But, once, if not before, the initial elections are held and the governments formed, media freedom then runs the risk of destabilizing these fragile democracies. The two prime ways that this would seem to occur are: the delegitimization of the government and the fomenting of divisive nationalism in ethnically divided countries or countries with weak identities.

In all societies coming out of authoritarianism, the public has learned to read between the lines and rely on palace gossip. It has not learned to hear political conflict, that problems are insoluble or solutions not sure, or that leaders have personal faults. Their media, as well, have often had severe limits on what cultural and social information or images they can publish. Journalists, because they have been barred from reporting these things, tend to focus on this "new" information when they have the opportunity. Whether what they report is the truth or exaggerated, they report it and emphasize it. Furthermore, in the search for profit, newspapers and the broadcast media fill themselves with advertisements. That can only expose the population to images of what they would like to have but can not get from the system, increasing their sense that the system does not work for them.

The result would seem to be (and here research is clearly needed to see if the correlations are accurate) that the public gets a very negative image of its new leadership and the system which it is creating. This could be one of the chief causes for the low level of political and economic satisfaction even in countries where there has been relative economic and political success as in Poland and Hungary.

The other line opened by the newly freed media breeds nationalism. Even if they do not do so consciously journalists coming out of a controlled press emphasize national interests and report about differences in their societies. This can not help but draw attention to those differences and create a clear sense of haves and have-nots that then may be played out in ethnic conflicts and a sense of relative deprivation. It is not, then, surprising that with the freeing of the press and the other changes from democratization, societies have fragmented and leaders have been able to target scapegoats to explain policy failures.

What the exact role of the media has been in consolidating and deconsolidating democracies remains, as in this chapter, basically a matter of speculation. The impetus is clear. What is not clear is how much of a part media messages actually play in this process. We know from research done on nationalism in the prewar period in new countries like Slovakia and in the Third World that the media have always been a leading force in developing a sense of nationalism. We also know that, however much their systems have improved and however many people support the basic concepts of democracy and freedom, there is a high level of dissatisfaction and de-politization even in the most successful democratizing societies. Clearly, this disaffection needs to be studied with a clear focus on the role of the disseminators of information.

3.2. The Who Dilemma

There are in the communication process three key actors whose actions and responses to marking and using "free" media need to be considered. They are the makers of the media, the receivers and the rulers. Change or freeing communications does not simply involve the journalists, editors, and publishers who make it. In fact, so far, with or without reschooling and aid, both those from the former establishment press and those from the dissident press as well as their few colleagues trained abroad have been remarkably able to switch to free journalism. The real problem groups in creating a free and democratic system of communication have been the users and the governing elites. Again, though, all of our attention both in terms of foreign aid and in terms of what little research has been done has been on the journalism profession.[1]

3.2.1. The Media Makers

What research there has been on the journalism profession has shown that journalists coming out of authoritarian societies and even in authoritarian systems have values not unlike their colleagues in Western democratic systems. Journalists in virtually all societies tend to rank as their most important roles: reporting news quickly, giving analysis, and being watchdogs of the government[2]. Where there are differences, these tend to reflect cultural rather than political differences. Ironically, on the issue of accuracy, it is the journalists of Britain and the Pacific Islands who are least likely to see this as important. Those from Germany, Finland, and Taiwan (where the press has been strongly controlled) see it as most important. In terms of how they do their work, again, cultural differences are more important than political ones.

Where the journalism profession, from my own interviews in Poland, seems to reflect its past history is in the perception of many journalists that they need to guide or teach the public, not simply to inform or to interpret.[3] Former journalists from the underground press tended to see their media as educators to prepare the public to be different and to see the public as mere ciphers for the regime in the past. Those who came from the establishment press, similarly, still voice evaluations which harken back to the days when the press was to lead and translate to the population.

Journalists also seem to "fall apart" as a profession in the initial democratization process and then be brought back to professional standards and organization by the negative impact of the commercialization of the press and broadcast media. Initially, the open market leads to "anything goes" but, by the end of the initial commercialization phase, there is such turnover in the media that journalists find themselves out of work. They also find themselves embroiled in conflicts over what should be reported and how. As a result, rather than let all of this be decided by the market, there has been in Poland at least a recreation of journalistic institutions.

Finally, for journalists from both the former opposition and the former government media, there is an initial melting of professional and political. Because they have name recognition, journalists are often elected to representative posts in the new government. Initially, some try to do both. That makes the line of objectivity even vaguer. What appears to have happened, though, in the consolidation phase is that some journalists cut their ties with journalism and remain in politics while the vast majority turn back to full time professional work, leaving politics as too restrictive of their ability to speak their minds and too "complicated".

3.2.2. The Rulers

For all rulers in systems that are democratizing, the media, by definition, are a necessary evil. While that is true of how most rulers in established democracies see the media as well, there is a clear difference: the rules of the game and the lines between media freedom and ruler rights are established both in law and in the sense of what is possible among the rulers. However much they would like to keep negative information out of the public's eye, they recognize that they cannot do so directly. Rulers who are just beginning to rule in emerging democracies are not nearly as clear about the worth of the media and the limits on their ability to control it. They liked it when it criticized the authoritarian system and touted the new democracy. They are not ready to "like" or even tolerate it when it is criticizing them or presenting alternatives or negative information.

I know of no democratizing rulers, except Nelson Mandela, who have felt so secure in their positions and their ability to fill their population's expectations that they have not chafed at press criticism and tried to limit negative information. Indeed, the tendency has been to want "their own" media either as a party press or as media that supported them. While this urge has decreased as the media have grown more regularized, there are still conflicts between what the media want and what the rulers are willing to accept. The "truce" seems to come about because rulers come to realize that the media cannot truly destablize the democratization process and that their attempts to control do not end well. So, the Vaclav Havel conflict with Ben Bradlee over how he, as president, would close journals for threatening national security when Bradlee maintained that was unacceptable, made sense in 1990 when the media conference was held in Prague. But, as democratic politics have evolved, Havel has proved to be or learned he had to be tolerant of media which called for Slovak independence and have criticized him as well as revealing corruption and other problems in the government.

What need to be studied is how this rapprochement is reached and what the lines are that emerge in rulers' minds between media freedoms and the needs of the rulers or the state, as they see it. So too does the process of professionalization of the relations and roles of both the rulers and their reporters.

3.2.3. The Users

Probably the most problematic actors in the role of the media in democratization are its recipients. The users of the media come to the free media hungry for information but with clear cultural and experiential senses of what is appropriate. For the literate and politically active populations, the freedom of discussion is a wonderful gain. But, however much this is, for them, a symbol of democracy emerging, their "take" on the media is not the same as that of people who have grown up reading free media which report the rough and tumble of politics and economic life.

It seems that, when the media begin to report social problems and battles in politics, these initially seem disproportionately large to users who are used to a perfect, if false picture of their societies and the political process. Suddenly now, given negative information about the institutions that are subject to the most criticism (the police) and the institutions that are in the business of political conflict (the parliament), in Eastern Europe even the most educated readers are overwhelmed by the problems and attacks. They do not see these as normal but as indications of serious problems in the society.

Beyond this, readers who used the controlled media in the past have to learn to read for content rather than between the lines. This clearly would require an unlearning of the reading strategies that come from the authoritarian press: looking for ties between sources and politicians, looking not at the information but for some indication of why it was allowed or written and looking outside the media for the "truth". Only time and experience with free media seems to have begun to "undo" some of these tendencies. And, that depends on the ability of the media establishment to do its new job and not to become enmeshed in politics.

Here, attitudinal studies need to be done on where users get their information and how they process it. Much of the "time" has been lost in the most successful democratizing countries, but there remain countries and areas in which the transformation is in process, where this kind of research was done when scholars focused on modernization and development rather than democracy, and found that the increased communication and communication channels were crucial to this process.

Finally, the media explosion of freedom and investment, when that occurs, does touch the less developed parts of the population. Their demands and consciousness of their position in society are clearly raised. The question then is how a free media can, without losing their freedom, school them and bring them into the political and economic process in a way that consolidates their democracies rather than destabilizing them.

4. The How Question

The processes of democratization and consolidation as well as the role of the media in these processes have been eminently more complicated in the postwar and postcomputer periods than it was in earlier periods in which democratization occurred. There are simply more ways of communication that cross international lines, can not be filtered through the professional establishment, and allow for interactive communication where the role of reporter and receiver are blurred or turned into reporter and respondent. Although these new methods of communication clearly offer chances to integrate and reach out to various segments of the society and the world, they also are potentially divisive in societies where access is unequal or where the system can not respond to the demands or pressures exerted.

We know from past research on development that the insertion of modern messages has raised expectations before the elite or economy were prepared to respond. It has also destabilized traditional ways by putting forth and highlighting new "modern" ways when there was no avenue for facilitating the new ways. Finally, we also know that it was the introduction of international norms of "the right to vote" that both stimulated popular demand and unrest even in developing systems.

There is no doubt that the new communication methods are already playing key roles. Nor is there any lack of theoretical interest in what can and can not be done with this new technology. What we need to study and know is how they actually affect the process of democratization. Whom do they affect and reach? How are their messages taken? What kinds of interaction actually occur when there are interactive channels available as they were in the constitution writing process in South Africa and Hungary? Where are the lines between the spread of information and technology and the transformation of political systems? And, what impact does this have on the social, educational and economic differences in societies as well as the development of their sense of being part of a "global village" or of their own nationalism?

5. The Where and When Questions

The answer to the "when" question is simple: now. These studies are already delayed in their initiation. In key model countries, the democratization process and the role of communications in it are well along. In this area, it is hard to go back and ask people who are adjusting or have adjusted what they did and what they thought initially. But, the issue is not over. There are other countries that are just beginning to travel this path. Models need to be developed before more millions of dollars in "media aid" are spent on apparently good projects that may or may not work and that may, in fact, do more harm than allowing a natural flow to occur.

There is, of course, much that can be done from the existing documentation. But, the reality is that the kind of data that is needed comes from public opinion surveys that ask where do you get your information, how do you understand this, and what are the triggers for your actions? It also needs to come from journalists and elites over time to see how and why these key players change their actions and relations to the media.

The research needs also to take into consideration the differences between systems not only in their levels of development and the extent of the social and economic differential in the society. It also needs to provide for models that differ in the development of nationalism and the level of ethnic and visible social differentiation in the society.

Finally, this research needs to be done in a way that "apples" are not compared with "oranges". Political and media systems all enter the democratization period with different historical legacies out of which different speeds and modes of transformation of both the media and polity occurred. These are crucial in how the media function in democratization. As a result, to come to any conclusion about the interaction of the media and its transformation with democratization and democratic consolidation, we need to consider systems in which the media were both controlled and directed (tightly and less tightly) as they were in communist states and systems where the media are controlled but not directed as they tend to be under more authoritarian rule. We also need to consider states where there are universal media that reach most of the population and where there are layered media with different messages and uses for different groups in the population. Finally, we need to consider the different ways in which the transition occurred: fast, slow, negotiated, or free-floating. In this, of course, it is important to look at systems were the release of the media was a planned part of the democratization and laws to regulate it were implemented apace as well as those where foreign buyers and market demand as opposed to law set the process.

6. Conclusion

This chapter is, in no way, a statement that the media and their freedom are not something that needs to be nurtured and furthered in the democratization process or that there does not need to be free media for the consolidation. It is only to suggest that knowing what should be for an ideal democracy to work is not the same as knowing what works in making democracy and how it works.

This research has much to teach us about how the media work even in established democratic states where communications research is well established, but where there is still an open question of "how do we know what we know" and what the real flow of information and impact of the media itself is as opposed to what the impact of social and personal factors is. In the process, it will shift our attention from either abstract flow charts, or media management agents. This will make us look at the relations between the environment and journalism and journalism/the media as actors in the political process overall.

For those who study and work in democratization, these kinds of studies are even more crucial. The media and its freedom are, after all, areas where millions of dollars have been invested with, to my knowledge, virtually no study of what this all means and whether it "worked" (if its goals were clear) or not. The roles that journalists trained in the old school of communism, for instance, have played in free media would suggest that schooling is not so necessary but that journalists naturally chafe under control and research out to play the roles of traditional democratic media when they can. At the same time, the difficulty the elites and the population have had in taking in their messages and accepting them for what they are would indicate that the problem is not in the same place as we are placing our monies.

Finally, the issue is simply a theoretically interesting one. "Givens" are not acceptable in research on change. No element "happens" without a story and without an effect. We need to research and tell that story for the media just as we are doing about party systems and party development or economic transformation. Indeed, we almost need to know the story of communications in democratization more. Without the media, parties and party systems would not function. Nor would we know what is happening. The media, in the case of economic transformation, have been one of the more interesting models and motors. But, in no case are they a "given", just a cog in the process, or a case like any other part of the democratization process.

Notes

1 The main study of the journalism profession in democratic, non democratic, and democratizing societies is The Global Journalist, ed. by Dennis Weaver (Cresskill, New Jersey: Hampton Press, 1998).

2 Weaver, pp. 466-467.

3 See for a quantitative report that touches on these issues, "The Polish Journalism Profession Views Itself in Transition" by J.L. Curry and Jerzy Oledzki in Vom Instrument der Partei Zur 'Vierten Gewalt' ed. by Eduard Mühle (Marburg: Verlag Herder-Institut, 1997).

Party Systems in Central East Europe: Dimensions of System Stability

ALGIS KRUPAVICIUS

1. Introduction

No one doubts that a multi-party system is a constituent element of every contemporary democracy. However, there are many ways to look at and evaluate the emerging party systems in new democracies, and in particular in Central East Europe (CEE). It is most easy to observe and to generalize party system development using only few variables and by speculative judgements on general (macro) issues. However, another way seems to be more fruitful and appropriate in that situation. It is an instrumental view on party systems on the basis of many variables.

From a comparative perspective, the Central East European countries represent the most successful cases of democratic transition after 1989. For this reason, it is important to explore more deeply the processes of the institutionalization and stabilization of the Central East European systems. From a traditional point of view, it might be useful to look at the development and stabilization of the Central East European party systems employing the seminal theory of social cleavages developed by Lipset and Rokkan. From an operational and instrumental point of view, however, it is better to concentrate on quantitative indicators and measures of party systems in the region.

The CEE party systems in this chapter are evaluated and measured along only one dimension, i.e. system stability vs. system instability. In other words, the task is to find out and identify sources and factors of party system stability and instability in Central East Europe.

Among the indicators used in this evaluation are the following: voter turnout or more broadly electoral participation as a major precondition of party system stability; the number of effective or relevant parties; indices of proportionality, party aggregation and electoral exclusion; ideological distribution of political parties and relative strength of different party groups within a particular country and in comparative perspective; electoral volatility. Finally, the indicators are divided into two groups: a) those which reflect the electoral bases of party system stability or instability, and b) those which primarily are helpful to identify structural causes of party system stability. From the focus of this analysis we have thus purposefully excluded electoral rules and institutional designs which inevitably are also shaping the structure of new party systems. To what extent these variables produce party system stability remains an open question.

The selection of countries was based on geographical regional criteria and the availability of empirical data for comparative analysis. Among the countries covered are Bulgaria, the Czech Republic, Slovakia, Slovenia, Romania, Poland, Hungary, Estonia,

Latvia, and Lithuania. Two of them, i.e. Bulgaria and Romania, do not entirely coincide with the CEE region. However, it was worth to include these countries for comparative reasons.

2. Electoral behavior and party systems in the CEE

Without any doubt, electoral behavior is a crucial factor, which shapes the structure and composition of multi-party systems as far as modern democracies are based on the principle of representative government. The first variable, to be considered, therefore, is the average rate of voter turnout. Of course, there are certain variations of voter turnout even in stable and advanced Western democracies (Table 1).

Table 1. ***Voter turnout in Western democracies 1992- 1996***

Country	National elections	Elections of European parliament	Country	National elections	Elections of European parliament
Belgium	90.7 (1995)	90.7	Austria	86.0 (1995)	67.7
Luxembourg	88.5 (1994)	88.3	Denmark	83.3 (1994)	52.5
Italy	85.0 (1996)	74.8	Germany	79.1 (1994)	60.1
Sweden	83.3 (1994)	41.6	Spain	78.1 (1996)	59.6
Netherlands	78.3 (1994)	35.6	Greece	76.4 (1996)	71.2
Great Britain	77.7 (1992)	36.4	France	69.0 (1993)	52.7
Finland	71.8 (1995)	58.8	Portugal	66.3 (1995)	35.6
Ireland	68.5 (1992)	44.0	USA*	48.5 (1996)	-
			Average	76.90	44.38

*) % of all eligible voters;

Source: Hickersberger M., Lutter J. (1996) Die Europaparlamentswahlen 1996 in Oesterreich und die Europaeische Normalitaet. -*SES Rundschau*- Vol. 36 (4), p. 393; Gans C.B. (1997) Why Citizens Shun the Polling Booth: An Interview with Curtis B. Gans [Director of the Committee for the Study of the American Electorate]" - *The Public Perspective*- February/March, pp. 41- 44.

Note: Elections to the European Parliament were held in 1994, except Sweden in 1995 and Austria in 1996.

However, participation in national parliamentary elections is a much more complicated mater in the new democracies. High variations of voter turnout may be observed in the CEE not only on a cross-national basis, but also from a time perspective. The latter factor seems to be most important in new democracies. Because of the plebiscitarian character of the founding elections and the democratic opening of political participation for citizens of the CEE countries, the voter turnout here slightly exceeded the level of Western democracies in the early 90-s on the average (see Figure 1).

Figure 1. ***Voter turnout in the CEE: time factor***

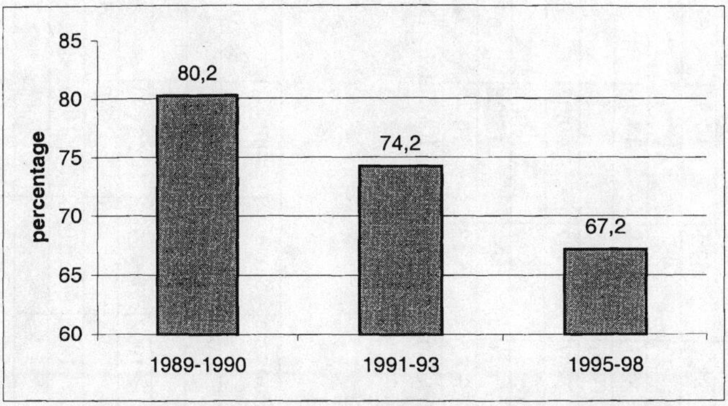

But two further remarks seem to be appropriate in this context. Electoral choice during the founding elections in the CEE was shaped not by traditional political parties in the Western sense, but by ideologically and organizationally heterogeneous mass political movements. Moreover, only a disintegration of these movements paved the way towards the institutionalization of genuinely representative, more or less ideologically coherent political parties. A paradox is that the founding elections introduced an element of competitiveness into the electoral process in new democracies without real parties. There were exceptions, of course, which were based on different degrees of articulation of party interests and organizations during the late period of communist liberalization. Hungary's exceptionalism is the most striking example. In this case the founding elections may be considered as the first multi-party elections, too.

The general trend of voter activity is clearly moving downward in the new democracies after a plebiscitarian explosion during the constituent elections. The voter turnout during the last five or six years declined by 13 percent on the average compared to the constituent elections, which means that almost one-third of the total electorate has been ignoring the national elections (Table 2).

The downward trend did not stop after the second multi-party elections, usually held in the countries of the region in 1994-1996. But a good message is that the level of voter turnout tends to stabilize in the majority of Central East European countries after the last round of parliamentary elections. Moreover, the CEE states succeeded to develop a "two-thirds" participating electorate on the average as can be concluded from the turnout data during the national elections in 1996-1998.

Certainly, the causes of low voter turnout rates are very complex. On the one hand, they might be found and explained through a concept of political socialization, i.e. inexperience of voters to make electoral choices, underdeveloped party alignments etc. On the other hand, the lack of political mobilization might be linked to political parties and party systems as a whole and their abilities to shape electoral decisions. This latter way of thinking seems to be more reasonable in the context of the weakness and strength of the new party systems in the CEE. To be sure, the political party is an active subject of the electoral process which is interested to mobilize as many as possible supporters in the elections, voters are the most passive elements in this game. A major but quite straightforward conclusion is, therefore, that political parties are still lacking the capabilities to mobilize a substantial part of the electorate, which was active during the founding elections. In general, the recent decline of voter turnout is an indication of

Table 2. ***Voter turnout in the CEE countries, 1989- 1998***

	Bulgaria	Czech Republic	Slovakia	Estonia	Latvia	Lithuania	Poland	Romania	Slovenia	Hungary	St.deviation	Median	Average
Founding elections	1990	1990	1990	1990	1990	1990	1989	1990	1990	1990			
	90,8	96,7	83	78	81,3	71,7	62,1	86,2	83,1	69,5	10,31	82,15	80,24
First multi-party elections	1991	1992	1992	1992	1993	1992	1991	1992	1992	1994			
	83,9	85,1	84,2	66,8	89,9	75,3	43,2	76,1	85,7	68,9	13,79	80	75,91
Second multi-party elections	1994	1996	1994	1995	1995	1996	1993	1996	1996	1998			
	75,2	76,4	75,6	68,9	71,9	52,9	52,1	76	73,7	57	9,97	72,8	67,97
Third multi-party elections	1997		1998		1998		1997						
	62,9		84,2		71,8		47,9				15,28	67,35	66,70
Average	78,20	86,07	81,75	71,23	78,73	66,63	51,33	79,43	80,83	65,13	10,42	78,46	73,93

Sources: Rose R., Munro N., Mackie T. (1998) Elections in Central and Eastern Europe since 1990. University of Strathclyde; PARLINE Database, Inter-Parliamentary Union, http://www.ipu.org

Table 4. ***Proportionality index in the CEE, 1990- 1998 (percentage)***

	Bulgaria	Czech Republic	Slovakia	Estonia	Latvia	Lithuania	Poland	Romania	Slovenia	Hungary	st. deviation	Average
Founding elections	1990	1990	1990	1990	1990	1990	1989	1990	1990	1990		
	95	81	92	-	-	-	-	96	94	78	7,79	89,33
First multi-party elections	1991	1992	1992	1992	1993	1992	1991	1992	1992	1994		
	75	81	76	83	90	90	88	84	85	79	5,38	83,10
Second multi-party elections	1994	1996	1994	1995	1995	1996	1993	1996	1996	1998		
	84	90	86	87	87	77	63	85	84	88	7,87	83,10
Third multi-party elections	1997		1998		1998		1997					
	92	-	97	-	94	-	81	-	-	-	-	91,00
Average	86,5	84	87,7	85	90,3	83,5	77,3	88,3	87,6	81,6	3,79	85,21

Calculated from: Rose R., Munro N., Mackie T. (1998) Elections in Central and Eastern Europe since 1990. University of Strathclyde, p.116- 117; PARLINE Database, Inter-Parliamentary Union, http://www.ipu.org

potential (rather than actual) party system instability in the Central East European countries.

Cross-national comparisons of voter turnout also allow to discern a few more positive developments. Voter turnout slightly increased in Estonia and Poland, for example, during the latest elections. Relatively stable patterns of electoral participation were demonstrated in the Czech Republic, Slovakia, Estonia and Romania since 1992.

One more interesting observation is the religious cleavage as a deeply rooted traditional cultural phenomenon in the CEE societies. All the countries with dominant Orthodox or Protestant religions (Bulgaria, Romania, Estonia, Latvia and the Czech Republic) enjoy the highest levels of voter turnout (78.7 per cent). By contrast, countries with Roman Catholics as the dominant religious group (Lithuania, Poland, and Hungary) have substantially lower voter turnouts (61 per cent on the average). An exception from this rule is Slovenia with an average turnout of almost 81 per cent. All other traditional cleavages such as urban-rural differences, varieties in economic development (including recent economic successes or failures), or differences in ethnic composition do not have any significant links with levels of voter turnout in the CEE countries.

The index of volatility is not only a good indicator to observe voter switches from one party to another in subsequent elections, but it is also an indicator of the relative strength and social basis of the leading parties as well. As far as West European democracies are concerned, the index of volatility is relatively low and does not exceed 21 points (Rose et al. 1998: 119). Only few countries of the CEE have a volatility index similar to the Western European one, i.e. Slovakia - 20 (1990-1994) and Romania - 15.5 (1990-1996) points (calculated from: Rose et al. 1998:119). In general, the index of volatility is more than twice as high in the CEE countries compared to Western Europe. Again it is a clear sign that multi-party and competitive party systems in the region are still relatively unstable. Moreover, the index of volatility demonstrates well that some major parties are unable to mobilize supporters on a permanent basis, or they are lacking stable social support in the society (Table 3).

Table 3. ***Index of volatility in the CEE countries, 1994- 1997***

	Index of volatility		Index of volatility
Bulgaria	49 (1997)	Romania	22 (1996)
Czech Republic	38 (1996)	Slovenia	50 (1996)
Slovakia	14 (1994)*	Hungary	48 (1994)
Estonia	53 (1995)	standard deviation	16,2
Latvia	65 (1995)**	Median	49,5
Lithuania	56 (1996)	Average	45,4
Poland	59 (1997)	West Europe	21

* After the 1998 parliamentary elections volatility index exceeded 60 per cent; ** in 1998 volatility index was around 50 per cent.

Source: Rose R., Munro N., Mackie T. (1998) Elections in Central and Eastern Europe since 1990. University of Strathclyde, p.119.

Another dimension related more to the electoral system than directly to voter behavior is the degree of proportionality, i.e. the difference between the vote percentage and seat percentage of a particular party received in competitive elections. However, as far as democratic elections are based on the preposition that every vote counts, the proportionality of an electoral system is an important factor to convince individual voters that their participation in elections is an important act of citizen awareness and responsibility. After all, it signalizes to parties and voters that the electoral process is fair. In general, proportionality is a substantial element of legitimacy not only of democratic elections but of the democratic political order as such. Because of the overall higher sensitivity of citizens to issues of legitimacy of the political system in the new democracies compared to stable and advanced ones, this problem has much higher importance than just being a formula translating votes into seats.

In spite of the fact that the CEE countries introduced proportional or mixed electoral systems (theoretically most conducive to the fair translation of votes into seats) in the early 90-s, again reality and election outcomes reveal some negative trends, which in the longer run may affect the stability of the party systems. Lijphart pointed out that proportionality might be evaluated by two different methods, i.e. as "the absolute differences between the vote percentages (v) and seat percentages (s) of all parties (n) that have received at least one-half percent of the total votes" (Rae index of disproportionality); or as "the difference between the vote and seat percentages of all the overrepresented parties together" (Loosemore & Hanby index) (see Lijphart 1984: 162). Instead, because of shortcomings of both indices, Lijphart proposes to base the proportionality index on "the average vote-seat share deviation of the two largest parties in each election" (Lijphart 1984: 163). Another measure is "the arithmetic difference between a party's share of the popular vote and its share of the total seats in Parliament, summed, divided by two and subtracted from 100" (Rose et al. 1998: 116).

This measure indicates that the founding elections have had mostly proportional results (Olson 1998: 36), despite the fact that the majority formula was in use to translate votes into seats in most countries of the CEE in 1989-1990 (see Figure 2).

Figure 2. ***Index of Proportionality in the CEE: time factor***

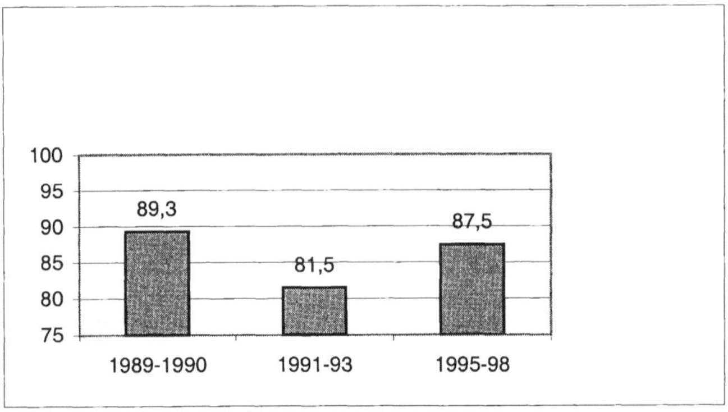

The overall decline of the proportionality index was less than 2 points comparing the third and/or fourth democratic elections in 1994-1998 with the founding elections of 1989-1990. This course of developments cannot be explained only by the introduction of proportional electoral systems with relatively high thresholds (4-5 per cent of total votes) in the new democracies. Certainly, a good message is that "the post-Communist elections remain more proportional than most first-past-the-post elections" (Rose et al. 1998; 116). Another sign of increasing party system stability is that the proportionality index tends to go up in the majority of countries (Bulgaria, the Czech Republic, Slovakia, Romania, Hungary) after the setback in the second democratic elections. Still, the latest average level of the proportionality index of the CEE of 91 points (calculated on the basis of the 1997-1998 elections in Latvia, Poland, Slovakia and Bulgaria) is slightly behind the Western European mean (96 points) (Table 4).

Some uncertainty of developmental direction is reflected by a comparison of the index of proportionality with an index of "wasted" votes or the mean of electoral exclusion in the words of David Olson. The index of electoral exclusion is calculated by summing up the total vote not represented in parliament (Olson 1998: 35). The critical points here seem to be the first and second sets of multi-party elections in the CEE countries. The absolute highest level of wasted votes (42.2 per cent) was registered during the 1993 parliamentary elections in Poland. Because the third multi-party elections were held only in 4 countries (Bulgaria, Slovakia, Latvia and Poland) so far, it is hard to predict that these elections will become a final transitional point towards an increase of electoral representation in the CEE.

The absolute numbers of electoral exclusion in some countries even after the last parliamentary elections are high (Lithuania - 32.7, concerning "proportional" formula; Romania - 19.8; Slovenia - 17.7; Estonia - 12.7 per cent). Among the direct outcomes of a high level of electoral exclusion may be a decrease of voter turnout, increased volatility and a general lack of party system stability. Certainly, we have to explore the correlation between electoral exclusion and confidence in the democratic order as well. In general, it is possible to conclude that the level of electoral exclusion tends to decrease considerably in the CEE countries in 1995. 1998. Nevertheless, the current level of exclusion is still higher by almost 4 percent compared to the founding elections (Table 5).

Figure 3. ***Electoral exclusion in the CEE countries***

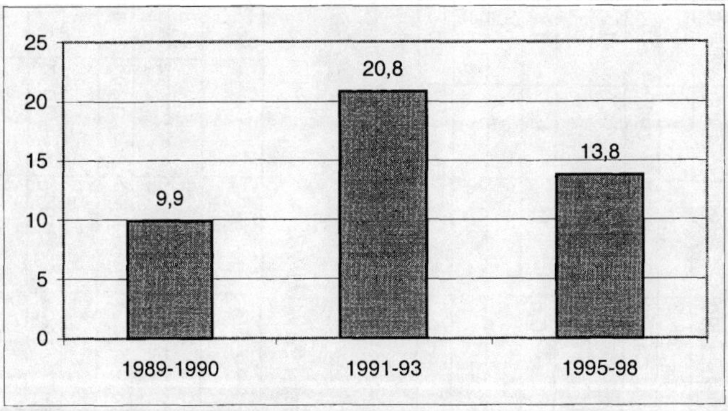

The overall picture of party system stability in the CEE from the perspective of electoral behavior thus is quite mixed. The data reveal some kind of a "fifty-fifty" situation, when two of four indicators allow to speak of a stabilization of party systems, i.e. first, the voter turnout tends to stabilize on lower levels than in the majority of Western European countries, but the trend toward stability is quite clear; second, the index of proportionality is coming very close to Western European standards. Two other indices employed in this evaluation - the index of volatility and the index of electoral exclusion - show, however, some sources of potential or even actual instability of the CEE party systems. Voter volatility is high compared to the advanced democracies, and it is a significant indication that in almost all countries there is a broad space for party exchange on the basis of shifting party loyalties. Another problem is the relatively high level of electoral exclusion in the CEE democracies.

Table 5. ***Index of electoral exclusion in Central East Europe, 1990- 1998***

	Bulgaria	Czech R. R.	Slovakia	Estonia	Latvia	*Lithuania	Poland	Romania	Slovenia	*Hungary	st. deviation	Average
Founding elections	1990	1990	1990	1990	1990	1990	1989	1990	1990	1990		
	2	18,8	7,8					7	7,8	16	6,26	9,90
First multi-party elections	1991	1992	1992	1992	1993	1992	1991	1992	1992	1994		
	24,9	19,2	23,6	14,6	10,9	14,1	7,08	20	17,7	12,6	5,64	16,47
Second multi-party elections	1994	1996	1994	1995	1995	1996	1993	1996	1996	1998		
	15,6	10,6	15,6	12,7	12,2	32,7	42,4	19,8	17,7	8	10,74	18,73
Third multi-party elections	1997		1998		1998		1997					
	7,6		4		11,9		12,8				4,07	9,08
Average	12,5	16,2	12,7	12,7	11,6	23,4	27,6	15,6	14,4	12,2	6,68	

* Only concerning proportional formula;
Source: Rose R., Munro N., Mackie T. (1998) Elections in Central and Eastern Europe since 1990. University of Strathclyde; PARLINE Database, Inter-Parlimentary Union, http://www.ipu.org

Table 6. ***Number of parliamentary parties, 1989- 1998***

	Bulgaria	Czech Republic	Slovakia	Estonia	Latvia	Lithuania	Poland	Romania	Slovenia	Hungary	Average of the CEE
Founding elections	1990	1990	1990	1990	1990	1990	1989	1990	1990	1990	
	4	4	7	3	2	2	4	18	4	7	5,5
First multi-party elections	1991	1992	1992	1992	1993	1992	1991	1992	1992	1994	
	3	8	5	9	8	13	27	10	8	8	9,9
Second multi-party elections	1994	1996	1994	1995	1995	1996	1993	1996	1996	1998	
	5	6	7	7	9	14	7	8	7	7	7,7
Third multi-party elections	1997		1998		1998		1997				
	5		6		6		6				5,75

Source: Rose R., Munro N., Mackie T. (1998) Elections in Central and Eastern Europe since 1990. University of Strathclyde; PARLINE Database, Inter-Parliamentary Union, http://www.ipu.org

3. Structural dimensions and party system stability in the CEE

Among the indicators of structural analysis of the CEE party systems are the following: number of parliamentary parties, strength of largest party, strength of socialist and bourgeois parties, influence of class-based, agrarian, religious, ethnic and non-cultural parties, effective number of parties, party aggregation index.

The number of parliamentary parties is a traditional indicator to investigate party systems. An increase in numbers of parliamentary parties occurred during the first multi-party elections in all countries, except Slovakia, Bulgaria and Romania. Large numbers of new political actors entered the political stage during the founding elections, because the old regime had collapsed leaving a political vacuum, which was filled by colorful opposition and semi-opposition political forces. In Slovakia, however, the Movement for a Democratic Slovakia was one of the driving forces of the break-up of former Czechoslovakia in 1992 and successfully monopolized power institutions of the country after it. The MDS led by Meciar used even some non-democratic means to constrain the development of opposition parties in 1992-98. In the case of Bulgaria the main reasons of limited fragmentation of parliamentary parties are rooted in the preservation of two major umbrella transitional players - the Bulgarian Socialist Party and the Union of Democratic Forces during the following multi-party elections. Furthermore, the overall slowdown of political as well as social and economic transformations in the country were factors of the limited party fragmentation in Bulgaria (Table 6).

But in general, a "hundred party system" was a short-lived phenomenon in the CEE countries, and a clear trend towards a decrease in the number of parliamentary parties could be observed as early as during the second set of multi-party elections. The most explicit exception here was Lithuania. But this exception is only partly true, as the "naked" numbers of parliamentary parties are highly misleading. This exception mostly resulted from effects of a mixed electoral formula. During the 1992 and 1996 Seimas elections the same number of parties - only five - entered parliament through the proportional formula, but in both cases in total more than ten parties succeeded to get mandates with the help of the majority formula. But the leading parties in the proportional system in 1992 and 1996 were able to secure most of the votes along the majority formula as well. Comparing the CEE and Western Europe it is worth noting that the absolute average number of parliamentary parties after the second multi-party elections was almost the same, i.e. 7.7 and 7.9 parties respectively (1989). Moreover, whereas the average number of parliamentary parties in Central East Europe was equal to 7.2 parties during the entire 1989-1998 period, the average number in West Europe was 7.0 parties in 1945-1989 (Lane & Ersson 1994: 183).

Unstable party formations are a common phenomenon in the early developmental stages of democratic party systems but elections here are an action-forcing event (Olson 1998: 12). An additional criterion to reflect the degree of party exchange in new democracies is the share of new parties in parliament (in absolute numbers): parties are considered as "old" if they were able to enter the national legislature in two subsequent elections. This perspective confirms that the most stable party systems are in the Czech Republic and Hungary, where no new political players entered parliament after the last parliamentary elections. The second group of countries includes Poland, Lithuania, and perhaps Romania, where the share of new parties is no more than one fourth of the total number of parliamentary parties. However, the exchange between new and old parties is especially high in Latvia (50% in 1998) and Bulgaria (40% in 1998). This picture is, however, not complete without a calculation of the relative parliamentary strength of new and old parties (Table 7).

Nevertheless, the overall party fractionalization on the parliamentary level in the CEE is quite comparable to Western European variations (Lane & Ersson 1994: 183). Despite of this fact and, for instance a success of Green and New Left parties in Western Europe since the 80-s, the political weight of new parties in the CEE countries after every new round of parliamentary elections is substantially higher than in the old democracies. Moreover, the electoral influence of new parties in the CEE is hardly explainable exclusively by institutional or electoral features, i.e. district magnitude, federalism or legislative-executive relations, as it is possible to do in the case of the Western democracies (see Wiley 1998: 236-239). The relative strength of new parties in the CEE countries is rather based on underdeveloped and changing party attachments mainly affected by short-term factors, i.e. social and economic conjuncture, performance by party in government etc. (Table 8).

The strength of the largest parliamentary party reflects structural opportunities and choices for cabinet formation and signalizes the stability of parliamentary majorities rather than overall party system stability. Nonetheless, the share of the largest party mirrors aggregation capacities of the leading political parties, which is an element of party system stability, too. Only in two countries - Bulgaria and Lithuania - the largest parties were able to secure one-party parliamentary majorities without major interruptions since 1990. In all other countries stable parliamentary majorities were produced only on a basis of party coalitions. Coalition governments are a reality in all the CEE countries. During the first and the second set of multi-party elections the average share of the largest party stabilized around 37.5 per cent of seats in the lower house of the national legislatures. This leads towards the establishment mainly of minimal winning coalitions in these states. However, the practical implementation of coalition potentials depends on many different but interrelated factors. One of them is the ideological composition of parliament. This aspect can be discussed by using the distinction between bourgeois and socialist parties.[1]

The nature of transition in the CEE to liberal democracy and market economy brought to power bourgeois parties almost everywhere in the early phase of democratization.[2] However, a definition of mass popular movements as bourgeois parties is dubious for the founding elections. In fact, the umbrella popular movements were extremely colorful organizations from an ideological point of view. D. Olson described them as a "rainbow coalition", which lost the basis of unity after achieving their goal - the removal of the Communist government (1998: 17). For reasons of simplification and because of the fact that all major reform movements advocated system change, pro-market economic reforms and in many cases these organizations later developed mainly into parties to the right of the political center, they may be identified with the bourgeois political camp even during the founding elections.

After a clear advantage of the bourgeois parties in the founding elections, a landslide victory of bourgeois parties (looking at the share of parliamentary seats) was achieved during the second set of democratic elections, except for Lithuania in 1992, Poland in 1993 and Hungary in 1994. Moreover, a trend toward a predominance of bourgeois parties is still strong in the CEE even after the last set of elections in 1997-1998, which is in sharp contrast to the Western European trend to bring back social democratic parties to power. A positive aspect of the right wing party dominance and a certain ideological homogeneity of the new power elite is that it may ease internal tensions between the leading political parties finally helping to achieve a broader consensus on policy priorities and to foster inter-party co-operation (Table 9).

Table 7. ***Share of new parties in the CEE parliaments, 1989- 1998***

	Bulgaria	Czech Republic	Slovakia	Estonia	Latvia	Lithuania	Poland	Romania	Slovenia	Hungary	Average
Founding elections	50%	50%	100%	67%	50%	50%	25%	89%	25%	71%	58%
First multi-party elections	0%	63%	20%	100%	100%	54%	96%	50%	25%	13%	52%
Second multi-party elections	40%	0%	43%	43%	44%	21%	14%	25%	29%	0%	26%
Third multi-party elections	40%		33%		50%		17%				35%
Mean	33%	25%	49%	70%	61%	42%	38%	55%	26%	28%	43%

Calculated from: Rose R., Munro N., Mackie T. (1998) Elections in Central and Eastern Europe since 1990. University of Strathclyde; PARLINE Database, Inter-Parliamentary Union, http://www.ipu.org

Table 8. ***Strength of largest parliamentary party, 1989- 1998 (percentage of seats)***

	Bulgaria	Czech Republic	Slovakia	Estonia	Latvia	Lithuania	Poland	Romania	Slovenia	Hungary	The CEE average
Founding elections	52,8	63,5	32	46,6	65,2	70,2	37,6	66,4	17,5	42,5	49,43
First multi-party elections	45,8	38	49,3	28,7	36	51,7	13,5	34,3	24,4	54,1	37,58
Second multi-party elections	52	34	40,7	40,6	18	51,1	37,2	35,2	27,8	38,3	37,49
Third Multi-party elections	57,1		28,6		24		43,7				
Average	51,93	45,17	40,67	38,63	35,80	57,67	33,00	45,30	23,23	44,97	41,64

Source: PARLINE Database, Inter-Parliamentary Union, http://www.ipu.org ; Rose R., Munro N., Mackie T. (1998) Elections in Central and Eastern Europe since 1990. University of Strathclyde.

What about the socialist parties? Do they see a light at the end of the tunnel? The CEE countries can be divided into three groups according to the criteria of socialist party influence. First, these are states as Bulgaria, Hungary, Poland and Romania where the socialist parties occupy no less than 30 per cent of parliamentary seats on a permanent basis. The second group is represented by the Czech Republic, Slovakia and Slovenia where the share of these parties tends to increase but still their share of seats in parliament is relatively small (little more than 20 per cent). In the third group of countries the role of socialist parties is rather insignificant as in Estonia (the most explicit case) and Latvia.[3] The case of Lithuania is a deviant one, because of the highly fluctuating influence of the socialist parties in parliament (see Tables 9 and 10).

The relatively low share of socialist parties corresponds with a weakness of other class-based parties as well. The average share of votes of the class-based parties was 27 per cent after the second set of multi-party elections in CEE. It was thus about 12 per cent less than in Western Europe on the average (see: Lane & Ersson 1994: 186).

However, the influence of a second group of structural parties, i.e. the aggregate strength of ethnic, religious and agrarian parties, is almost the same as in the West European democracies. It was equal to 23.9 per cent in CEE and 23.8 per cent in Western Europe. Cross-national variations here are important, too. The share of ethnic, agrarian and religious parties is quite significant in Poland, Estonia, Slovenia, and even dominant in Slovakia. As far as most of these parties were "manufactured" by historical circumstances and traditional social cleavages, it is important not to deny the roles of historical subcultures in the new democracies of Central East Europe.

In contrast to Western Europe where the average support of ethnic parties is low, this is not the case in some countries of the CEE. Of course, here the most obvious example is Slovakia (Table 11). Even though the bourgeois parties have been in leading positions in the CEE parliaments for almost a decade since 1990, the strength of non-structural parties, defining them as conservative and liberal parties, is not so indisputable compared to other party groups. The non-structural parties are in relatively dominant positions in the Czech Republic, Estonia, Latvia, Lithuania, Hungary and Poland, but the average strength of these parties is 39.7 per cent of total votes, and was slightly lower than the Western European average of 42.3 per cent in 1985-1989 (Lane & Ersson 1994: 188). From this situation it is possible to hypothesize that the conservative and liberal parties in order to preserve stable parliamentary majorities need to invite as coalition partners other right wing parties, mostly religious and nationalist ones.

The most common quantitative indicator to evaluate competitive party systems during a longer period of time is the index of the effective number of parties developed by Markku Laakso and Rein Taagepera in 1979. This index takes into account not only the total number of political parties taking part in competition for votes and seats, but also measures their relative parliamentary strength. In addition, the effective number of parties reflects well the degree of party system concentration. Looking at all countries together, we can observe three different waves of changes in the effective number of parties in CEE (Table 12). The first wave coincided with the founding elections which may be called a "limited pluralism" because the average of the effective number of parties was relatively low - only 2.8 parties. As has been mentioned before, political competition in many countries involved only two or three political subjects, i.e. the non-communist opposition, reform communists and hard-line communists during the early phase of transition to democracy. The second wave started with the first multi-party elections and the number of relevant parties increased almost twofold to 4.9 parties on the average. This phase may be called an "oversized pluralism" (or segmented pluralism in Steins Rokkan's terminology). It is interesting that a growth in party numbers was

Table 9. ***Strength of bourgeois parties, 1989- 1998 (percentage of seats)***

	Bulgaria	Czech Republic	Slovakia	Estonia	Latvia	Lithuania	Poland	Romania	Slovenia	Hungary	st. deviation	Average
Founding elections	1990	1990	1990	1990	1990	1990	1989	1990	1990	1990		
	42,1	73	72,1	46,6	65,2	70,2	35	15,4	56,35	89,6	21,94	56,56
First multi-party elections	1991	1992	1992	1992	1993	1992	1991	1992	1992	1994		
	55,8	60,5	71,3	88,1	93	45,4	67,4	50,1	72,2	45,9	16,64	64,97
Second multi-party elections	1994	1996	1994	1995	1995	1996	1993	1996	1996	1998		
	30,8	49,5	68	94,1	79	81,7	24,4	46,1	65,6	65,3	22,46	60,45
Third multi-party elections	1997				1998		1997					
	70				86		58				14,05	71,33
Mean	49,7	61,0	70,5	76,3	80,8	65,8	46,2	37,2	64,7	66,9	13,71	61,9

Calculated from: Rose R., Munro N., Mackie T. (1998) Elections in Central and Eastern Europe since 1990. University of Strathclyde; PARLINE Database, Inter-Parliamentary Union, http://www.ipu.org

Table 10. ***Strength of socialist parties, 1989- 1998 (percentage of seats)***

	Bulgaria	Czech Republic	Slovakia	Estonia	Latvia	Lithuania	Poland	Romania	Slovenia	Hungary	st. deviation	Average
Founding elections	1990	1990	1990	1990	1990	1990	1989	1990	1990	1990		
	56,8	16	14,7	53,4	29,4	19,8	37,6	68,2	31,25	8,5	20,15	33,57
First multi-party elections	1991	1992	1992	1992	1993	1992	1991	1992	1992	1994		
	44,2	25,5	19,3	11,9	7	51,8	24,3	38,1	20	54,1	16,48	29,62
Second multi-party elections	1994	1996	1994	1995	1995	1996	1993	1996	1996	1998		
	59,2	41,5	20,7	5,9	13	17,6	74,8	42,2	22,2	34,7	21,69	33,18
Third multi-party elections	1997				1998		1997					
	30				14		41,6				13,86	28,53
Mean	47,6	27,7	18,2	23,7	15,9	29,7	44,6	49,5	24,5	32,4	12,03	31,4

Calculated from: Rose R., Munro N., Mackie T. (1998) Elections in Central and Eastern Europe since 1990. University of Strathclyde; PARLINE Database, Inter-Parliamentary Union, http://www.ipu.org

also a feature of democratizing Germany (in 1945-49 the effective number of parties was 4.9, but it was reduced to 2.8 in the second half of the 50-s), Spain (4.3 in the late 70-s and 3.4 in early 80-s respectively), and Greece (3.7 in 1975-79 and 2.7 in 1980-84) (Lane & Ersson 1994: 184).

The second and third multi-party elections brought a new trend and initiated a third wave of changes, i.e. a reduction of the effective number of parties by one point to 3.9 parties on the average. Hopefully, this is an initial step to the phase of a "stable pluralism". Of course, this does not mean that the number of relevant parties will stay frozen. But it will be hard to expect that their number in the next few years will rise to more than 10 parties, or that in the next elections it will be reduced to less than 4 relevant parties as happened in Poland in the mid-nineties. Moreover, the current average in ten countries equal to 4 relevant parties correlates well with the Western European mean of 4.3 parties in 1989.

The effective number of parties shows substantial variations on a country-by-country basis. After the last set of democratic elections a higher number of relevant parties compared to the average of CEE could be found in Latvia, Slovakia, Slovenia and Romania. All other countries, excluding Poland, have had lower indices of effective parties than the region's mean. Poland is clearly a deviant case, because of sharp fluctuations from one election to another. David M. Olson calculated the effective number of parties using a two-way method: basing the index on the share of party votes as well as on the number of party seats in the legislature. The effective number was higher basing the indicator on share of party votes compared to the number of seats in all Central East European countries. But one thing is even more remarkable. In some instances, the distance between differently calculated indices was almost double - Bulgaria, Hungary, or even higher - Poland (1998: 37). However, in both calculations an overall decrease in the effective number of parties is evident after the third set of elections.

The last indicator to be used in this evaluation of party system stability is an index of party aggregation. The original index of aggregation is calculated as A=100(S/L)/P, where A= the aggregation index, S= the seats held by the largest party in the government coalition, L= the total number of seats in the lower house of the legislature, and P= the number of parties holding at least one seat in that house. The higher the score, the more aggregated the party system. But here a modified version of the aggregation index is used, i.e. A=S/P, where S= the percentage of votes by the largest parliamentary party, and P= the total number of parties in the lower house of the national legislature.

As is obvious in Table 12 and Table 13, the indices of effective number of parties and party aggregation are inter-related, i.e. a lower number of effective parties means a higher level of party aggregation. In both cases it seems important to look not only at absolute figures for every individual country but also to consider the standard deviations of both indicators as far as they reflect the fluctuation of party choices during the parliamentary elections. Only in case of 4 countries out of 10 (the Czech Republic, Lithuania, Romania and Hungary) both indicators are relatively stable and the standard deviation is lower than the CEE average. Slovenia and Bulgaria represent deviant cases because the standard deviations indicate different trajectories of party system development. The situation is especially interesting in Bulgaria. Here the effective party number is low with a low standard deviation, but the index of aggregation is high and the standard deviation is among the highest in the region.

Table 11. ***Average shares of structural and non-structural parties, 1989-1998 (percentage of votes)***

	Bulgaria	Czech Republic	Slovakia	Estonia	Latvia	Lithuania	Poland	Romania	Slovenia	Hungary	The CEE mean	W. Europe mean, 1945-89
Class- based parties	38,40	26,57	17,18	24,33	14,65	28,90	27,80	50,33	25,67	30,03	28,39	39,30
Ethnic, religious and agrarian parties	15,33	20,77	54,38	25,13	23,28	16,37	26,18	17,10	32,07	8,87	23,95	23,80
Non-structural parties	38,28	46,00	22,08	42,17	57,90	45,43	38,10	20,43	29,77	57,43	39,76	36,90

Calculated from: Rose R., Munro N., Mackie T. (1998) Elections in Central and Eastern Europe since 1990. University of Strathclyde; PARLINE Database, Inter-Parliamentary Union, http://www.ipu.org

Table 12. ***Number of effective parties, 1989- 1998 (seats)***

	Bulgaria	Czech Republic	Slovakia	Estonia	Latvia	Lithuania	Poland	Romania	Slovenia	Hungary	The CEE average
Founding elections	2,4	2,2	4,9	3	1,9	1,87	3,4	2,19	2,5	3,7	2,80
First multi-party elections	2,4	4,7	3,2	5,9	5,1	3	10,7	4,75	6,6	2,9	4,92
Second multi-party elections	2,7	4,2	4,6	4,15	6,1	3,3	3,9	4,3	5,5	3,45	4,22
Third multi-party elections	2,5		4,8		5,5		3				3,95
St. deviation*	0,15	0,35	0,87	1,24	0,50	0,21	4,21	0,32	0,78	0,39	0,50
Mean	2,50	3,70	4,38	4,35	4,65	2,72	5,25	3,75	4,87	3,35	

* standard deviation calculated only since the first multi-party elections in each country.

4. Quantitative profiles of the CEE party systems

The most common way to evaluate party systems is to classify them along the numbers and relative sizes of political parties. Jean Blondel pioneered this field by proposing a four-dimensional classification along the mentioned criteria, i.e. two-party, two-and-a-half party, multiparty with a dominant party, multiparty system without a dominant party.

Table 14. ***Classification of Party Systems Based on the Numbers and Relative Sizes of Political Parties***

Party Systems	*Hypothetical examples of seat shares*	*Effective number of parties*
Two-party system	55-45	2.0
Two-and-a-half-party system	45-40-15	2.6
Multiparty system with a dominant party	45-20-15-10-10	3.5
Multiparty system without a dominant party	25-25-25-15-10	4.5

Source: Lijphart A.(1984), Democracies. Patterns of Majoritarian and Consensus Government in Twenty-One Countries. Yale University Press, p. 119.

A few questions remain important in the analysis of the CEE party systems in this context: a) the numerical profile of party systems itself; b) the extent of system changes or number of party system turnovers. However, one additional remark is appropriate here. Because of the non-party character of the founding elections (except, maybe, Hungary), it is relevant to look on party system profiles only starting from the first multi-party elections.

Surprisingly, the numerical profiles of the CEE party systems are relatively stable from the very first multi-party elections. Only few countries changed party systems in a more drastic way, including Poland which moved from a multiparty system without a dominant party in 1991 to a two-and-a-half party system in 1997, or Latvia from a multiparty system with a dominant party in 1993 to the same system but without a dominant party in 1998.

Table 15. ***Typology of party systems in Central East Europe***

Party system	*First multi-party elections*	*Second multi-party elections*	*Third multi-party elections*
Two-party system	Bulgaria (1991)	Bulgaria (1994)	Bulgaria (1997)
Two-and-a-half party system	Romania (1992)	Romania (1996)	Hungary (1998) Poland (1997)
Multiparty system with a dominant party	Czech (1992) Hungary (1990) Slovakia (1992) Latvia (1993) Lithuania (1992)	Czech (1996) Estonia (1995) Hungary (1994) Slovakia (1994) Lithuania (1996) Poland (1993)	Slovakia (1998)
Multiparty system without a dominant party	Estonia (1992) Poland (1991) Slovenia (1992)	Latvia (1995) Slovenia (1996)	Latvia (1998)

Table 13. ***Index of aggregation in the Central East Europe, 1989- 1998***

	Bulgaria	Czech Republic	Slovakia	Estonia	Latvia	Lithuania	Poland	Romania	Slovenia	Hungary	The CEE average
Founding elections	11,8	12,4	4,2					3,7	4,3	3,5	6,6
First multi-party elections	11,4	3,7	7,4	2,4	4,1	3,3	0,5	2,8	2,9	4,1	4,3
Second multi-party elections	8,7	4,9	5,0	4,6	1,7	2,2	2,9	3,8	3,9	4,7	4,2
Third multi-party elections	10,5		4,5		3,5		5,6				6,0
St. deviation*	1,4	0,8	1,6	1,6	1,2	0,8	2,6	0,7	0,7	0,4	1,2

* standard deviation calculated only since the first multi-party elections in each country.

Table 17. ***Dynamics of profiles of party systems in CEE, 1990- 1998***

	Bulgaria	Czech	Slovakia	Estonia	Hungary	Latvia	Lithuania	Poland	Romania	Slovenia
First multi-party elections	2	3.5	3.5	4	3	3.5	3	4	2.5	4
Second multi-party elections	2	3	3.5	3.5	3	4	3.5	3	2.5	4
Third multi-party elections	2		3		2.5	4		2.5		
Average	2	3.25	3.33	3.75	2.83	3.83	3.25	3.16	2.5	4
Average number of effective parties*	2.5	4.2	4.8	4.15	3.45	5.5	3.3	3	4.3	5.5

2= two-party system; 2.5= two-and-a-half system; 3= multiparty system with two dominant parties; 3.5= multiparty system with one dominant party; 4= multiparty system without dominant party;

Note: a higher mean (3.5) in evaluation of multiparty system with one dominant party compared to multiparty system with two dominant parties (3.0) was introduced, because examples of Poland and Hungary show that a likelihood of moving from multiparty system with two dominant parties to a party system with a smaller number of relevant parties is greater than *vice versa.*

*After the last parliamentary elections in every country.

Clearly, the two-party system is the least common system type. Two-and-a-half party systems seem to be established at the moment in three countries of the region: Hungary, Poland and Romania. Quite steadily Latvia and Slovenia are moving along the lines of multiparty systems without a dominant party. Meanwhile, the most common system in the CEE countries is a multiparty system with a dominant party. This dominant profile of the CEE party systems partially may be evaluated as an outcome of the introduction of one or another form of proportional representation in all newly democratic countries. However, Blondel's party system typology is hiding a number of dominant parties in the multiparty system as well as the actual number of relevant parliamentary parties (which can establish a single parliamentary faction in the legislature). In that situation it should be appropriate to merge Blondel's typology with a classification developed by Giovanni Sartori (1976). In particular, there is a need to divide the multiparty system with a dominant party into two subgroups: a) with one party, and b) with two parties.

This classification of multiparty systems with a dominant party illustrates well that system stability is slightly lower, because all the countries, except Hungary, were moving between one party and two party subgroups. In the case of Hungary, the development of a two-and-a-half party system after the 1998 elections is much more logical knowing that from the first democratic elections electoral competition was dominated by two major political players (Table 16).

Table 16. ***Typology of multiparty systems with a dominant party in CEE***

Multiparty system with a dominant party	*First multi-party elections*	*Second multi-party elections*	*Third multi-party elections*
One party	Czech(1992) Slovakia (1992) Latvia (1993)	Slovakia(1994) Estonia(1995) Lithuania (1996)	
Two parties	Lithuania (1992) Hungary (1990)	Czech(1996) Hungary(1994) Poland (1993)	Slovakia (1998)

The quantitative party system changes can be described sufficiently well using arithmetic means (Table 17).

The range of party system changes in most CEE countries is only 0.5 points, which is low in relative terms. Of course, a diversity of party systems is a natural feature in CEE as well as in Western Europe. What are the directions of party system changes? Most unstable is a multiparty system with one dominant party. This party system tends to transform either to a multiparty network with two dominant parties, or into an equally divided multiparty system (Table 17).

Table 18. ***Frequency of different party systems in CEE***

Party Systems	*Number of country cases*
Two-party system	1 (Bulgaria)
Two-and-a-half-party system	3 (Hungary, Poland, Romania)
Multiparty system with a dominant party: With one party With two parties	 5 (Czech, Estonia, Latvia, Lithuania, Latvia) 4 (Czech, Hungary, Lithuania, Poland)
Multiparty system without a dominant party	4 (Estonia, Poland, Latvia, Slovenia)

After the last elections in only two cases, i.e. Slovakia and Romania, the effective number of parties was higher by more than one point from the hypothetical effective number of parties attributed by A. Lijphart to multiparty systems with a dominant party (Tables 14 and 17). This means that there is a significant potential of party system exchange in these countries.

How many party system turnovers have been experienced? Only three countries escaped from major party system reshuffling after the first multi-party elections, i.e. Bulgaria, Romania and Slovenia. All other CEE states have had one significant party system turnover, except Poland, but only half of the countries have held the third set of multi-party elections so far (Table 17).

5. Conclusion

In general, aspects of electoral behavior and the structural conditions of the CEE party systems are favoring further system stabilization and consolidation. However, this conclusion is not entirely a straightforward one. A decline in the numbers of parliamentary and relevant parties leads to a consolidation and stability of new party systems. The established conservative - liberal or bourgeois consensus with a leadership of bourgeois parties may be evaluated as a factor of the systems as well. But it is impossible to say the same about the still high proportion of new parties after each parliamentary election in such countries as Bulgaria, Latvia or even Estonia. On the contrary, it is a good basis to speculate about the underdeveloped social bases of relatively old parties. The underdevelopment of class-based parties may be a good argument, but not a sufficient one without further investigation in order to confirm that parties in some countries have no stable social (or electoral, in order not to overemphasize the need of some social homogeneity of their supporters) bases, and their electoral support may decrease by more than six times from one election to another, as it happened to the Lithuanian Democratic Labor Party in the elections of 1996 (Krupavicius 1997: 547).

High rates of electoral volatility may be the potentially most dangerous factor to party system stability in its current configuration. Because it signifies that even major parties lack the capabilities to mobilize stable numbers of supporters, not speaking about the attraction of undecided voters. A substantial part of this group has been simply removed from the electoral process and political participation for an indefinite period of time since 1989-1990. At the institutional level there are also some things to be improved. The proportionality indices could be higher, if the electoral thresholds were lower. The same is possible to say about significant levels of electoral exclusion.

Of course, these remarks on stability of the CEE party systems have to be supplemented, at least, by three more aspects: the stability and contents of the ideological discourse; the coalition-building strategies by leading parties (the distribution of party parliamentary shares forces them to enter coalitions, as well as because "a party system is a system of elements with relationships" (Lane & Ersson 1994: 191)); the study of internal organizations of political parties. Moreover, the indicators used in the evaluation of the CEE party systems need some rethinking, especially in the sense of developing more coherent scales within each indicator.

An illustrative example (already mentioned earlier) about a need of precision in party system measurement may be the case of Lithuania in comparing the numbers of efficient and parliamentary parties because the result was clearly the opposite according to the two indicators since the parliamentary elections of 1992. The opposing estimations resulted from the majority formula in the mixed electoral system, which produced high party fragmentation in Lithuania.

Table 19. ***Cumulative indicators of party system stability***

	Electoral factors of stability:				Structural factors of stability:				Outcome
	Voter turnout	Volatility	Proporti onality	Electoral exclusion	Number of parliamentary parties (fragmentation)	Strength of new parties	Effective number of parties (concentration)	Strength of largest parliamentary party	
Bulgaria	low (-1)	high (-1)	medium (0)	low (+1)	low (+1)	Medium (0)	low (+1)	high (+1)	0,25
Czech Republic	high (+1)	medium (0)	medium (0)	low (+1)	low (+1)	Low (+1)	medium (0)	low (-1)	0,375
Slovakia	high (+1)	low (+1)	high (+1)	low (+1)	low (+1)	Medium (0)	medium (0)	low (-1)	0,5
Estonia	medium (0)	high (-1)	medium (0)	low (+1)	medium (0)	High (-1)	medium (0)	medium (0)	-0,125
Hungary	low (-1)	high (-1)	medium (0)	low (+1)	medium (0)	Low (+1)	low (+1)	medium (0)	0,125
Latvia	medium (0)	high (-1)	medium (0)	low (+1)	low (+1)	High (-1)	high (-1)	low (-1)	-0,25
Lithuania	low (-1)	high (-1)	low (–1)	high (-1)	high (-1)	Low (+1)	low (+1)	high (+1)	-0,25
Poland	low (-1)	high (-1)	medium (0)	high (-1)	low (+1)	Low (+1)	low (+1)	high (+1)	0,125
Romania	high (+1)	low (+1)	medium (0)	medium (0)	high (-1)	Low (+1)	medium (0)	medium (0)	0,25
Slovenia	medium (0)	high (-1)	medium (0)	medium (0)	medium (0)	Medium (0)	high (-1)	low (-1)	-0,375

Methods of evaluation: *Voter turnout*: High (+1) equals 73.9 per cent or a total average of electoral activity in CEE since 1990; medium (0)- is no less than the CEE average, i.e. 67.9 %, after the second multi-party elections; low (-1)- is less than 67.9 per cent. All data only of the last parliamentary elections in each separate country.

Index of volatility: Low (+1) equals to 21 per cent or to an average of West Europe in early 90-s; medium (0) – is less or equal to an average of CEE countries; high (-1) – is higher than average of CEE. All data only of the last parliamentary elections in each separate country.

Proportionality index: High (+1) equals to 96 per cent or more, i.e. an average of Western Europe; medium (0)- is not lower than total average of the CEE, i.e. 85 per cent; low (-1)- is less than total average of CEE. Evaluation is based only of data of the last parliamentary elections in each separate country.

Table 19. ***Cumulative indicators of party system stability***

	Electoral factors of stability:				Structural factors of stability:				Outcome
	Voter turnout	Volatility	Proporti onality	Electoral exclusion	Number of parliamentary parties (fragmentation)	Strength of new parties	Effective number of parties (concentration)	Strength of largest parliamentary party	
Bulgaria	low (-1)	high (-1)	medium (0)	low (+1)	low (+1)	Medium (0)	low (+1)	high (+1)	0,25
Czech Republic	high (+1)	medium (0)	medium (0)	low (+1)	low (+1)	Low (+1)	medium (0)	low (-1)	0,375
Slovakia	high (+1)	low (+1)	high (+1)	low (+1)	low (+1)	Medium (0)	medium (0)	low (-1)	0,5
Estonia	medium (0)	high (-1)	medium (0)	low (+1)	medium (0)	High (-1)	medium (0)	medium (0)	-0,125
Hungary	low (-1)	high (-1)	medium (0)	low (+1)	medium (0)	Low (+1)	low (+1)	medium (0)	0,125
Latvia	medium (0)	high (-1)	medium (0)	low (+1)	low (+1)	High (-1)	high (-1)	low (-1)	-0,25
Lithuania	low (-1)	high (-1)	low (–1)	high (-1)	high (-1)	Low (+1)	low (+1)	high (+1)	-0,25
Poland	low (-1)	high (-1)	medium (0)	high (-1)	low (+1)	Low (+1)	low (+1)	high (+1)	0,125
Romania	high (+1)	low (+1)	medium (0)	medium (0)	high (-1)	Low (+1)	medium (0)	medium (0)	0,25
Slovenia	medium (0)	high (-1)	medium (0)	medium (0)	medium (0)	Medium (0)	high (-1)	low (-1)	-0,375

Methods of evaluation: *Voter turnout*: High (+1) equals 73.9 per cent or a total average of electoral activity in CEE since 1990; medium (0)- is no less than the CEE average, i.e. 67.9 %, after the second multi-party elections; low (-1)- is less than 67.9 per cent. All data only of the last parliamentary elections in each separate country.

Index of volatility: Low (+1) equals to 21 per cent or to an average of West Europe in early 90-s; medium (0) – is less or equal to an average of CEE countries; high (-1) – is higher than average of CEE. All data only of the last parliamentary elections in each separate country.

Proportionality index: High (+1) equals to 96 per cent or more, i.e. an average of Western Europe; medium (0)- is not lower than total average of the CEE, i.e. 85 per cent; low (-1)- is less than total average of CEE. Evaluation is based only of data of the last parliamentary elections in each separate country.

Index of electoral exclusion: Low (+1) is less than 13,5 per cent, i.e. total average in CEE in 1990- 1998; medium (0)- is higher than 13,5 but less than 18,7 or the highest average in CEE (see Table 5,); high (-1)- is higher than 18, 7 per cent. Evaluation is based only of data of the last parliamentary elections in each separate country.

Number of parliamentary parties: Low (+1) is less than an average of West Europe, i.e. 7 parties; medium (0)- is no less than 7 parties but not higher than 7.7- the CEE average after the second multi-party elections (because the data is available for all countries); high (-1)- is higher than 7.7 parties. Evaluation is based only of data of the last parliamentary elections in each separate country.

Strength of new parties: Low (+1) is less than 26 % - the CEE average after the second set of multi-party elections; medium (0)- is no less than 26 per cent but no more than 43 per cent the CEE mean since 1989; high (-1)- is higher than 43 per cent. Evaluation is based only of data of the last parliamentary elections in each separate country.

Effective number of parties: Low (+1) is less than 4 – West European average in 1945-89; medium (0)- is more than 4 but no less than 4,9- the highest CEE mean since 1989; high (-1)- is higher than 4.9. Evaluation is based only of data of the last parliamentary elections in each separate country.

Strength of largest parliamentary party: High (+1) more than 41,64 per cent the total CEE mean since 1989; medium (0)- is no more than 41,64 but no less than 37,49 the lowest CEE mean since 1989; low (-1)- is lower than 37,49 per cent. Evaluation is based only of data of the last parliamentary elections in each separate country.

Table 20. ***Cumulative indicators of party system stability: quantitative aspect***

	Voter turnout	Volatility	Proportionality	Electoral exclusion	Mean of electoral stability:	Number of parliamentary parties	Strength of new parties	Effective number of parties	Strength of largest parliamentary party	Mean of structural stability:	Total mean
Bulgaria	-1	-1	0	1	-0,25	1	0	1	1	0,75	0,25
Czech Republic	1	0	0	1	0,5	1	1	0	-1	0,25	0,375
Slovakia	1	1	1	1	1	1	0	0	-1	0	0,5
Estonia	0	-1	0	1	0	0	-1	0	0	-0,25	-0,125
Hungary	-1	-1	0	1	-0,25	0	1	1	0	0,5	0,125
Latvia	0	-1	0	1	0	1	-1	-1	-1	-0,5	-0,25
Lithuania	-1	-1	-1	-1	-1	-1	1	1	1	0,5	-0,25
Poland	-1	-1	0	-1	-0,75	1	1	1	1	1	0,125
Romania	1	1	0	0	0,5	-1	1	0	0	0	0,25
Slovenia	0	-1	0	0	-0,25	0	0	-1	-1	-0,5	-0,375
Average:	-0,1	-0,5	0	0,4	-0,05	0,3	0,3	0,2	-0,1	0,175	

parties was high, but the proportional formula, by contrast, limited the number of relevant parties to 4 or 5. The final result is that the efficient number of parties in Lithuania is still one of the lowest in Central East Europe.

The stability of parliamentary factions is one more missing element in this analysis. It is true that after each new parliamentary election party factions still are not stable enough, and in some cases the difference between number of parties, which took part in the national elections and the number of parliamentary factions is highly significant. However, the congruence between parties participating in elections, and parties which establish single-party factions as well as the overall survival of unchanged party factions in the national legislature during a parliamentary term tend to increase with the consolidation of democracy. But strength of parliamentary factions is also indicator of party system stability and an enforcing factor of democratic consolidation itself.

In spite of all challenges that the new CEE party systems are still facing, there is no danger that general principles of competitiveness and multipartyism might be rejected by one or another party, or voted out by citizens favoring an authoritarian system in the foreseeable future. On the contrary, major parties seem to understand better and better that they depend on permanent supporters, a stable party electorate as far as their ideological identities and organizational institutions are becoming sufficiently developed.

A few last observations: the CEE party systems and the Western European ones are different. In some cases a perspective of system reorganization may be predictable, but in most CEE countries centripetal forces leading to some sort of party system stability are more powerful than centrifugal ones. In general, only the party systems of Slovenia, Latvia, Lithuania and Estonia have totally negative scores along our two sets of indicators, the electoral and structural variables, and this may be an indication that their systems still lack stability. On the other hand, even the negative scores are relatively low, because they tend to be close to zero. However, such a generalization may be misleading because most indicators are based on data of the parliamentary elections in each single country.

Because all variables were initially divided into two different groups, indicators of electoral and structural stability, it is important to compare results in both groups of indicators separately (Table 20). Moreover, a separate evaluation of indicators can show in a more comprehensive way potential sources of party system instability. Looking in this way, only one country - Slovenia - has negative means in both groups.

Other leading countries with respect to a potential of electoral instability are Lithuania and Poland, because of low voter turnout and high levels of volatility and electoral exclusion. But voter participation is not an indicator which poses an immediate threat to the developing party system. Hopefully, all the indicators of electoral instability have more or less a latent character and impact on party systems in CEE, excluding voter volatility (this index has the highest total negative mean across all the countries) which directly reveals instability of party preferences. All electoral indicators tend to have negative values in the countries of Central East Europe, and the average of electoral stability is equal to minus 0-05 points here.

From a structural point of view, the highest potential of instability is in Latvia, Slovenia and Estonia. But structural stability is based more on subjective party building strategies and the general logic of party legitimacy in new democracies (see: Krupavicius 1997: 584). Of course, structural factors might pose an immediate short-term danger to party system stability, especially if the strength of new parties and the effective number of parties are high. Fortunately, the overall mean of structural stability is high enough and equal to plus 0.175 points.

Occasionally, some researchers on party systems, especially those who are based in the transforming countries, are rather skeptical about the reliability and validity of Western instruments of investigation, including the application of various indices and formulas, to cope with the post-communist realities. Hopefully, this chapter could, at least partly, reassure and convince them that Western tools in party system studies are relevant and efficient to reflect basic changes even in very different social and cultural environments such as currently in Eastern Europe.

Notes

1 Bourgeois parties were defined as all non-communist, non-socialist parties, except Green, ethnic minority and single-issue parties. As socialist parties are described all socialist, social democratic and communist parties.

2 But it is not a general law of transformation of the post-communist countries. On the contrary, the ex-communist or reformed communist parties dominated the political stage of many of the post-Soviet states after the dissolution of the USSR in 1991.

3 After the 1998 elections the Latvian Social Democratic Party considerably increased its political weight getting important political positions in Latvia's Saeima, and striving to become a coalition partner in the new Cabinet.

References

Gans C. B. (1997) Why Citizens Shun the Polling Booth: An Interview with Director of the Committee for the Study of the American Electorate- "*The Public Perspective*", February/March, pp. 41- 44.

Hickersberger M., Lutter J. (1996). "Die Europaparlamentswahlen 1996 in Oesterreich und die Europaeische Normalitaet. *SES Rundschau*, Vol. 36 (4): 380- 402

Krupavicius A. (1997), The Lithuanian Parliamentary Elections of 1996.- "*Electoral Studies*", 16 (4), pp. 541- 549.

Lane J.-E., Ersson S. (1994) Politics and Society in Western Europe. Sage

Lijphart A. (1984) Democracies. Patterns of Majoritarian and Consensus Government in Twenty-One Countries. Yale University Press.

Olson D. (1998) Party Formation and Party System Consolidation in the New Democracies of Central Europe. In: Hofferbert R. (ed.) *Parties and Democracy: Party Structure and Party Performance in Old and New Democracies*. Blackwell Publishers, pp. 10- 42.

PARLINE Database, Inter-Parliamentary Union, http://www.ipu.org

Rose R., Munro N., Mackie T. (1998) Elections in Central and Eastern Europe since 1990. University of Strathclyde

Sartori G. (1976) Parties and Party Systems. A Framework for Analysis. Cambridge University Press.

Wiley J. (1998) Institutional Arrangements and the Success of New Parties in Old Democracies. In: Hofferbert R. (ed.) *Parties and Democracy: Party Structure and Party Performance in Old and New Democracies*. Blackwell Publishers, pp. 229- 246.

Democratic Governability in East-Central Europe - A Comparative Performance Account

ARTUR GRUSZCZAK

1. Introduction

A decade of transformation in East-Central Europe legitimates our intents to present a tentative, but in no way preliminary, account of the reforms and changes so far. After ten years of the systemic transformation, some of the former Communist bloc countries have reached quite an advanced level of regime stability, economic transformation and social change. In the realm of politics, the most spectacular achievement of those leading post-Communist states and societies has been a continuous and generally successful process of democratic consolidation. Various indicators, like the dynamics and scope of legislative changes, stability of party systems, level of social participation, stabilization of electoral patterns, show that in some East-Central European countries, namely Poland, the Czech Republic and Hungary, the consolidation of democratic structures, norms and values is well advanced (Rose, 1997).

However, these "new democracies" still experience a great number of problems, deficiencies and shortcomings, stemming mostly from the gap between the perception of democracy as an ideal and the practice of democracy, especially regarding the rule of law and political culture. Such is the case of Slovakia, for example. Hence, one of the biggest dilemmas and doubts persecuting societies of the new democracies is why democracy does not satisfy many social expectations and aspirations, does not prevent conflicts and cleavages, is not identified with judicious, responsible, just rule enjoying popular support and legitimacy. This apparently rhetorical question contains a germ of uncertainty, so typical for democratic regimes, but reflected in a special kind of structural relationship between state institutions and society. That special relationship may be called governability.

Governability has recently become one of the most discussed features of political systems, particularly in the context of systemic change and regime consolidation. Intertwined with the notion of governance, it used to be identified not only with problems of democratic transition and consolidation, but also with the management of a country's resources: economic, political, social, etc., regardless of regime form or the type of political system. The issue of governability had been taken up already in the sixties and seventies when Western democracies were facing various challenges of a political, cultural or socio-economic nature. In the eighties and nineties, it assumed a growing importance in the face of the rising wave of democratization in Latin America and then East Europe. Governability was regarded as a basic condition for a successful consolidation of democratic regimes. At that time the concept of governability acquired a new, modern meaning, reflecting directly civilizational shifts: globalization, supranationalism and interdependence. Due to that, international financial and economic institutions more and more frequently underlined a special connection between economic reforms and the capacity of particular governments to play an active role in managing the reform.

The present analysis comprises four countries of East-Central Europe: the Czech Republic, Hungary, Poland and Slovakia. The lively discussion about the prospects for successful consolidation, and especially the debate concerning ways and means of establishing, reinforcing and consolidating post-communist political systems, has been increasingly centered on conditions, ways, means and opportunities of effective fulfillment and successful accomplishment of the grand strategy of systemic transformation. The essence of that strategy laid in making the new political system governable and securing favorable conditions for stable, legitimate and efficient democratic rule. The concept of governability came to be applied as a criterion of "maturity" of transitory regimes, measuring the level of their consolidation. This is the position adopted in this chapter.

2. Governability and Governance

The theory of governability and governance has been enhanced in the present decade. First, the concept of governability has been widening its scope as far as the needs for a comprehensive theoretical and analytical approach to the processes of democratic consolidation have arisen. Growing failures, shortcomings and problems of new democratic regimes, particularly in Latin America and East Europe, were increasingly perceived in the context of government performance, its ability to manage successfully the complex processes of change and transformation in the fields of politics, society and economy.

Second, at the beginning of the nineties the issue of governability acquired a new, modern meaning, reflecting more universal shifts in the framework of "globalization". Therefore, officials and representatives of international financial and economic institutions stressed a peculiar relationship between the success of economic reforms, especially those requiring a profound restructurization of national economies, and the ability of the respective governments to play an active role in managing the reform. A new term was popularized: governance, for describing a process in which state authority is used for managing resources at its disposal.

Third, more and more scholars preferred to use the term "governance" instead of "governability" for describing similar conditions of rule and patterns of authority. In their mind, governability became an old-fashioned concept born in the early seventies for describing problems of state bureaucracy and excessive social, or better class, demands and pressures on the government and the power elite, expressed under the guise of the "crisis of democracy" (Crozier, Huntington, Watanuki, 1975; Alcántara Sáez, 1994: 7). The "modern" concept of governability highlights the growing complexity, diversity and variance of the social systems. Under such circumstances the ability of the state authorities to maintain stable conditions of rule and mobilize resources through systematically influencing large areas of activities of the population (Giddens, 1987: 322) became more and more difficult, if not impossible. Contemporary political (democratic) regimes turned out to be complex systems largely based on self-governing structures where government and the state administration can operate effectively on the macro-level of decision-making and rule enforcement. On the level of political community, governability becomes subject to various individual and group interactions based not only on rational choices but also, and sometimes mostly, on value-based functional attitudes. In this sense governability seems to be much closer to the concept of socio-political governance.

Figure 1. ***The systemic context of governability***

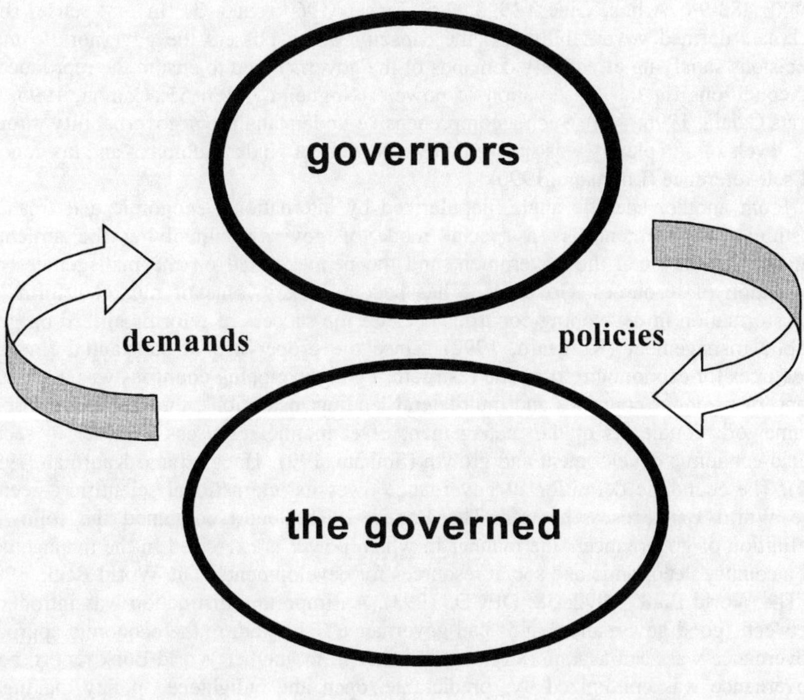

Obviously, governability and governance are all but identical concepts (Gruszczak, 1998: 29-30). In the original meaning, governability was about patterns of interaction between government and society (see Figure 1). It should be seen as a balancing process between governing needs and governing capacities (Kooiman, 1993a: 2). The most discussed issue was the scope, areas and levels of such an interaction as well as its subjects. For governability covers a large area of social, political and economic activities due to multiple functions of government as the authoritative expression of the state. However, what was basic for the "pure" governability, it was the structural relationship between state institutions and society organized along formal and informal rules of the game as well as patterns and channels of participation in politics. Another approach to the issue of governability was much closer to the modern concept of socio-political governance although it made strong references to the traditional perception of conditions and patterns of regime stability and permanence. It became evident that modern governability deals with problems resulting from social complexity, the special dynamics of complex modern societies. Taking governing as serial acts of intervention in the processes of self-reproduction and auto-renovation when their functioning is endangered or when their outcomes seem more and more problematic, governability may be seen as the capacity of societal actors to act in an organized way to facilitate or enable governing (Mayntz, 1993: 16-20; Kooiman, 1993b: 46-47; Rhodes, 1996: 652).[1] Therefore, the clue was to reach a dynamic equilibrium between societal needs/demands and state policies/capacities through certain forms, modes and channels of participation, and representation as well as decision making and rule enforcement securing socio-political stability based on legitimacy and efficiency (Linz, 1978: 16-23; Dahrendorf, 1990: 283-94; Arbós, Giner, 1993: 2-5; Lipset, 1960: chap. 3). In that sense, some scholars defined governability as "the capacity which possess the governors to make decisions satisfying effectively demands of the governed and to ensure the reproduction of conditions for the preservation of power" (Nogueira, 1995: 55; Camou, 1995: 30; Prats Català, 1996: 449). Such a comprehensive understanding of governability through the levels of complexity was suggested by followers of Niklas Luhmann and his concept of self-reference (Luhmann, 1990).

From another specific angle, popularized by international economic and financial institutions, governance is a special mode of governing involving the structural relationship between the government and the people based on the management and allocation of resources. Governance has become a key issue of market reform and transformation in developing countries because the success of reforms hinged on good public management (Klitgaard, 1992). Since the proper use of substantial financial resources for economic reform and restructuring in developing countries was a growing concern of donor countries and multilateral lending institutions, they established some framework conditions of the management of economic resources in order to secure socio-economic development and growth (Shihata, 1991; Haggard and Kaufman, 1995: 16). The economic definition of governance owes its international scientific career to the World Bank research staff. The Bank's 1991 Report contained the following definition of governance: "the manner in which power is exercised in the management of a country's economic and social resources for development" (The World Bank, 1991: i; The World Bank, 1992: 58; OECD, 1993). An important distinction was introduced between "good governance" and "bad governance", although in the economic approach governance was seen as a morally neutral concept. In another World Bank report, good governance was epitomized by "predictable, open and enlightened policy making, a bureaucracy imbued with a professional ethos acting in furtherance of the public good, the rule of law, transparent processes, and a strong civil society participating in public affairs". Bad governance was characterized by "arbitrary policy making, unaccountable bureaucracies, unenforced or unjust legal systems, the abuse of executive power, a civil society unengaged in public life, and widespread corruption" (The World Bank, 1994). The Bank's call for good governance seemed to encourage governments to create the legal and institutional framework for transparency, predictability and competence in the conduct of public affairs and the fostering of economic development.

Synthesizing the above-mentioned concepts and meanings of governability and governance, let us propose the following schematization:

Table 1. ***Modalities of the Concepts of Governability***

Variable	Governability	Socio-Political Governance	Economic Governance
level of analysis	Political	Societal	economic
systemic environment	Political system	Political culture	economics (global)
systemic area	Regime	Social system	economy
objectives	Legitimacy	Stability	efficiency
mechanisms	Representation	Collective choice	management
strategic resources	Political power	Values	economic goods
management of resources	Distribution	Exchange	allocation
failures	Overload, delegitimation	Distrust, unaccountability	waste, corruption

3. Governability and Democracy

As we have noticed, governability is a particular problem for democratic regimes because of the "difficulty of translating a mandate from voters in an election into workable policies" (Peters, 1987: 256). In this sense it may (and did) concern both mature stable democratic regimes and new "consolidating democracies" of post-authoritarian origins. As we have also said, governability consists in interactions between different social and political actors involved in the process of governing. Democracy in its turn consists in decision-making about rules and policies over which the people exercise political control (Beetham, 1993: 55).

Certainly, the meaning of democratic governability directly rests on the selected notion of democracy. Given the multiplicity of models and concepts of democracy, any attempt at defining democratic governability seems to be predetermined by the theory of democracy. To avoid falling into the trap of theoretization on the nature and substance of democracy, it seems reasonable to reduce the scope of analysis to the area limited by the two variables critical in the working concept of governability: legitimacy and efficiency.

Democratic legitimacy is based on the capacity of the system to maintain the general conviction that the political system is the most appropriate one, therefore the belief in adequacy, rightfulness and appropriateness of government policies is verified through current decisions, policy results and visible effects of long-term strategies. If governmental policies are qualified as inadequate to dominant societal interests and demands, society withdraws its support for the government and disengages from politics. Therefore, the sources of regime legitimacy may become exhausted. Delegitimization of the socio-political order is a dangerous phenomenon which produces harmful effects on a regime's institutional and normative bases (Habermas, 1975; Vidlich and Glassman, 1979; Lehman, 1987). In representative democracies, the legitimacy of the government stems mostly from regularly held, free and fair elections. Political action, within the limits established by democratic institutions, norms and procedures, involves developing identities of citizens and groups. The formation, maintenance and evolution of democratic identities are the principal responsibilities of governments (March and Olsen, 1995: 45-46). In a situation of instability, citizen alienation and societal demobilization, social support for the government is rapidly weakening, posing at the same time a crucial dilemma of continuity in power. Such a situation is characteristic of transitional and unstable regimes which cannot count on firm social, institutional and normative bases of their legitimacy.

Hence, they are facing a difficult choice: either to continue in power despite the erosion of legitimacy or submit their authority to verification through democratic procedures (Morlino, 1985). Society may either restrain from pressure until new elections are held or develop a whole range of activities aiming to replace the inefficient and delegitimized authorities by a new political formation. In contemporary stable democracies it is possible to accommodate government policies and societal actions through corporate patterns of governance or a dense institutional network of popular participation and representation.

In the case of non-consolidated democratic regimes, it turns out, however, that the intermediary structures and institutions (political society) are insufficient to secure democratic governability. The majority of political parties do not mediate between the state and civil society, nor do they anchor both popular demands and support to the state. Yet if they do function as vehicles of pressure and support, they soon acquire a populist bias, subject to certain radicalized and politically expansive groups. The fragmentation of the political arena and its "normalization" in accordance with the standards of democratic politics makes it impossible to fulfill in a short span of time basic interests and demands of numerous social groups. Dangerous tensions within a critical network of popular groups, political parties and state institutions generate a high dynamics of discontent and mutual resentments. To avoid this, it is important that the government be able to stabilize the system of interest representation around collective identities (Cirtautas, 1994: 37).

At the present-time, governability depends much on an active legitimacy developed by modern societies. Nevertheless, the dilemmas of legitimacy have much to do with the declining ability of national governments to meet citizens' expectations, the changing nature of the participation and representation processes, and the growing transparency of the decision-making process. Delegitimation, ungovernability and distrust may result from the difficulty of steering a society, managing societal conflicts or fulfilling increasing societal aspirations, or may ensue from the multiplicity of levels of governing and decision making, as modern societies become more decentralized, fragmented, heterogeneous, and with strong independent resources (Misztal, 1996a: 255-56). This may go together with the difficulties to carry out democratic processes and practices articulated within the complex arena of national and international policies. Moreover, processes of globalization do not necessarily lead to growing global integration; globalization can generate forces of both fragmentation and unification.

Democratic governability must concentrate on democracy, and next on governability (Linz and Stepan, 1996: 10-11). This is to say that for the legitimate and effective structural relationship between the state and society, the societal sphere is much more important than the organization of the state and the performance of its institutions. Society then, the civil and political one, is the key actor in the process of governing.

4. Evaluating Democratic Governability

Democratic governability is a multifaceted concept and its evaluation may and does present different problems. Firstly, governability is determined by many different factors, each one displaying distinct features. A simple operationalization of determinants is technically difficult and moreover may lead either to overestimation of factors of minor relevance or to underevaluation of first-priority determinants. Due to that, a reasonable approach should rely upon choosing the most important factors from the point of view of the basic elements of democratic governability: regime stability, participation and representation, distribution of strategic resources, international position.

The number of governments and their longevity, besides reflecting the overall stability of the political system, indicate the level of formal legitimization of given strategies and policies. Frequent changes of cabinets show that the formal democratic mandate granted to the government after regular parliamentary elections is insufficient for securing governability. Therefore, government changes reflect growing problems of effectiveness of government performance, which usually prompt societal response in the form of pressures and demands of change or policy corrections. On the other hand, the abuse of democratic procedures affects negatively popular support for democracy as a method of establishing state authorities. Frequent elections on local, regional and country-wide levels as well as popular referenda exhaust gradually possibilities of mobilizing the electorate and make it suspect that the government cannot perform effectively its functions without a frequent renovation of the sources of formal legitimacy.

Although stability is not necessarily a basic feature of democratic governability, it strongly contributes to establishing favorable conditions of governability. Therefore the basic indicators of socio-political order, like the level of social dissatisfaction, the intensity of dissent and protest, the level of criminality, provide evidence of effectiveness regarding the basic functions of the government: law enforcement and citizens' security, which in its turn affect strongly the level of popular support for the government and political regime.

One viewpoint prevailing among authors from developing countries is that democratic governability must involve the ability to cope successfully with the entire range of socio-economic problems like poverty, malnutrition, deprivation, striking inequalities in resource distribution, etc. (Commission on Global Governance, 1995; Tomassini, 1996: 51; Kohli, 1990; Falk, 1995). Therefore, the basic socio-economic indicators also may provide an interesting outlook on human/existential bases of democratic governability. Measuring democratic governability cannot omit macro-economic indicators. Economic performance has a direct impact on socio-economic stability and may influence the popular support for the government.

Since participation is considered to be one of the main aspects of democratic governability, particularly in the light of models of participatory democracy, political activity of citizens must be also made operative. Hence voter turnout, membership in political parties and organizations, involvement in public enterprises are the principal indicators of political participation. In democracies, most public activities of the citizens take place on the level of political society and political parties play the most important role within the structural relationship between the state and its citizens. The characteristics of the party system may illustrate the overall nature of the political system in the context of chances and prospects for its governability.

Finally, one has to take into account the external dimension of a country's governability since the modern states do not function in a vacuum but quite to the contrary, they are active participants of international relations in various dimensions and at different levels. Moreover, one of the important components of legitimacy of a given political regime is the quality of relations with international actors who may provide external legitimacy.

Table 2. ***Indicators of Democratic Governability***

Variable	Systemic Area	Governability Indicators
political stability	State authority	Number of governments, average longevity
	Social system	Number of strikes and social protests
	Rules of the political game	Number of elections and referenda, number of constitutional changes
economic stability	Economic performance	main macroeconomic indicators
	Income distribution	Gini coefficient, index of equality
political participation of the society	Party system	Number of political parties (legal and illegal); percentage of votes for anti-system parties; index of volatility
	Civil society	Voter turnout; membership in political parties and organizations; participation in public enterprises
political culture	Social consciousness	level of trust/confidence in state institutions
		index of corruption
law and order	Institutions of internal security	Number of crimes, percentage of efficiency of enforcement agencies
	Justice	Average duration of juridical process, number of law suits
external security	Institutions of external security	Structure of the armed forces
	Foreign service	Intensity of diplomatic relations; number of international agreements

5. Governability in East-Central Europe - A Preliminary Balance Sheet

Problems of governability are inherent not only in stable mature democratic regimes but also, which is more important in the context of the present chapter, in "new democracies" emerging after a long period of totalitarian or authoritarian rule. A logical reaction to the overloaded, over-extended or simply ineffective governments of authoritarian regimes seemed to be a drastic scaling down of the scope and scale of government (Gamble, 1996: 124). This conviction backed up the rationale of the neoliberal approach to the transformation and resulted in growing problems of governability of the emerging political and economic systems.

Governability is intertwined with democratic consolidation inasmuch as legitimacy, efficiency and accountability are subject to the establishment, reinforcement and stabilization of the new democratic regime as well as the construction, enhancement and consolidation of the institutional framework. The specific nature of the system transformation in East-Central Europe consists in its multidimensionality. Governability seems to be the result of varied processes and phenomena occurring in every area of the transformation. Any balance of governability and of comparative performance of governments in the post-communist period must take into account the dynamics of transition as well as structural determinants specific for each country.

5.1. Stability of the political system

Efforts to secure political stability accompanied democratic transition form its very beginning. The strategies adopted by the principal actors of the transitions to democracy in Poland, Hungary and even Czechoslovakia aimed at avoiding destabilization, popular revolt or violent confrontation. The choice of a consensual mode of political change - via political pact (Poland), elite settlement (Hungary) and power cession (Czechoslovakia) - was predetermined by the consequent striving to secure relatively stable conditions of rule and maintain the minimum of governability (Bozóki, 1994: 137-43; Csanadi and Bunce, 1991: 55-75; Friedheim, 1993).

The making of a new democratic polity, institutionalization of the new norms and rules of the political game, restructuring of the social system as well as changes in political consciousness, had to provoke instability and undermine governability of the transitory regimes. The dynamics of political transition were heightened by the social and political consequences of market reforms. High costs of the economic transformation along with poor short-term effects of the reforms shook the socio-economic bases of systemic stability and as a result diminished popular support for the new regimes, weakening their legitimacy. This was particularly evident in Poland, in the period 1990-93, while in Hungary a milder character of the economic reform helped to avoid the eruption of discontent and in Czechoslovakia the low level of popular mobilization, especially of labor, was maintained due to a strategic compromise between the government and trade unions (Tõkés, 1991: 259-61, 1996: 188-99; Enríquez González, 1993: chap. 7; Csepeli and Örkény, 1992; Zbořil, 1995: 205-09; Wheaton and Kavan, 1992; Bruszt and Stark, 1992: 45-52; Clark and Wildavsky, 1990; Kamiński, 1991; Sanford, 1992, Bunčák et al. 1996). Later economic difficulties, especially in Hungary in 1995 and the Czech Republic in 1997, did produce an outburst of protests and unrest. The generally positive macroeconomic performance of the Polish and Slovak economies contributed to appeasing social discontent.

Table 3. ***Stability of Governments in East-Central Europe***

Country	Number of governments	Avg. longevity (months)	Number of elections
Poland	8	14.75	10
Hungary	4	25.50	7
Czech Rep.	4	26.75	6
Slovakia	7	15.30	7

Poland, since the establishment of the Mazowiecki cabinet in September 1989, has experienced frequent government changes, almost in an Italian style. Even the relatively strong parliamentary majority (initially Solidarity-born political parties, next the stable leftist coalition SLD-PSL) did not prevent government crises and needs of alteration. Poles were also the most frequently mobilized society, going as much as 10 times to the polls since June 1989. The "voting fatigue" had to influence the citizens' attitude towards such an "electoral democracy". In a 1992 Times Mirror Survey, only 41 percent of the Poles agreed that elections matter for governmental policy. A similar answer was given by 49 percent of the Hungarians, 58 percent of the citizens of Czechoslovakia, but 76 percent of the Bulgarians and 76 percent of the French (quoted in Beyme 1996: 154). A similar characteristic has become apparent in Slovakia, although after the October 1994 parliamentary elections the pattern of instability was replaced by the domination of HZDS and Vladimír Mečiar (Mesežnikov, 1996: 12-17, 1997: 18; Kusý, 1997: 27-28; Szomolányi, 1997). The political systems of Hungary and the Czech Republic present themselves as much more stable, where governments have been based on a disciplined parliamentary majority (Jičínský and Škaloud, 1996: 90-109; Dvořáková and Kunc, 1996: 159-66; Kéri and Levendel, 1995: 134-35; Tőkés, 1997: 109-49; Malová, 1998).

Party systems, however, have not contributed significantly to the enhancement of governability. Rather to the contrary, they were "the weak chain" on the intermediary level of the political system. Although some authors, like Kopecký, claim that political parties gradually assumed a central role among the new institutions playing also a decisive role in the governance of the new democratic regimes (Kopecký, 1995: 515-16), various surveys confirm that it is still a postulate bordering on "wishful thinking". As the "New Democracies Barometer" showed, political parties were seen as the least trusted political institutions. Another survey conducted at the end of 1993 revealed the low evaluation of efficiency. Only 22 percent of the Hungarians, 39 percent of the Slovaks and 41 percent of the Czechs see a positive effect of working through a political party (Wyman et al., 1995: 540). Gábor Toká states that party systems of all four countries remained relatively unstable due to an unfinished institutionalization meaning specifically the independence of party organizations with respect to their leaders (Tóka, 1996: 100-25; 1997: 96). Institutional instability provides another source of weakness contributing to ideological polarization and fragmentation of the party systems (Elster et al., 1998: 146; Olson, 1998).

5.2. Interest representation

An interesting experience and contribution to the issue of governability in East-Central Europe has been the application of neocorporatist mechanisms of interest representation. This is an important aspect in studying the post-communist transformations since some authors have maintained that in certain transitory circumstances corporatist structures could serve as the main channel and mechanism of social participation and representation in transition from totalitarian/authoritarian regimes to pluralist democracy. Trends towards neocorporatism were a common feature of social change in the post-communist environment (Elster et al., 1998: 235-44; Brokl, 1997: 65). The main reason was the necessity to secure appropriate and relatively efficient channels of societal participation regarding the changing peculiar relationship between the state and civil society during the transition to democracy.

The deficits of the "revolution from above" had a direct and negative impact on fulfilling the superior tasks of political transition. Rebuilding the state and consolidating civil society was carried out under the conditions of a powerful though inert state, a weak, petrified civil society and an emerging chaotic new party system (Misztal, 1996b: 120-28). Mechanisms and instruments of interest representation had to suffer certain institutional and social limits while the dynamics of social protests, rising expectations and needs threatened not only a successful realization of market reforms but also undermined the socio-political bases of stability. Overload and delegitimation were logical consequences of this situation. Neocorporatist models, especially the Austrian model of social partnership, seemed particularly appealing to the new democratic governments in East-Central Europe (Tatur, 1994: 99-100; Brokl, 1997: 90).

Hungary was the first country where a tripartite forum was established. Still under the communist regime, in December 1988 the National Interest Reconciliation Council had been set up and, having experienced transition turbulences, was revitalized in August 1990. According to Mária Ladó, corporativist patterns have contributed positively to the transformation in Hungary. They facilitated the economic and social changes, fostered the structural transformation of the society and helped the state to withdraw gradually from the economy (Ladó, 1996: 166-67). This was, however, the result of the Antall government's policy of "dividing and conquering" organized labor, excluding its influence on government policies (Stark and Bruszt, 1998: 186).

In the Czech Republic the corporatist scheme, modeled after the Austrian and Scandinavian "social partnership", was organized around the Council of Economic and Social Accord formed in September 1990 (Mansfeldová, 1997: 101-108; Antoszewski and Herbut, 1997: 179). According to some authors, the corporatist system of labor relations was the key to the socio-economic stability under the Klaus government. It made possible a strategic compromise between the government and trade unions as to the low-wage, low-unemployment and low-inflation policies of the Czech government (Orenstein, 1996: 177; Stark and Bruszt, 1998: 185).

Poland is a special case due to the extraordinary political role of the Solidarity trade union in the transition from communist rule. This role increased after setting into motion the radical market reform (the Balcerowicz plan) in 1990, when Solidarity with Lech Wałęsa at the head was "keeping an umbrella" over the Mazowiecki government securing social stability and order necessary to carry out the reform policies. Political costs of Solidarity's policy, growing popularity of the former communist OPZZ trade union and the radical Solidarity '80 syndicate, as well as the increasing disappointment of the "basis" of Solidarity with the neoliberal economic strategy, which culminated in the wave of strikes in summer 1992, inclined the Suchocka government to work out the Pact on the State Enterprises, a purely corporatist agreement (Gardawski, 1996). Likewise, the leftist SLD-PSL coalition introduced neocorporatist arrangements, centered on the Trilateral Commission, which in spite of Solidarity's suspicion and distrust was reinforced as a forum of consultation and socio-political discussion. The emergence of AWS and its electoral victory in 1997 heralded the return to an "ultra-political role by a trade union" (Wesołowski, 1997: 234; Zagórski, 1998: 114-15).

Slovakia's case is distinct given the developments of political transition after the consolidation of HZDS's domination in the country's political system. The introduction and reinforcement of corporatist patterns of mediation and interest representation before 1993, within the federalist scheme of tripartism, was followed by the decisive shift toward "party-state corporatism" promoted by the ruling HZDS (Malova, 1997: 100-109). This model of interest representation was based on clientelism and political patronage, on the domination of the ruling party and the government over the affiliated organizations and loyal social groups through conceding political and social privileges and providing them with resources from the state budget. In this request, it was much closer to the mass-society model than pluralist societal corporatism.

5.3. Social conflicts

The multiplicity of transition strategies in East-Central Europe and the widening scope of political freedom, going together with the mobilization of societies, favored strong dynamics of contentious actions and affected negatively the democratic governability of the new political regimes. The institutionalization of conflicts, depending on the institutionalization of democratic politics, was strongly determined by cultural factors. "Rebellious" societies, like in Poland, displayed a pronounced tendency towards open, mass, ardent and sometimes vehement forms of discontent. "Consensual" societies, like in the Czech Republic, preferred negotiated solutions and compromise avoiding radical actions.

On the political stage, the formation and establishment of the network of institutions were progressing at an uneven pace. In the early phase of democratic transition the institutionalization of democratic politics advanced rapidly, except for Poland, where a constant struggle between opposite visions of the emerging socio-political order, symbolized by the so-called "war at the top", effectively hindered the progress of transformation and had harmful effects on governability. Similar consequences for Slovakia's politics saw the rise of the Movement for Democratic Slovakia (HZDS) under the leadership of Vladimír Mečiar. Nationalist and populist rhetoric, personal conflictiveness and excessive political ambitions initially destroyed the social consensus, then provoked growing polarization over different issues, starting from the division of the Czechoslovak federation, and finally resulting in abuses of constitutional prerogatives by the Prime Minister, a permanent conflict with the opposition and the decline in Slovakia's international prestige.[2]

Hungary and the Czech Republic have been relatively more stable than the other two countries although they did not avoid many conflicts that weakened democratic governability. The long-term strategy of the Czech rightist government linked socio-political governance with economic stability and development. Therefore problems appeared when the economy began suffering growing tensions due to the dangerous deficit in trade and current account balances in the spring of 1997. Delegitimation of the ruling coalition was accelerated by corruption and financial scandals, splits in the dominant Civic Democratic Party (ODS) as well as in the government and ruling coalition ODS-KDU-ČSL, and finally brought about the fall of the Klaus government in November 1997 (Čermák and Sotona, 1997).

Hungarian society preferred a pragmatist attitude, seeking cooperative formulae rather than conflictive issues on the path of transformation (Urbán, 1991: 306-08;

"Negative consensus" (Stark and Bruszt, 1998: 183; Lengyel, 1995: 19-20; Bunce and Csanádi, 1993: 255-56) sometimes erupted into radical civil protest (the taxi drivers' blockade of autumn 1990), elite quarrel (the "war over the media" 1992-93) or country-wide strikes (railway strikes in autumn 1994) (Gombár et al., 1995; Bozóki, 1992). Interestingly enough, despite the highest level of popular dissatisfaction with the changes, the intensity of social protest in Hungary was clearly lower in comparison with the other countries (Ekiert and Kubik, 1997).

5.4. Minority rights

One of the most vulnerable elements of the governability of Hungary and Slovakia, at least the most exposed one, has been the conflictive issue of ethnic and national minorities. The capacity to prevent and resolve conflicts as an important feature of democratic governability is frequently underlined by scholars. This comes out of the functionalist approach to conflict theory, recently propagated by Adam Przeworski. Democracy then is "a particular system of processing and terminating intergroup conflicts", so effectiveness of a democratic government rests on specific institutional arrangements taking into account interests and reasons of the conflicting groups while legitimacy of conflict resolution procedures should result from consent to accept unforeseen outcomes of conflicts (Przeworski, 1986: 56-58; 1988: 64; Gruszczak, 1996: 17-28).

The problem of the Hungarian minority in Slovakia as well as the policies of Hungarian governments towards Hungarian minority groups abroad undermined both internal and external bases of governability. Its roots touched the very nature of the post-communist formation of the nation-state in both Slovakia and Hungary. Slovakia was particularly touchy on the issue of independence, calls for the defense of minority rights, especially in local self-government, education and language, formulated by the representatives of the Hungarian community were perceived as a direct threat to the cohesiveness and integrity of the newly born Slovak sovereign state. Grounded on the political culture of nationalist populism, the Mečiar government (1994-98) pressed by the key coalition party, the nationalist SNS, took the Hungarian postulates as demands of autonomy blaming the Hungarian representatives, especially the Coexistence (Együttelés), for acting to the disadvantage of Slovakia's national interest as well as damaging Slovakia's reputation in Europe and image in the world (Marko and Martinický, 1996; Fábry, 1997; Dostál, 1997a: 63-74). The invitation for the Hungarian Coalition to enter the ruling coalition after the recent parliamentary elections of September 1998 augurs well, nevertheless the controversies heightened during the coalition talks around the participation of the Hungarian minority in the new cabinet make the chances for improving governability still uncertain.

Hungary in its turn, particularly under the Antall government, was seized with the moral and spiritual ideal of greater Hungary, fanned by the nationalist-right wing of the ruling MDF, identified with István Csurka. Antall's messages of "ten million Hungarians" abroad as constituting "Hungaria Minor" were ill-received especially by Slovak and Romanian authorities and brought about conflicts and quarrels. The Horn government eliminated that messianic flavor seeking consensual arrangement of conflictive minority issues in its efforts to get closer with the European and Euro-Atlantic international institutions (EU and NATO).

6. Conclusions (Governability and Consolidation of the New Democracies)

The scrutinized countries represent basically two variants of governability. The first included Poland, Hungary and the Czech Republic, which have exhibited remarkable efforts on their way to consolidated democracy, political stabilization and socio-political governance. The second variant dealt with the negative case of Slovakia, where the strategy carried out by the ruling HZDS and its leader, Prime Minister Vladimír Mečiar, rooted in a specific parochial-nationalist political culture, undermined democratic governability and damaged socio-political order.

Transformative processes in East-Central Europe have shown the changing dynamics of the three main approaches to the issue of capacity of governing. At the early stages of democratic transitions in Poland and Czecho-Slovakia there was a predominance of economic governance over democratic governability given the importance of economic stabilization and market reform intermingled with characters and outlooks of the leading policy-makers: Balcerowicz in Poland and Klaus in Czecho-Slovakia. Hungary was bound up in legitimizing formally the outcomes of the "negotiated revolution" as well as securing socio-economic stability. In the second half of 1990 Poland rapidly turned to the democratic governability issue, as a result of the efforts of Solidarity's right wing to break up with the Round-Table political pact and convoke free presidential elections. This stage was closed with the free parliamentary elections of October 1991. Next Polish governments and political parties sought to secure socio-political governance depending on macroeconomic performance, and this was a common feature shared by the Czech Republic in the years 1992-96 and in Hungary 1991-94. Economic problems in Hungary 1994-95 as well as in the Czech Republic 1996-97 shifted the governments' attention towards macroeconomic stabilization. After the fall of the Klaus government, Czech politics evolved towards greater governability through early parliamentary elections. The outcomes of the 1998 voting helped going back to socio-economic governance as the primary objective of the ČSSD-ODS coalition. A similar situation emerged in Poland in 1997 when problems of formal legitimization of the new constitution as well as the popular need for verifying the SLD-PSL rule at the polls brought up the issue of democratic governability. Independent Slovakia was initially concentrated on securing socio-economic governance but promptly the problem of democratic governability came to the fore. Frequent cabinet changes and the political maneuvering of the HZDS and Mečiar made Slovakia crossing the line between governability and ungovernability. Only the recent parliamentary elections and the triumph of the anti-Mečiar coalition enabled the return to the politics of democratic governability concatenated with the need to guarantee socio-economic governance (through political inclusion of the Magyar minority) as well as the urgent necessity to stabilize the economy.

Comparing East-Central European countries according to criteria of democratic governability, we can thus distinguish the following features:

1. The predominance of political elites. This is the main reason underlying various problems and dilemmas of democratic governability, both in positive as well as negative aspects. Given strong inclinations of the ruling elites towards oligarchization, popular support granted via democratic procedures was frequently abused leading to delegitimization of the executive and the legislative.
2. Politicians as points of reference. Social identification with individuals in power helped to cope with cognitive disorientation in the transitory circumstances but at the same time endowed them with excessive popular capital, which was often

abused. The spectacular careers of Mečiar, Wałęsa or Klaus prove that charismatic leaders may easily turn to petty dodgers or cool cynics.

3. The weakness of civil society. The predominance of elites and leaders on the level of the state institutions stems mostly from the feebleness of civil society, low citizens' activity, and a generally negative civic potential, strengthened by the remnants of political culture under communist rule. These weaknesses are particularly visible in the local communities, where participatory patterns of authority are replaced with clientelism and political patronage.
4. The necessity to combine democratic governability with socio-economic governance. This seems particularly challenging because of some inherent difficulties or even contradictions between the contents of both processes. The biggest problem lies in the conflict between democratic procedures of legitimacy and social bases of systemic stability based on good macroeconomic performance.

Theoretically, democratic governability should be secured by the government counting on a strong majority coalition in the parliament. Formal legitimacy of such a government, supposed efficiency of the law-making process, and law enforcement alike, cooperative relations between the executive and legislative, all these should contribute to an efficient, competent governing performance. Majority rule, however, may evoke various threats to governability. The major one lies in efforts to stabilize the socio-economic field and secure governability to the disadvantage of minority interests. It corresponds with "political consolidation" meaning the establishment and reinforcement of those regime elements which devoid of a democratic nature contribute to stabilizing the political system and increasing chances for constant reproduction of its structures. The efficiency factor, constitutive for consolidated democracy from the point of view of governability, may turn out to be incompatible with legitimacy, as a functional minimum of a stable democratic regime, in the face of growing challenges, threats and difficulties. The example of Slovakia's state consolidation strategy carried out by the ruling HZDS-led coalition illustrates the dangers provoked by the forced political consolidation.

Another mode of enhancing governability through political consolidation deals with building strong ruling coalitions on the basis of elite agreements concerning the division of areas of power and influence excluding almost totally the other political actors. The elite arrangements usually took the form of meticulous written pacts due to a high level of distrust between the coalition partners. The most striking example was the coalition agreement between the parties currently ruling in the Czech Republic - ČSSD and ODS. Cold pragmatism in spite of earlier hostility, personal animosity between the leaders and ideological divisions, as well as the overtly exclusionary verbal and political meaning of the pact aroused understandable criticism and fears among the remaining parties of a marginalization of the opposition as a result of the "majority dictatorship" (Drake, 1998). Similar pacts even among kindred parties, like the leftist SLD-PSL coalition formed in Poland in 1993 or the Solidarity-rooted AWS-UW coalition established after the recent elections in Poland, also shared that characteristic. This had much to do with the political culture of democracy as well as the strength and maturity of civil and political societies. Anyhow, the need for the classical balance of powers seems to get a peculiar relevance for the democratic governability of the new democracies.

Why should governability be seen as an important, even as a critical indicator of democratic consolidation in East-Central Europe? My hunch is that the present challenge of democratic governability to this group of states is similar to that confronting Western societies a decade ago. The basic reason is the growing complexity, diversity and dynamics of modern societies resulting from globalization processes and a civilizational shift. By introducing political democracy, market economy and cultural opening, the countries of East-Central Europe expected to recuperate the ability to reproduce their resources and maintain a continuous progress, development and growth in all areas. Moreover, the systemic change involved the transformation of functioning structures and their adaptation and adjustment to their local and international environments.[3] The constant contrast between the projected civilizational paradigm and the sober reality was translated also into the formation and stabilization of patterns of governability and democratic consolidation. Democratic governability, as well as socio-political governance, became the main indicators and relevant features of the civilizational shift in East Europe.

Summing up, governability in East-Central Europe is not so much the function of efficiency of the governmental decision making and policy enforcement and of popular support for its policies, but of its ability to respond satisfactorily to varied, often contradictory, interests, demands and aspirations of the major political actors. Paradoxically enough, the rise of social participation in democratic politics poses a certain obstacle to governability, and not an enhancement factor.

Notes

1 J.N. Rosenau (1992; 4-5) rightly claims that "governance is always effective in performing the functions necessary to systemic persistence". As soon as problems and difficulties arise with reference to system reproduction, it is hardly legitimate to continue speaking about governance or governability of that system. Instead, some specific terms have been introduced to the subject literature: inefficient (bad, poor) governance or, better, ungovernability.

2 An interesting analyses of Mečiar's personality is found in Leško, 1997. See also critical essays by Chelemendik, 1996.

3 For the author's further comments, see Gruszczak, 1994.

References

Alcántara Sáez, M. 1994. "De la gobernabilidad", *América Latina Hoy*, 8, 7-13.

Antoszewski, A. and R. Herbut, eds. 1997. *Demokracje Europy Środkowo-Wschodniej w perspektywie porównawczej*, Wrocław, Wydawnictwo Uniwersytetu Wrocławskiego.

Arbós, X. and S. Giner. 1993. *La gobernabilidad. Ciudadanía y democracia en la encrucijada mundial*, Madrid: Siglo Veintiuno.

Beetham, D. 1993. "Liberal Democracy and the Limits of Democratization", in *Prospects for Democracy: North, South, East, West*, ed. by D. Held, Cambridge: Polity Press, 55-73.

Beyme, K. von. 1996. *Transition to Democracy in Eastern Europe*, Houndmills and London: Macmillan Press.

Bozóki, A. 1992. "Democrats Against Democracy? Civil Protest in Hungary Since 1990" in *Flying Blind. Emerging Democracies in East-Central Europe*, ed. by G. Szoboszlai, Budapest: Hungarian Political Science Association, Budapest, 382-398.

Bozóki, A. 1994. "From Soft Communism to Post-Communism (Authoritarian Legacy and Democratic Transition in Hungary)", in *Transition to Capitalism? The Communist Legacy in Eastern Europe*, ed. by J.M. Kovács, New Brunswick and London: Transaction Publishers, 121-146.

Brokl, L. 1997. "Pluralitní demokracie nebo neokorporativismus?" in *Reprezentace zájmú v politickém systému České republiky*, ed. by L. Brokl & co., Prague: SLON, 11-97.

Bruszt, L. and D. Stark. 1992. "Remaking the Political Field in Hungary: From the Politics of Confrontation to the Politics of Competition", in *Eastern Europe in Revolution*, ed. by I. Banac, Ithaca and London: Cornell University Press, 13-55.

Bunčák, J. et al. 1996. *Politická zmena v spoločenskej rozprave*, Bratislava: VEDA.

Bunce, V. and M. Csanádi. 1993. "Uncertainty in the Transition: Post-Communism in Hungary", *East European Politics and Societies*, 7 (2), 240-275.

Camou, A. 1995. "Gobernabilidad y democracia", *Espacios*, 3, 23-33.

Čermák, M. and J. Sotona. 1997. *Klaus je mrtev, ať žije Klaus*, Praha: DUEL.

Chelemendik, S. 1996. *Európa alebo Mečiar. Moc utópií a utópie moci*, n.p.e.: Edícia Zrkadlo.

Cirtautas, A.M. 1994. "In pursuit of the democratic interest. The institutionalization of parties and interests in Eastern Europe", in *The new great transformation? Change and continuity in East-Central Europe*, ed. by C.G.A. Bryant and E. Mokrzycki, London and New York: Routledge,36-57.

Clark, J. and A. Wildavsky. 1990. *The Moral Collapse of Communism. Poland as a Cautionary Tale*, San Francisco: ICS Press.

Commission on Global Governance. 1995. *Our Global Neigbourhood. The Report of the Commission on Global Governance*, Oxford: Oxford University Press.

Crozier, M., S.P. Huntington, J. Watanuki. 1975. *The Crisis of Democracy*, New York University Press, New York 1975

Csanadi, M. and V. Bunce. 1991. "A Systematic Analysis of a Non-System: Post-Communism in Eastern Europe", *Sisyphus*, VIII (1), 55-75.

Csepeli, G. and A. Örkény. 1992. *Ideology and Political Beliefs in Hungary. The Twilight of State Socialism*, London and New York: Pinter Publishers.

Dahrendorf, R. 1990. "On the Governability of Democracies" in *Comparative Politics. Notes and Readings*, ed. by R.C. Macridis & B.E. Brown, 7th edition, Pacific Grove: Brooks/Cole, 1990, 283-94 (reprinted from: "Effectiveness and Legitimacy: On the `Governability' of Democracies", *The Political Quarterly*, October-December 1980, 393-410).

Dostál, O. 1997. "Minorities", in *Global Report on Slovakia. Comprehensive Analyses from 1995 and Trends from 1996*, ed. by M. Bútora and P. Hunčík, Bratislava: IVO / Sándor Márai Foundation, 63-74.

Drake, J. 1998. "Deal is OK with ODS", *The Prague Post*, 15 July.

Dvořáková, V. and J. Kunc. 1996. "The Czech Party System and Its Dynamics" in *Grappling with Democracy. Deliberations on Post-Communist Societies (1990-1995)*, ed. by E. Matynia, Prague: SLON, 159-166.

Ekiert G. and J. Kubik. 1997. *Contentious Politics in New Democracies: Hungary, Poland, Slovakia, and the Former East Germany Since 1989*, Cambridge: Program on Central and Eastern Europe, Working Paper Series no. 41, Harvard University.

Elster, J. et al. 1998. *Institutional Design in Post-communist Societies. Rebuilding the Ship at Sea*, Cambridge-New York-Melbourne: Cambridge University Press 1998.

Enríquez González, C. 1993. *Crisis y cambio en Europa del Este. La transición húngara a la democracia*, Madrid: CIS / Siglo XXI.

Fábry, V. 1997. *O Slovákoch a Maďaroch. 100 otázok a 99 odpovedí*, Bratislava: Kubko-Goral.

Falk, R. 1995. *On Humane Governance. Toward a New Global Politics*, Cambridge: Polity Press.

Friedheim, D.V. 1993. "Bringing Society Back into Democratic Transition Theory after 1989: Pact Making and Regime Collapse", *East European Politics and Societies*, 7 (3).

Gamble, A. 1996. "The Limits of Democracy", in *Reinventing Democracy*, ed. by P. Hirst and S. Khilnami, Oxford and Cambridge: Blackwell Publishers, 117-131.

Gardawski, J. 1996. *Przyzwolenie ograniczone. Robotnicy wobec rynku i demokracji*, Warszawa: PWN.

Giddens, A. 1987. *The Nation-State and Violence*, Berkeley and Los Angeles: University of California Press.

Gombár, Cs. et al. 1995. *Question Marks: The Hungarian Government 1994-1995*, Budapest: KORRIDOR Centre for Political Research.

Gruszczak, A. 1994. "The Essence of Transformation: From One System to Another", paper to the Fifth International Karl Polanyi Conference, Vienna, 10-13 November.

Gruszczak, A. 1996. "Regulacja konfliktów w procesie konsolidacji demokracji - perspektywa funkcjonalna", *Studia Polityczne*, 5, 17-28.

Gruszczak, A. 1998. "Governability and Trust. Principles and Foundations of Transformation and Integration in Europe", in *Transformation und Integration in Europa*, ed. by K. Dicke and K. Schmitt, Berlin: Berlin Verlag, 25-36.

Habermas, J. 1975. *Legitimation Crisis*, Boston: Beacon Press.

Haggard, S. and R.R. Kaufman. 1995. *The Political Economy of Democratic Transitions*, Princeton, N.J.: Princeton University Press.

Jičínský, Z. and J. Škaloud. 1996. "Transformace politického systému k demokracii", in *Transformace české společnosti 1989-1995*, ed. by. V. Šafaříková et al., Brno: Nakladatelství Doplněk, Brno 1996, pp. 50-113.

Kamiński, B. 1991. *The Collapse of State Socialism. The Case of Poland*, Princeton, N.J.: Princeton University Press.

Kéri, L. and A. Levendel. 1995. "The First Three Years of a Multi-party System in Hungary", in *Party Formation in East-Central Europe. Post-communist politics in Czechoslovakia, Hungary, Poland and Bulgaria*, ed. by G. Wightman, Aldershot and Brookfield: Edward Elgar, 134-153.
Klitgaard, R. 1992. *Economic Development*, San Francisco: ICS Press.
Kohli, A. 1990. *Democracy and Discontent: India's Growing Crisis of Governability*, Cambridge: Cambridge University Press.
Kooiman, J. 1993a. "Social-Political Governance: Introduction", in *Modern Governance. New Government-Society Interactions*, ed. by J. Kooiman, London - Thousand Oaks - New Delhi:Sage Publications, 1-6.
Kooiman, J. 1993b. "Governance and Governability: Using Complexity, Dynamics and Diversity", in *Modern Governance. New Government-Society Interactions*, ed. by J. Kooiman, London -Thousand Oaks - New Delhi: Sage Publications, 35-48.
Kopecký, P. 1995. "Developing Party Organizations in East-Central Europe. What Type of Party is Likely to Emerge?", *Party Politics*, 1 (4), 515-534.
Kusý, M. 1997. "Slovakia: A Democracy Without Democrats", *The New Presence*, December, 27-28
Ladó, M. 1996. "Continuity and Changes in Tripartism in Hungary", in *Parliaments and Organized Interests: The Second Steps*, ed. by A. Ágh and G. Ilonszki, Budapest: Hungarian Centre for Democracy Studies, 158-172.
Lehman, E.W. 1987. "The Crisis of Political Legitimacy: What Is It? Who's Got It? Who Needs It?, *Research in Political Sociology*, 3 (2), 203-21.
Lengyel, L. 1995. "The Mousetrap", in *Question Marks: The Hungarian Government 1994-1995*, ed. by Cs. Gombár et al., Budapest: KORRIDOR Centre for Political Research, 13-50.
Leško, M. 1997. *Mečiar a mečiarizmus (Politik bez škrupúľ, politika bez zábran)*, Bratislava: VMV.
Linz, J.J. 1978. "Crisis, Breakdown, and Reequilibration" in *The Breakdown of Democratic Regimes*, ed. by J.J. Linz and A. Stepan, Baltimore and London: The Johns Hopkins University Press.
Linz, J.J. and A. Stepan. 1996. *Problems of Democratic Transition and Consolidation. Southern Europe, South America, and Post-Communist Europe*, Baltimore and London: The Johns Hopkins University Press.
Lipset, S.M. 1960. *Political Man. The Social Bases of Politics*, Garden City: Doubleday.
Luhmann, N. 1990. *Essays on Self-Reference*, New York: Columbia University Press.
Malova, D. 1997. "The Development of Interest Representation in Slovakia After 1989: From `Transmission Belts' to `Party-State corporatism'?" in *Slovakia: Problems of Democratic Consolidation*, ed. by S. Szomolányi and J.A. Gould, Bratislava: Slovak Political Science Association and Friedrich Ebert Foundation, 93-111.
Malová, D. 1998. "Neľahká inštitucionalizácia parlamentnej demokracie na Slovensku", *Politologická revue*, IV (1), 43-59.
Mansfeldová, Z. "Sociální partnerství v české republice" in *Reprezentace zájmů v politickém systému české republiky*, ed. by L. Brokl & co., Prague: SLON, 99-150.
March, J.G. and J.P. Olsen. 1995. *Democratic Governance*, New York: The Free Press.
Marko, A. and P. Martinický. 1996. *Slovensko-maďarské vzťahy- história a súčasnosť vo faktoch*, 2nd edition, Bratislava: Slovenská spoločnosť na obranu demokracie a humanity.
Mayntz, R. 1993. "Governing Failures and the Problem of Governability: Some Comments on a Theoretical Paradigm", in *Modern Governance. New Government-Society Interactions*, ed. by J. Kooiman, London- Thousand Oaks - New Delhi: Sage Publications, 9-20.
Mesežnikov, G. 1996. "Vnútropolitický vývoj a politická scéna SR v roku 1995", in *Slovensko 1995. Súhrnná správa o stave spoločnosti*, ed. by M. Bútora and P. Hunčík, Bratislava: Nadácia Sándora Máraiho, 11-25.
Mesežnikov, G. 1997. "Vnútropolitický vývoj a politická scéna", in *Slovensko 1996. Súhrnná správa o stave spoločnosti a trendoch na rok 1997*, ed. by M. Bútora, Bratislava: IVO, 15-37.
Misztal, B.A. 1996a. *Trust in Modern Societies. The Search for the Bases of Social Order*, Cambridge: Polity Press.
Misztal, B.A. 1996b. "Postcommunist ambivalence: becoming of a new formation?", *Archives Européennes de Sociologie*, XXXVII (1), 104-140.
Morlino, L. 1985. *Como cambian los regímenes políticos*, Madrid: Centro de Estudios Constitucionales.
Nogueira, M.A. 1995. "Gobernabilidad democrática progresiva. Dilemas y requisitos", *Análisis Político*, 25, 55-68.
OECD. 1993. *DAC Orientations on Participatory Development and Good Governance*, Paris: Development Assistance Committee, OECD.
Olson, D.M. 1998. "Party Formation and Party System Consolidation in the New Democracies of Central Europe", *Political Studies*, XLVII (3), 432-464.

Orenstein, M. "The Czech Tripartite Council and its Contribution to Social Peace", in *Parliaments and Organized Interests: The Second Steps*, ed. by A. Ágh and G. Ilonszki, Budapest: Hungarian Centre for Democracy Studies, 173-189.

Peters, B.G. 1987. "Governability" in *The Blackwell Encyclopaedia of Political Institutions*, ed. by. V. Bogdanor, Oxford: Basil Blackwell, 256-257.

Prats Català, J. 1996. "Gobernabilidad democrática en la América Latina finisecular. Instituciones, gobiernos y liderazgos", *Estudios Internacionales*, XXIX (116), 447-492.

Przeworski, A. 1986. "Some Problems in the Study of the Transition to Democracy" in *Transitions from Authoritarian Rule*, ed. by G. O'Donnell et al., Baltimore and London: The Johns Hopkins University Press, vol. II, 48-63.

Przeworski, A. 1988. "Democracy as a contingent outcome of conflicts", in *Constitutionalism and Democracy*, ed. by J. Elster and R. Slagstad, Cambridge: Cambridge University Press, 59-80.

Rose, R. 1997. *Where Are Post-Communist Countries Going?*, Glasgow: Center for the Study of Public Policy, University of Strathclyde.

Rhodes, R.A.W. 1996. "The New Governance: Governing without Government", *Political Studies*, XLIV (4), 652-667.

Rosenau, J.N. 1992. "Governance, Order, and Change in World Politics" in *Governance without government: order and change in world politics*, ed. by J.N. Rosenau & E.-O. Czempiel, Cambridge: Cambridge University Press, 1-29.

Sanford, G. 1992. "The Polish Road to Democratization: From Political Impasse to the 'Controlled Abdication' of Communist Power", in *Democratization in Poland, 1988-90*, ed. by G. Sanford, Houndmills and London: St. Martin's Press, 1-34.

I. Shihata, *The World Bank in a Changing World. Selected Articles*, Martinus Nijhoff, Dordrecht 1991.

D. Stark and L. Bruszt. 1998. *Postsocialist Pathways. Transforming Politics and Property in East Central Europe*, Cambridge: Cambridge University Press.

Szomolányi, S. 1997. "Identifying Slovakia's Emerging Regime", in *Slovakia. Problems of Democratic Consolidation*, ed. by S. Szomolányi and J.A. Gould, Bratislava: Slovak Political Science Association / Friedrich Ebert Foundation, 9-33.

Tatur, M. 1994. "Corporatism as a Paradigm of Transformation", in *W poszukiwaniu paradygmatu transformacji*, ed. by J. Staniszkis, Warszawa: ISP PAN, 93-130.

The World Bank. 1991. *Managing Development: The Governance Dimension*, Washington, D.C.: The World Bank.

The World Bank. 1992. *Governance and Development*, Washington, D.C.: The World Bank.

Governance: The World Bank's Experience, The World Bank, Washington, D.C. 1994

Tóka, G. 1996. "Parties and electoral choices in east-central Europe", in *Stabilising fragile democracies. Comparing new party systems in southern and eastern Europe*, ed. by G. Pridham and P. Lewis, London and New York: Routledge, 100-25.

Tóka, G. 1997. "Political parties in East Central Europe" in *Consolidating the Third Wave Democracies*, ed. by L. Diamond et al., Baltimore and London: The Johns Hopkins University Press, 93-134.

Tőkés, R.L. 1991. "Hungary's New Political Elites: Adaptation and Change, 1989-1990", in *Democracy and Political Transformation. Theories and East-Central European Realities*, ed. by Gy. Szoboszlai, Budapest: Hungarian Political Science Association, 226-286.

Tőkés, R.L. 1996. *Hungary's Negotiated Revolution. Economic reform, social change and political succession, 1957-90*, Cambridge-New York-Melbourne: Cambridge University Press.

Tőkés, R.L. 1997. "Party politics and political participation in postcommunist Hungary" in *The consolidation of democracy in East-Central Europe*, ed. by K. Dawisha and B. Parrott, Cambridge-New York-Melbourne: Cambridge University Press, 109-49.

Tomassini, L. 1996. "La gobernabilidad en América Latina", *Síntesis*, 25, 47-56.

Urbán, L. 1991. "Why was the Hungarian transition exceptionally peaceful?", in *Democracy and Political Transformation. Theories and East-Central European Realities*, ed. by Gy. Szoboszlai, Budapest: Hungarian Political Science Association, 303-309.

Vidlich, A.J. and R.M. Glassman. 1979. *Conflict and Control: Challenge to Legitimacy of Modern Governments*, Beverly Hills and London: Sage.

Wesołowski, W. 1997. "Political Actors and Democracy: Poland 1990-1997", *Polish Sociological Review*, 3, 227-248.

Wheaton, B. and Z. Kavan. 1992. *The Velvet Revolution. Czechoslovakia 1988-1991*, Boulder-San Francisco-Oxford: Westview Press.

Wyman, M. et al. 1995. "The Place of `Party' in Post-communist Europe", *Party Politics*, 1 (4), 535-560,

Zagórski, K. 1998. "Transformation, Reforms and Attitudes to Neo-Corporatism in Poland, Finland and Australia", in *Values and Radical Social Change*, ed. by E. Wnuk-Lipiński, Warsaw: ISP PAN, 111-140.

Zbořil, Z. 1995. "Impediments to the Development of Democratic Politics: a Czech Perspective", in *Party Formation in East-Central Europe. Post-communist politics in Czechoslovakia, Hungary, Poland and Bulgaria*, ed. by G. Wightman, Aldershot and Brookfield: Edward Elgar, 202-216.

Democracy and Civil Conflict after the Cold War

SCOTT GATES, HÅVARD HEGRE and
NILS PETTER GLEDITSCH

1. Introduction

The wave of democratization since 1974 (Huntington, 1991) has raised hopes for a more peaceful world. It is commonly expected that extending democracy will lead to a reduction in interstate wars (Gleditsch & Hegre, 1997). Yet, war is not primarily a matter of conflict between states. Most wars are now civil wars. A common perception is that civil war has been on the increase after the Cold War, and that this might be related to political change. In this article we investigate the effects of the level of democracy as well as democratization on the outbreak of civil war.

During the period 1989-97, a total of 103 armed conflicts occurred in 70 different countries. Only six of these were classic interstate conflicts and only one of these interstate conflicts surpassed the level of violence conventionally used to classify it as a war (Wallensteen & Sollenberg, 1998: 621-34). Civil wars are not just more likely to occur than interstate wars, but they are just as bloody, and they tend to last longer.

Are certain regime types more likely to experience civil conflict than others? Previous studies have indicated that established democracies and harshly authoritarian states have few civil conflicts, whereas semi-democracies (or semi-authoritarian states, if you will) are the most conflict-prone (Muller & Weede, 1990). Contrasting West European democracies and the totalitarian states in the Soviet system with the imperfect democracies left behind by the colonial powers in Africa, illustrates this point. Other studies (Jakobsen, 1996) have concluded that political change, whether towards greater democracy or greater autocracy, increases the probability of armed conflict.

In this chapter we combine these two insights and investigate their joint effect in the post-Cold War period. We focus on the post-Cold War period because of a well-known body of thought that argues that the conflict-dampening effect of democracy is not found outside the Cold War period (Farber & Gowa, 1995). If this argument is correct, the on-going wave of democratization should not offer much hope in terms of a further reduction of conflict.

2. Regime Type and Civil Conflict

Organized civil violence is causally related to two factors, opportunity and grievance. *Grievance* refers to the extent of dissatisfaction with the state among different oppressed groups, dissatisfaction so severe that a group is willing to engage in civil conflict to address these issues. Grievance is particularly evident in authoritarian political systems, where a large number of people suffer from war, hunger, disease, or displacement. Such grievances are typically the result of "deformed, exclusionary, and undemocratic politics" (Väyrynen, 1997: 12-13). Such deficiencies of a political system may result in total state failure or in severe rent-seeking and predatory politics at the expense of the population at large. These are factors that induce groups to rebel against the state. Established legitimate democracies, alternatively, offer political mechanisms that can serve to mitigate grievances. Serious grievances are prevalent in authoritarian systems and rare in democracies.

Opportunity relates to a dissatisfied group's ability to organize against the state. The more open the state, the greater the opportunities for organized rebellion. Closed authoritarian or totalitarian states offer few opportunities for revolt. Organized rebellion and political violence, such as civil war and armed conflict, are rooted in the interactions between a protesting group and the government (Tilly, 1978). How a government responds to protesters plays a big role in determining whether protests can be organized and whether they become violent.

Both grievance and opportunity are a function of the institutional structures of a political system. State repression leads to grievance, reflected in a group's interest in protesting against the state. Dissatisfied groups with a history of grievance are more likely to rebel. Opportunity, in turn, reflects state openness and a lack of repression. Closed and repressive systems are less prone to rebellion, since protest is never allowed in the first place. According to resource mobilization theory (Tilly, 1978), violent revolt occurs when rebellion is a viable and salient option. Autocratic repression can stifle rebellion of any sort, making armed civil conflict or any variety of organized rebellion nonviable. Democracies, on the other hand, permit non-violent forms of protest, thereby making civil violence less salient. Armed civil conflict is therefore most likely when non-violent options of protest are closed off and repression is present but limited. In other words, conflict is most likely to occur in semi-democracies, when there is both opportunity and grievance. Neither established democracies nor strong autocracies are very likely to experience civil conflict. This inverted U-curve is illustrated in Figure 1.

The figure shows the hypothesized probability of civil conflict for different regime types, relative to the baseline hazard. Democracy is measured as Democracy minus Autocracy in Polity IIId (McLaughlin et al., 1998). The data on civil conflict are from the Uppsala conflict project (Wallensteen & Sollenberg, 1998). The inverted U-curve is evident with the highest risk of civil conflict for the semi-democracies (those regimes near zero on the democracy scale).

Ellingsen & Gleditsch (1997) confirmed the inverted U-curve using data on violent domestic conflict for the period 1945-94.[1] They expected to find less violence in democracies and in autocracies, but more in the in-between regime types. They also expected the most serious domestic violence, civil war, to be virtually non-existent in the most highly developed democracies. All these expectations were confirmed. Highly democratic states, even in the Third World, experience civil war very rarely. First-world democracies had *no* civil war over the period 1973-92. The lower probability of violent conflict in democracies as compared to autocracies is also reflected in Figure1, where the parabola is skewed, with the lowest values on the right-hand side.

Figure 1. **Relative Risk of Civil Conflict as a Function of Democracy, 1989-94**

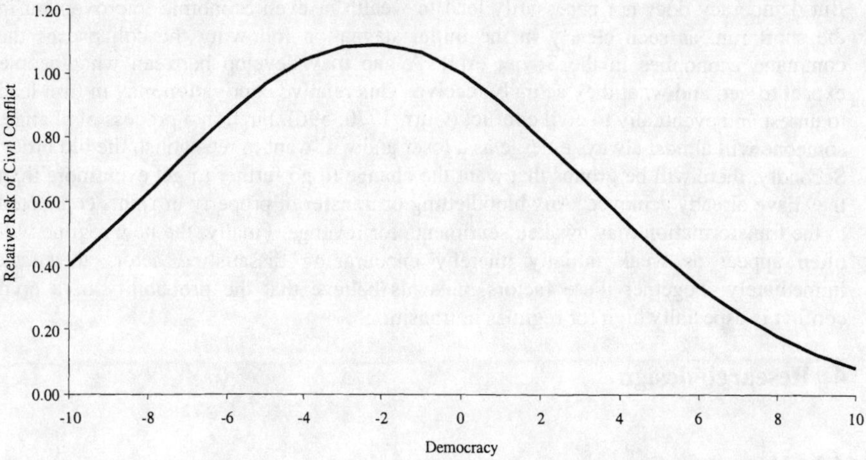

The relative risk is the probability of civil conflict relative to a baseline probability. The baseline here is Democracy = 0. A relative risk of 0.50 means that the probability of civil conflict is only half of the baseline. 'Democracy' is the Democracy-Autocracy index in Polity IIId (McLaughlin et al., 1999). Data for civil conflict are taken from Wallensteen & Sollenberg (1998).

3. Political Change and Civil Conflict

Transitions from authoritarianism to democracy do not occur overnight. They usually go through a rocky transition, in which mass politics mixes with authoritarian elite politics in a volatile way.[2] Wallensteen & Sollenberg (1998) report an increase in armed conflict immediately after the Cold War (1989–92). During this period democracy continued to spread – particularly to countries previously polarized by the Cold War. Many political transitions have been coupled with political violence, bloodshed, and ethnic conflict. In Africa there have been major tragedies in countries such as Rwanda, Algeria, and Sudan; the former Soviet Union has experienced major violent conflicts in the Caucasus and in Central Asia; even in Europe violent internal strife has torn Yugoslavia apart. Has the wave of democratization been a factor in generating these conflicts?

As de Tocqueville (1856/1955: 182) pointed out, 'revolutions do not always come when things are going from bad to worse … Usually the most dangerous time for a bad government is when it attempts to reform itself.' Huntington (1991) echoes this finding when he concludes that political violence is frequently coupled with democratization. Such changes are unlikely to occur without serious conflicts, especially in countries where different ethnic minorities share the same territory (Horowitz, 1993). Gurr (1993: 165) argues that communal groups in democratizing autocracies have substantial opportunities for mobilization, but that such states usually lack the institutional resources to reach the kind of accommodation that is typical of established democracy. The collapse of authoritarianism followed by ineffectual efforts to create democracy creates an interim period of relative anarchy during which ethno-national leaders may organize rebellion rather than wait for democracy.

The transition to democracy may give rise to widespread hopes for a better future. But democracy does not necessarily lead to wealth or even economic improvement in the short run, as seen clearly in the initial stagnation following the collapse of the command economies in the Soviet orbit. A gap may develop between what people expect to get, and what they actually receive. This relative deprivation may in turn lead to unrest and eventually to civil conflict (Gurr, 1970: 596). First, in a process of change, someone will almost always emerge as a loser and will want to reestablish the old order. Secondly, there will be groups that want the change to go further to get even more than they have already achieved. Any bloodletting or transfer of property or rights connected to the transformation may awaken sentiments for revenge. Finally, the new regime will often appear as weak initially, thereby encouraging dissatisfied actors to attack immediately. Together these factors make us believe that the probability of a civil conflict is especially high for regimes in transition.

4. Research design

4.1. Hypotheses

We posit the following hypotheses:

H_1 Fully developed democracies and stark autocracies seldom experience civil conflict and semi-democracies are much more likely to experience civil conflict than either democracies or autocracies.

H_2 Fully developed democracies experience civil conflict significantly more rarely than semi-democracies.

H_3 Countries that have undergone a political transition are more likely to experience civil conflict than countries where the political system has remained stable.

4.2. The dependent variables

In our analysis, the dependent variable is the outbreak of armed conflict as coded by the Department of Peace and Conflict Research at Uppsala University (Wallensteen & Sollenberg 1999). Here, an armed conflict is defined as 'a contested incompatibility that concerns government and/or territory where the use of armed force between two parties, of which at least one is the government of a state, results in at least 25 battle deaths'. The starting date of the armed conflict is defined as 'the first day of use of force with the intention to kill'.[3]

In contrast to the better known civil war dataset from the Correlates of War Project, the Uppsala dataset allows more than one ²armed conflict simultaneously in a country at a particular time. For instance, from October 1993 to December 1994 there were three armed conflicts in Bosnia and Herzegovina: One in the Serb part of the country, one in the Croat area, and one in the Bihac territory.

4.3. Regime type and regime change

For regime type, we use Polity IIId (McLaughlin et al., 1998), the newest version of the Polity dataset originally generated by Ted R. Gurr and his associates (Gurr, Jaggers & Moore, 1990; Jaggers & Gurr, 1995). The Democracy–Autocracy index used by Jaggers & Gurr (1995) and others ranges from –10 (most autocratic) to 10 (most democratic).

Earlier versions of Polity III suffer from having an annual format of the regime change. This made it difficult to pinpoint regime change relative to the outbreak of civil war. In Polity IIId the regime change is recorded to the exact day wherever possible.[4] When a regime change occurred in the same year as the outbreak of a civil war, the new data set enabled us to code the regime score for the day before the civil war outbreak. With these data we were also able to count the number of days since the last regime change (if any such change had occurred) for all countries for each time-point with outbreak of civil war. A regime change is defined as a change in an existing state greater than or equal to two in the Polity Democracy-Autocracy index, or as the creation of a new state.

4.4. Control variables

Civil conflict occurs more frequently in poor, underdeveloped countries (Collier & Hoeffler, 1999; Hibbs, 1973). We include in our model energy consumption per capita as a measure of the level of development. The variable is log-transformed since we expect the impact of one unit's increase to be larger for a country with a low level on the variable than for a country with a high level. The highly skewed nature of the variable makes this correction more important than for other variables. We also enter the square term of this variable. The data were taken from the Correlates of War National Capabilities dataset (Singer & Small, 1993).

Civil war occurs more frequently in countries having substantial ethnic, linguistic, or religious minorities. Vanhanen (1999) has demonstrated an association between ethnic heterogeneity and ethnic conflict. As our measure of heterogeneity we use $1\text{-}s^2$, where s is the share of the population in the country that belongs to the largest group.

The probability of civil war also depends on the country's conflict history. We expect, however, that time heals old wounds, and have constructed a variable on the lines of the Time Since Regime Change variable.

War against another state may also engender war within. If a country is involved in an international war, we expect this to affect the probability of internal violence as well: An international war may provide an opportunity for dissident groups to attack a weakened regime, or the other country's government may incite a revolt. On the other hand, international war may also reduce the probability of civil war as potentially conflicting groups come together against a common enemy. Thus, we remain agnostic as to the direction of this relationship. To test it, we include a dichotomous variable 'International War in Country' which is coded as 1 if the country was involved in an interstate war (as defined in the Correlates of War Interstate War dataset) the day before the day of observation.

Likewise, civil war may spread from one country to its neighboring countries. The variable Civil War in Neighboring Country has the value 1 if there was a civil war going on in a neighboring country the day before the day of observation.

To model diffusion of conflict from one region to another, we have coded a variable 'Civil War in Another Region', which has the value 1 if an armed conflict is active in the country at the day of observation, and 0 if there is no armed conflict.

Finally, we have added a variable called Time Since Independence. The idea is that new states may be assumed to be less settled, and thus more conflictual. Since the declaration of independence is coded as all countries' first regime change, this variable is correlated with Time Since Regime Change, but not very highly. We may expect a newly independent country to have many changes of governments that are not regime changes in the sense defined here. For instance, if one dictator replaces another, the country is classified as being under stable autocracy, but even such a change may lead to violence.

4.5. Model

In order to account for the effects of regime changes, we will use an event-history approach with a proportional hazard model used in earlier studies (Hegre et al., 1999; Raknerud & Hegre, 1997). This analytical method allows us to deal with issues of statistical dependence between cases. Standard regression techniques (ordinary least squares) cannot do this. To get a better understanding of the statistical non-independence across cases, consider a civil war that continues over several years. Subsequent country-years at war will be highly dependent on the first year at war for that country. But correspondingly, consecutive years of peace in a country are just as dependent on the first year of peace.

The proportional hazard model works by taking a 'snap-shot' of the international system each day an armed conflict breaks out somewhere. With each 'snap-shot', we assess the risk of civil conflict by comparing the characteristics of the country experiencing conflict to all other countries that are system members and not already at war. In this way, we can assess the factors that are associated with the outbreak of civil conflict. Essentially, the Cox regression (proportional hazard) model compares the country that erupted in conflict to all countries that were at risk of doing so. Thus, all information for the time between different armed conflicts is ignored. From the combined information about all war outbreaks during the six years that we study, we can estimate the relative hazard for any set of explanatory variable values.

5. Analysis

Our results are presented in Table I. In this analysis the inverted U-curve is confirmed: Democracy Squared is negatively related to Civil War and highly significant. The relationship between Democracy and Civil War is also slightly negative and significant. In addition to the parabolic relationship, we find that Democracy itself is significantly associated with reducing the risk of civil conflict. One unit's change in Democracy reduces the risk of civil conflict to 93%. One unit's change in Democracy Squared, which is used to assess the inverted U relationship, reduces the risk of war to 98%. These estimates are easier to interpret when visualized, and in fact Figure 1 was produced using these data. Both the parabolic relationship and the pacifying effects of democracy are evident in this figure. As noted, the parabolic relationship between Democracy and Civil War in Figure 1 deviates somewhat from symmetry, with fully-fledged democracies being the most peaceful internally.

The estimate for Time Since Regime Change is not significantly different from 1: regime changes do not increase the risk of civil violence. The estimate even implies that regime changes reduce this risk. This is contrary to the results for a longer time period obtained in Hegre et al. (1999). Possibly, the post-Cold War period could be different than the longer time periods (1816-1992 and 1946-92) analyzed in that article. But as the estimate for the Time Since Independence variable suggests, a large fraction of the civil conflicts after the Cold War took place in newly independent states (i.e., in the states that were formed with the break-up of the Soviet Union and Yugoslavia): The Time Since Independence variable is significant for the 1989-94 period, and the substantive effect of this variable is strong. Countries that have recently become independent are more than six times more likely to experience civil conflict than countries that have existed for 30-40 years. We observe this pattern among some of the new states that emerged out of Yugoslavia and the Soviet Union. The results are not that inconsistent with each other after all, since the creation of a new state is the largest regime change of all.

Turning now to the control variables, the estimates for the Development variables change dramatically from those reported in Hegre, et al. (1999) for the post-World War II period (1946-92): Although not significantly different from zero, the parameter estimates are positive. The reason for this is probably that a large portion of the conflicts originated with the breakdown of the Soviet Union and Yugoslavia. These conflicts represent a pent-up release after the strict discipline (within and between states) of the Cold War. Former Yugoslavia and the former Soviet Union, as well as their constituent parts, were well above the world average in wealth, but not in democracy. In addition, the Soviet Union had a great deal of oil, but not much environmental consciousness. Therefore, using energy consumption as our measure of development probably exaggerates the level of development of the countries of the former Soviet Union. If we exclude the 12 conflicts in the former Soviet Union and Yugoslavia, the parameter estimate for the Development variable is negative, consistent with Hegre, et al. (1999) and Collier & Hoeffler (1999).

Table 1. ***The Relative Risk of Civil War, 1989-94***

Risk Factors	Relative hazard
Democracy	0.925*
Democracy Squared	0.983**
Time Since Regime Change	0.81
Time Since Last Civil Conflict	0.25
Time Since Independence	6.39*
Civil Conflict in Other Region	3.39**
International War	3.60
Neighboring Civil War	1.13
Development	1.22
Development Squared	1.07
Ethnic Heterogeneity	0.63
Likelihood Ratio Test (11 df)*	26.2**
Number of Events	30

The relative hazard measures the change in the probability of civil conflict when increasing the explanatory variable with one unit.

* Statistically significant, $p < 0.05$. **Statistically significant, $p < 0.01$. For the Democracy variable, the *p*-value refers to a two-sided test. For the other variables, they refer to one-sided tests. The Likelihood ratio test refers to 2 times the ratio of the log likelihood function values for the restricted and the unrestricted model.

The ethnic fragmentation variable for the Uppsala conflicts is non-significant and even in the opposite direction of what we expected. The same applies to the Time Since Last Civil Conflict. Significant support was found for these cofactors to increase the likelihood of civil wars in Hegre et al. (1999) for the 1946–92 and 1816–1992 periods. We found no support for the idea that countries that are involved in an international war have a higher probability of civil conflict. This negative result reflects the ambiguous findings of the literature on the internal-external conflict nexus (Heldt, 1997; Levy, 1988). An international war may be seen as an opportunity for dissenting groups to rebel, but also as a means for the government to unite the country against an external enemy. The Neighboring Civil War variable is even less significant. We find no clear evidence for the hypothesized diffusion of civil war. Civil war does occur more frequently in some parts of the world than in others, but this is due to other factors in the model; mainly development and democracy. The Civil War in Other Region variable is positive and clearly significant. Internal armed conflicts within the same country are rarely independent.

6. Towards a Democratic Civil Peace after the Cold War?

Our analysis clearly confirms that democracies have less domestic armed conflict than autocracies and autocracies less than semi-democracies. Thus, we have a parabolic relationship between democracy and armed civil conflict with the lowest risk of armed conflict at the high democratic end of the scale. Countries with a middle score on the Democracy-Autocracy scale have a significantly higher probability of civil war than either democracies or autocracies.

This result holds when we control for Time Since Independence, Time Since last Civil War, International War, Civil War in a Neighboring Country, Energy Consumption per Capita (Development), and Heterogeneity. The relationship is tested using a more appropriate statistical model than in most previous studies, with considerably more reliable estimates for statistical significance.

In the short run regime change does not clearly increase the probability of armed civil conflict during this period. This may, however, be due to a masking effect: A large fraction of the civil conflicts in this period took place in the new states that were formed after the break-up of the Soviet Union and Yugoslavia. Our results imply, then, that the age of the polity by no means can serve as an explanation for the higher level of civil war in semi-democracies. The combination of opportunity and grievance found in semi-democracies makes them more prone to violent domestic conflict, even when they have had time to stabilize from independence.

Although a high level of domestic conflict has persisted after the Cold War with some new conflicts arising in areas with major political change, we conclude on a fairly optimistic note: There is a democratic civil peace. Although political change will continue to move formerly autocratic countries through a zone of semi-democratic turmoil, the long-run prospects are that further democratization will reduce the amount of civil violence.

Notes

1 A number of works support the hypothesis of an inverted U-curve between democracy and domestic violence. Such empirical support in the literature is discussed in Hegre et al. (1999).

2 Bratton & Van de Walle (1996), Casper & Taylor (1996), Gates & Humes (1997), Przeworski (1991).

3 The start dates are not recorded in the published version of the dataset. They have been added by us based on information from Margareta Sollenberg, to whom we record our thanks.

4 In many cases, the Polity IIId coders were not able to date the regime change precisely (see McLaughlin et al., 1998: 236). To avoid erroneously coding regime changes as preceding civil wars, we changed the Polity IIId dates in these cases. In cases where only the month of the change is

reported, we use the first instead of the 16th of the month as the day of change. In cases where only the year of the change is known, we use 1 January instead of 1 July of that year.

References

Agress, Renee & Scott Gates, 1999. 'Potential Pitfalls on the Pathways: Authoritarian Transition and Civil Conflict'. Presented at the 40th Annual Convention of the International Studies Association, Washington, DC, 16-20 February.

Bratton, Michael, & Nicholas van de Walle, 1996. *Democratic Experiments in Africa: Regime Transitions in Comparative Perspective*. Cambridge: Cambridge University Press.

Casper, Gretchen & Michelle M. Taylor, 1996. *Negotiating Democracy: Transitions from Authoritarian Rule*. Pittsburgh, PA: University of Pittsburgh Press.

Cohen, Youssef; Brian R. Brown & A.F.K. Organski, 1981. 'The Paradoxical Nature of State-making', *American Political Science Review* 75: 901-910.

Collier, Paul & Anke Hoeffler, 1999. 'Justice-seeking and Loot-seeking in Civil War' Presented at the World Bank Workshop on the Economics of Civil Wars, Crime and Violence in Developing Countries, Washington, DC, 22-23 February.

Ellingsen, Tanja & Nils Petter Gleditsch, 1997. 'Democracy and Armed Conflict in the Third World', in *Causes of Conflict in Third World Countries,* Ketil Volden & Dan Smith, eds. Oslo: North-South Coalition & International Peace Research Institute.

Farber, Henry S. & Joanne Gowa. 1995. 'Politics and Peace', *International Security* 20(2): 123-146.

Fearon, James D. & David D. Laitin, 1996. 'Explaining Interethnic Cooperation', *American Political Science Review* 90: 715-735.

Gates, Scott & Brian D. Humes, 1997. *Games, Information & Politics: Applying Game Theoretic Models to Political Science*. Ann Arbor, MI: University of Michigan Press.

Gleditsch, Nils Petter & Håvard Hegre, 1997. 'Peace and Democracy: Three Levels of Analysis.' *Journal of Conflict Resolution* 41(2): 283-310.

Gurr, Ted Robert, 1993. 'Why Minorities Rebel: A Global Analysis of Communal Mobilization and Conflict Since 1945' *International Political Science Review* 14: 161-201.

Gurr, Ted Robert; Keith Jaggers & Will H. Moore, 1990. 'The Transformation of the Western State: The Growth of Democracy, Autocracy, and State Power Since 1800', *Studies in Comparative International Development* 25: 73-108.

Hegre, Håvard; Tanja Ellingsen, Nils Petter Gleditsch & Scott Gates, 1999. 'Towards a Democratic Peace? Opportunity, Grievance, and Civil War 1816-1992', Presented at the World Bank Workshop on the Economics of Civil Wars, Crime and Violence in Developing Countries, Washington, DC, 22-23 February. http//www.worldbank.org/research/conflict/papers/peace.htm.

Heldt, Birger, 1997. 'The Dependent Variable of the Domestic-External Conflict Relationship: Anecdotes, Theories and Systematic Studies', *Journal of Peace Research* 34: 101-106.

Hibbs, Douglas A., 1973. *Mass Political Violence. A Cross-National Causal Analysis.* New York: Wiley.

Horowitz, Donald L., 1993. 'Democracy in Divided Societies', *Journal of Democracy* 4: 18-38.

Huntington, Samuel P., 1991. *The Third Wave: Democratization in the Late Twentieth Century.* Norman, OK & London: University of Oklahoma Press.

Jaggers, Keith & Ted R. Gurr, 1995. 'Transitions to Democracy. Tracking Democracy's Third Wave with the Polity III Data', *Journal of Peace Research* 32(4): 469–482.

Jakobsen, Monica S., 1996. 'Peace and Prosperity or Democratic Chaos? A Study of Regime Transitions and Civil War 1945–92', Presented at the 37th Annual Convention of the International Studies Association, San Diego, CA, 16-20 April.

Levy, Jack S. 1988, 'Domestic Politics and War.' *Journal of Interdisciplinary History* 28: 653-673.

McLaughlin, Sara; Scott Gates, Håvard Hegre, Ranveig Gissinger, & Nils Petter Gleditsch, 1998. 'Timing the Changes in Political Structures: A New Polity Database.' *Journal of Conflict Resolution* 42: 231-242.

Muller, Edward & Erich Weede, 1990. 'Cross-National Variations in Political Violence: A Rational Action Approach', *Journal of Conflict Resolution* 34: 624-651.

O'Donnell, Guillermo; Philippe C. Schmitter & Laurence Whitehead, 1986. *Transitions from Authoritarian Rule. Prospects for Democracy.* Baltimore, MD: Johns Hopkins University Press.

Przeworski, Adam, 1991. *Democracy and the Market: Political and Economic Reforms in Eastern Europe and Latin America*. Cambridge: Cambridge University Press.

Raknerud, Arvid & Håvard Hegre, 1997. 'The Hazard of War: Reassessing the Evidence for the Democratic Peace', *Journal of Peace Research* 34: 385-404.

Rummel, Rudolph J., 1995. 'Democracy, Power, Genocide, and Mass Murder', *Journal of Conflict Resolution* 39: 3-26.

Scott, James C., 1976. *The Moral Economy of the Peasant*. New Haven, CT: Yale University Press.

Singer, David J. & Melvin Small, 1993. '*Correlates of War Project: National Material Capabilities Data, 1816–1985*'. Ann Arbor, MI: Inter-university Consortium for Political and Social Research.

Singer, David J. & Melvin Small, 1994. '*Correlates of War Project: International and Civil War Data, 1816–1992*'. Ann Arbor, MI: Inter-university Consortium for Political and Social Research.

Skocpol, Theda, 1979. *States and Revolutions*. Cambridge: Cambridge University Press.

Sørensen, Georg, 1993. *Democracy and Democratization. Processes and Prospects in a Changing World*. Boulder, CO & Oxford: Westview.

Taylor, Michael, 1988. *Rationality and Revolution*. Reading: Cambridge University Press.

Tilly, Charles, 1978. *From Mobilization to Revolution*. Reading: Addison-Wesley.

Tocqueville, Alexis de, 1856/1955. *The Old Régime and the French Revolution*. New York: Doubleday.

Vanhanen, Tatu, 1999. 'Domestic Ethnic Conflict and Ethnic Nepotism', *Journal of Peace Research* 36(1):55-73.

Väyrynen, Raimo, 1997. 'How the Humanitarian Emergencies End', Presented at the 17th World Congress of the International Political Science Association, Seoul, 17-21 August.

Wallensteen, Peter & Margareta Sollenberg, 1999. 'Armed Conflict, 1989-98', *Journal of Peace Research* 36(5): 593-606

IV. INTER-REGIONAL COMPARATIVE ASPECTS

Prospects of Democratic Survival Under Difficult Conditions - a View From India

SURINDER K. SHUKLA

1. Introduction

India with a population next only to China is today the largest democracy in the world.[1] Interestingly, India has historically little background of democracy.[2] The closest that India, in ancient days, moved towards democracy was the concept of *Panchayati Raj*. In ancient times there were small kingdoms in India, with the rule of absolute monarchy at the apex. However, it is said that there was some semblance of democracy at the local level in the shape of *Panchayati Raj*. Five village elders were chosen to solve the village disputes. These village elders operated under the apex rule of the autocratic king.

With the exception of Panchayati Raj *India has no tradition of national level democracy*. Politics never fully permeated the Indian ethos. India had a strong social system but a weak political system till the British came. In fact, India strayed into democracy as a result of a long association with the British as a part of the British Raj. The poverty[3] and illiteracy[4] in the country prodded the pundits of democracy to an early foregone conclusion of the failure of democracy in India. But quite "irrationally" democracy in India evaded a failure.

Democracy in India is the consequence of several inputs which took place both inside and outside the country. Democracy in India was almost non-existent during the British regime in the 18th and 19th centuries and virtually unknown earlier in the Mughal period. Late in the Nineteenth Century, one positive input of the British rule manifested itself in the introduction of an education system. The education system became instrumental in bringing about some awareness among the urban population. This made it ultimately possible to implant the notions of democratic thinking in free India. This awareness could not, however, percolate down to the grass-root level due to various factors, such as prejudice of the illiterate caste-ridden people against the system of education, poverty, non-availability of schools in villages etc. Education, thus, was not accessible to the vast multitudes. Therefore, in India one can say that political awareness preceded education as such. The wave against imperialism in the 19th century was another wind that blew on the Indian sub-continent and encouraged the participatory element of the populace. Close-by in the early twentieth-century a powerful revolution was building in Russia. The Russian Revolution was complete in 1917. A cry for independence became another input of India's national struggle.

Myron Weiner (1987) argues that "tutelary democracy" under British colonialism appears to be a significant determinant of democracy in the Third World. There were three components of the British model. First, the British created bureaucratic structures (civil services, judiciary, police, army) thereby legitimizing the role of state authority in maintaining social order through prescribed procedures and the rule of law. Second, the British introduced and professionally expanded the principles and institutions of representative government. Third, with regard to both the bureaucratic structures and representative institutions, the British incorporated large number of natives into the process of government. Thus by the time the British departed, they left behind political parties that had learnt to participate in competitive elections and an educated elite that had been socialized into the norms of democratic governance.

The successful establishment of democracy in India was built on the assets transmitted by the British rule. Congress got transformed from an elite into a mass party. It acted as a channel for the articulation of popular demands on the well-established bureaucratic structures. The satisfaction of voter demands in turn strengthened the social bases of the formation of other political parties, besides the Congress party. Democracy thus found its feet.

2. Adaptation of Democracy in India

The liberal democracy (combination of free market economy with universal adult suffrage) handed over to India in the early Twentieth Century, underwent a myriad of adaptations. The principles of liberal democracy (government by discussion, majority rule, recognition of minority rights and constitutional government) underwent a kaleidoscopic change due to the peculiarities of the social and geopolitical set up. The social peculiarities of India include such factors as caste, regionalism, language, communalism, secularism etc. Social conflict, sometimes violent at other times dormant, largely formed the background of the transition of democratic institutions.

India has adopted democratic institutions at two levels - the Union level and the state level. On the one hand there is *ideal* democracy (in India, it was projected by Gandhi[5] in his partyless democracy), on the other hand, there is *real* democracy as it actually exists. Between the two, the ideal and the real, there is a wide gap. Perhaps ideal democracy exists nowhere in the world. At the close of the Twentieth Century, India is in a stage of transition. The democratic institutions have to be adjusted in order to accommodate new demands for political participation and to solve serious socio-economic problems. Besides, there are innumerable shades of combination and permutations of India's democracy. It is relatively easy to see immediate results of these combinations; but not so easy to assess the long-term impact on the polity – both at the national and state levels.

In fact, the very existence of democracy in India has been threatened several times since its inception. In the 1980s due to the armed secessionist movements in Punjab, Kashmir and India's North-East and communal conflicts in other parts of the country whereas such incidents were relatively rare in the early Indian history. Yet, except for a short phase of emergency (1975-77), the Indian electorate has, by and large, very clearly voted for the sustenance of democracy. India has maintained its political freedom, there have been no unchecked Public Security Ministry, no street committees, no network of forced-labor camps, no persecution of whole groups of people because they were intellectuals or had relatives who had once been landlords, no destruction of libraries and universities.

The transitory phase is a phase of turmoil. There are some achievements, but these are yet indeed very far from the ideal. Indian democracy is young. Legally, it is equipped with the tools of democracy. In fact, the Constitution of India ensures democracy, that is, based on the one man one vote formula of universal suffrage. Elections are held at regular intervals. But this picture gets clouded when we see the actual practice. People come out for voting in large numbers during elections; but the voting pattern reflects the caste and local affiliations of the electorate. Either the caste and local affiliations color the voter's judgement or the reality of stark poverty makes them bow before some monetary gain held aloft by the elitist members of a political party. Such compromises that India's democracy had to make are discussed in some detail in the pages that follow.

Clearly, India has yet to adopt democracy as a way of life. Only a democratic society can have a democratic political system. But something can become 'a way of life' only after a long and gradual process involving generations. Nevertheless, despite the numerous trials and tribulations India has proved to be a shining example of democracy. India is surrounded by neighbors (Pakistan, Nepal, Burma and Sri Lanka) each one of whom adopted democracy at one time or the other. But their recent history reflects a see-saw of, sometimes a bend towards democracy and then a tilt towards authoritarianism. At least twice in India there were sharp possibilities of democracy turning into authoritarian rule. Prime Minister Nehru in the 1950s and 60s obtained a vast majority in the general elections. People reposed total faith in him, but it is on record that he remained a true parliamentarian and sincerely believed in the democratic principles. Again, India came close to authoritarian rule during the National Emergency declared by Mrs. Indira Gandhi in June 1975. But in support of democracy, it can be said, that Mrs. Gandhi herself announced the following general elections. All major democracies, including the USA, had to pass through a phase of turmoil before they finally settled down. Dankwart Rustow in his seminal article[6] in 1970 focused attention on *political conflicts* and *dynamic interactions* and suggests the struggle will lead to a *democratic compromise* (or pact). Further he says, that democracies "not forged in conflict might prove ephemeral".

The operational democracy in India may be broadly divided into two parts - the national level and the state level. However, no clear-cut lines can be drawn because issues of national importance may affect local politics and vice-versa. Understanding Indian politics is an endless challenge because newer political identities continue to emerge alongside some deeply enduring ones. Violent social conflict and democratic politics exist alongside each other giving rise to the 'Indian Paradox: "In most post-colonial regimes, political participation is restricted and leaders are not held accountable and in worst cases, governments are tyrannical, India.... is a notable exception".[7] Conflicts, concerning religion, caste, etc. continue, yet India's democratic political system continues to function.

3. The generally understood requisites of democracy are: Equality, Liberty, Tolerance and Freedom

Equality and freedom have been provided in the Constitution. Part III dealing with Fundamental Rights guarantees the Right to Equality (Articles 14-18) and the Right to Freedom (Articles 19-22). These are justifiable, which means these rights can be enforced by the courts of the country. In the Preamble of the Constitution, the people have solemnly resolved to constitute India into a sovereign, socialist, secular "democratic" republic which is secure for all its citizens. Liberty of thought, expression of faith and worship are guaranteed. Without such goals, politics becomes rudderless.

Besides, these national goals give directions to achieve national development. Without such goals, progress is bound to be lop-sided.

Democracy implies that power is in some sense accountable to those affected by its exercise. This is political democracy, but political democracy has no meaning in the absence of social democracy, especially when the society is caste-ridden and there is a marked difference between high and low, rich and poor. Unless there is social democracy which provides equal opportunities to all sections of society, irrespective of caste, color, creed, sex or religion, political democracy cannot be achieved. In this sense social democracy or equal opportunities for all, are a pre-requisite to true democracy.

The realization of such a democracy has been a difficult task and therefore adaptations had to be made. Democracy at the social level is limited by caste, religion, language, poverty, illiteracy, backward classes and tribes, or when women vote as their menfolk do. At the economic level, democracy is limited by scarce resources, feudal values, unemployment and violence.

The difficulties posed by the social and political interests of different sections of people at both national and state levels are further compounded by the lack of resources and an inhospitable climate[8]. The scarce resources factor complicates the economic development and sparks off a cut-throat competition. In a bid to compete for scarce resources, tempers run high and 'tolerance' (one of the requisites of democracy) is relegated to the background. Democracy is a rule of the majority. But democracy can function properly only if the party in power and the opposition parties cooperate and tolerate each other and work for the welfare of the people and country.

The notion of requisites rests on the conception that the transfer of institutions from one society to another are to be taken as a whole or rejected in toto on grounds of incompatibility. India's paradoxical democratic tradition, however, has made adaptations within the framework of caste, regionalism, language and religion. The tradition of acquiescence to authority so dominant in the Indian social system (starting from the family) was entirely contrary to democratic traditions. But acquiescence to authority exists alongside the large membership of political organization protest movements, strikes, and large turnouts during the elections. The *Plural Society* of India reflects a myriad of diversities in ethnic groupings, linguistic solidarity and caste associations. The prevalence of castes and classes leads to further stratification. As a result, politics gets fragmented and gives rise to regional consciousness, local parties (Akali Dal in Punjab, AIADK in Tamil Nadu) and state level identities.

4. Major Elements of of India's Democracy

4.1. Bureaucracy

The structure of the democratic state is supported by a large group of an elite official class. The Indian Constitution is distinctive for including provisions relating to the federal and state public services. This peculiar administrative burden sharing between the Union and the state governments distinguishes India from other federal systems like the US, Australia or Canada. Its advantage is that it confers a degree of uniformity of administrative structure and practice throughout the land. It is also one of the major integrative institutions in Indian politics.[9] India is a sub-continent, the mix of local and out-of-state staffing ensures a spread of talent all around the country. At the same time, there is also an attempt to strike a balance between national integration and localism (at least $1/5^{th}$ of IAS officers in a state must be recruited from within the states' own administrative service. But no more than half of any states IAS cadre can be from within the state). [10] The bureaucracy has been described as a body of competent, trained, honest and patriotic civil servants. Interestingly like the British 'sahibs', Indian bureaucracy has given rise to an exclusive elite class that is cut off from the people whom they administer.

But Indian democracy has led to what is termed a 'crisis of governability' (Atul Kohli 1991). This crisis encompasses a general rise in lawlessness, decline in the level of governance, breakdown of law and order, political instability, and a consequent decline in legitimacy. In the process of governing bureaucracy has played a key role. Like the British 'sahibs', who distrusted the people over whom they administered the law, the post-independent bureaucrat sits smugly in the bungalow which is cloistered from the ordinary citizen residing in the area under the officer's administration. The bureaucracy is open to criticism on other counts, too. It overestimates the rationality and efficiency of standard operating procedures of standing organizations staffed by faceless experts. Conversely, it downplays the element of `redtapism' of officials exemplified by 'Parkinson's Law' that work expands to fill the time available for its completion. There is also the related 'Peter's Law' that each person raises to his or her level of incompetence.

In post-independent India, a close proximity has been fostered between the bureaucracy and the politician, leading to a nexus of what is called 'neta-babu raj' (politician-bureaucrat rule). [11] The tentacles of the nexus do not allow the reforms that have been introduced in the system, to have a speedy affect on the political and economic situation in the country. The vested interests of the *'neta-babu raj'* allow only a slow movement towards the path of development. India is in a position to take tremendous advantage of the current economic crisis in East Asia but it is bogged down by bureaucratic red-tape.[12]

India lives in many layers and is a fine of tradition and modernity. India's exposure to modernity led to a renewed awareness and quickening of traditional identity, its reinterpretation and rejuvenation and its consolidation in the framework of new institutions and ideas. The Indian response to modern stimuli consisted of 'asserting the Indianness of India, reformulating the Indianness and giving it a modern character'. [13]

4.2. Consensus and Conflict

Whenever there has been a challenge to the nation (1962, 1965, 1971) there has been a consensus among the people and all political parties in order to face the situation amicably. In more recent times, examples like the issues of Assam, Kashmir, terrorism in Punjab have also been dealt with by national consensus. Yet there have been conflicts between states (inter-state boundary issues, canal water dispute) and also conflicts based on caste, regionalisms etc. Depending on the exigencies of the issue people have exhibited alienation or conversely identification with the issue. At the population level, a political party with its huge organizational legacy, its leadership and its control of institutional patronage alone can provide a politics of consensus.[14]

The concept of duality in Indian politics has led to difficulties in the actual functioning of democracy. For example, the democratic state carried out the re-organization of states (under Article 3-4 of the Constitution of India), but at the same time it was faced with the herculean task of forging national integration. Indeed, two divergent tasks are sought to be met with again and again.

Gandhian philosophy provides some answers to the question of duality. Gandhi[15] went beyond the traditional definition of democracy in three major respects, adaptations of which can foster the prospects of democracy in India:

1. Where traditional democracy lays emphasis on the structure of the political machinery, Gandhi lays stress on the widely accepted *technique of discussion and debate* and in that sense, brings the participative element to the fore. Reposing on an implicit faith in the common man, Gandhi, in case of a constitutional breakdown, suggests protest through demonstration and extra-constitutional methods of civil disobedience.
2. Secondly, Gandhi lays stress on *compromise*. By compromise, he suggested a willingness to adjust to realities and avoid conflicts, even at the cost of sacrificing some position taken originally, however sound it may have been.
3. Thirdly, whereas liberal democracy lays emphasis on decisions by the majority, Gandhi was deeply conscious of a 'tyranny of the majority'.

Lijphart[16] has argued that *consociational democracy* based on partnership is the suitable model for plural societies. Consociational democracy, a 'coalescent rather than an adversarial model', is characterized by a grand coalition government of segmental elites, a mutual veto based on concurrent majority rule, a proportionality in the allocation of public funds, parliamentary seats and public service positions and a high degree of autonomy for all significant segments of plural society. Since the 1993 General Elections, India has come close to a 'hung' Parliament again and again. In such an event, the consociational model becomes important. The principles of liberal democracy (government by discussion, majority rule, recognition of minority rights and constitutional government) have undergone a kaleidoscopic change in India due to the peculiarities of its social and geopolitical set up. Social conflict, sometimes violent at other times dormant, has largely formed the background for the democratic changes in India. Factors of social conflict or the "deeper structures" like caste etc. have influenced the democratic politics in India.

4.3. Caste

Caste in Indian society refers to a social group were membership is largely decided on the basis of birth. Embedded deeply in the psyche of the citizens of India, the caste[17] factor plays an important role in politics, right from making a choice for casting the vote during elections. To remove caste from Indian politics, as Rajni Kothari puts it, is to put cart before the horse. The importance of caste may be judged from the fact that, like a meandering rivulet the caste factor moves through the major aspects of Indian policy. Birth not worth has come to be the consideration on which quite a large number of people vote. This constitutes an integral part of the Indian political system.

Tatu Vanhanen's study[18] traces the origin of ethnic conflicts in multi-ethnic countries like India to 'our assumed universal behavioral predisposition shared by natural selection, to favor kin to non-kin'.

People are, therefore, easily organized along ethnic lines in the struggle *for scarce resources*. Vanhanen refers to this process as *'ethnic nepotism'*. He argues that it may be possible to mitigate ethnic conflicts by making political structures better adapted to the nature of ethnic nepotism. In other words, he proposes accommodation of ethnic conflict by political reform.

Caste is one of the most important aspects of social and political life. Caste is there to stay - it is futile to argue whether caste uses politics or politics use caste as Rajni

Kothari puts it. According to the late Jagjivan Ram, in Indian Society one can give up everything but he cannot give up his faith in caste.[19] Thus, any political analysis that neglects caste is not worth much. Caste as a social institution is strongly entrenched and inspite of the modernization trends (as a result of urbanization, improved means of communication and development of secular education) the caste factor remains. In fact, caste has also undergone a change - it has become a factor to be reckoned with.

The Indian Democratic State has been facing challenges on many fronts. It is threatened by the forces of casteism, religion, regionalism and even separatism. India has been witnessing rising intolerance, erosion of trust and greater willingness to participate in the politics of group exclusion. Some of the symptoms of frailty of India's democratic polity- the myriad forms of public protest, such as caste violence and political insurgency- are simultaneously indices of the upwardly mobile political groups being recruited into the political center. The rapid rise of Bahujan Samaj Party (BSP) is a case in point.

Kohli (1991) identifies several aspects of the eroding political order. India's democracy has been democracy from above. It has been more a gift from the elite to the masses rather than something that the masses have secured for themselves. It is true that the longer democracy is practiced the more difficult it becomes for the elite to take away basic democratic rights. But such a lot of power is concentrated in the hands of few leaders that there is a danger of it being misused (Mrs Gandhi almost did it). The elite-led democracy has also structured the pattern of political-mobilization. Whereas social mobilization is generally produced by economic development, elite-led mobilization often reflects intra-elite conflict.

Due to scare resources the state has to play a crucial role in the economy. The state has the dual role of being both an agent of political order and being responsible for socio-economic development. The scarce resources have forced India to adopt a developmental model that makes India an interventionist state. Besides this there are distributional conflicts. These are largely because of the developmental model that was chosen by India and it has exacerbated the existing inequalities along regional, rural vs urban, ethnic, class and caste lines. The scarce resources are controlled by politicians and bureaucrats. Competition among individuals and groups seeking economic improvements leads to intense conflict among them.

Furthermore, it is frequently argued that the broader the range of winning parties, the greater the ability of the party system to represent diversity of the electorate. Also the more proportional the translation of votes to seats, the less the electoral mechanism violates the electorate's expressed preferences.[20] However, a system that is too representative can result in deadlocks. Of late, anti-incumbency attitude of the voters has led to political instability resulting in marked fluctuations. Ever since the Emergency conferred by Mrs. Gandhi, the voters have started questioning the affairs and achievements of the successive governments. After the emergency, Mrs. Gandhi lost the elections, but after one year and a half won the election again by a 2/3rd majority in 1981. In almost each election the electorate has changed the government showing discontent against the incumbent party. This is good news and bad news. The good news is that the voters have become more and more aware and have become assertive. The bad news is that change in each election does not really lead to stability and development. Even in elections at the state level, changes have occurred almost every time the election has taken place. Political instability has its fall-outs.

Considering the size and problems of India, parliamentary and state level elections are held with regularity. There is a deep concern for maintaining dignity, maturity, accommodation and a sense of appreciation of each other's point of view lest the legislators should become 'objects of ridicule'.[21]

Another strange aspect of Indian democracy is the deep sense of gratitude and the inherent memory of the Indian voter towards those who made sacrifices for the freedom struggle. In the early elections Congress leaders who were prominent in the freedom struggle like Dr. Rajendra Prasad, Maulana Abdul Kalam Azad, Sardar Patel, Jawaharlal Nehru and others were and are national heroes of India. Their names and ideals are still used by political parties for promotion of the political views of the various parties. Subhash Chander Bose is still the heart throb of the millions of India. The political opinions of the people are still motivated by leaders of the National Movement of pre-independence days. Jawaharlal Nehru was a great leader of the national movement and became the first Prime Minister of India. Later his daughter Mrs. Indira Gandhi became the Prime Minister. Her son Rajiv Gandhi followed her as Prime Minister. Jawaharlal Nehru, Indira Gandhi and Rajiv Gandhi were elected as leaders of the Congress Party and the nation accepted the dynastic right of governing, through democratic means. The charisma of leadership in India has at times family background as the basis.

One problem distinctive to Indian democracy is that of sycophancy. A second problem is that of dissidence. Three consequences flow from this. First there is general instability. This is true even when the same party remains in power after the elections. A Chief Minister often has to spend as much time on political self-preservation as on policy matters. A common joke is that the cost of stability is actually the cost spent on it to keep it stable. Second, those who come laden with gifts are full of expectations. That is, financial corruption is the other side of financial sycophancy. Third, because of political instability, no person can presume to be in office for any length of time. Therefore whatever profits are to be made must be made speedily.

The net result is that one of the most resource- rich states of India (Bihar) is the poorest in terms of income, wealth-creation and productive economic activity. The first known instance of ballot-rigging was recorded in Bihar in the 1962 national elections. Since then it has become a regular process. The booth-capturing armies do not discriminate between ideologies, castes and parties, as they are pure mercenaries. Booth-capturing makes politicians beholden to the armed criminals thereby establishing an unholy nexus between them.

4.4. Coalition Formation

The diversity of India's social structure stands in the way of developing cohesive national parties. First at the State level and then at the Union Level, coalition formations have overtaken the democratic process in India. It is extremely difficult for Indian politicians and parties to accept the argument that a multi-party system and coalition governments are more natural and even more effective than one party majority governments and a British style two-party system that never really emerged in India.

The population of India is divided by factors such as language, religion, caste, regionalism etc. Thus divided, it has become extremely difficult for any single party to maintain a hegemonic political system. In fact, scholars (Varshney 1995, Vanhanen 1998) lay emphasis on the significance of ethnic cleavages from the perspective of democracy. According to them, the ethnic diversity of Indian population in fact supports democratic politics.

Political instability is exacerbated during times of coalition formation. For India's coalition politics, this is the best of times and the worst of times. Even the humblest farmer can now occupy the most powerful office in the land, but on the new coalition chessboard the loftiest of kings appear vulnerable and can be easily checkmated by the most puny of pawns. The distant provinces have regained their pre-eminence lost during the centrist phase under the Congress rule.

Finally, although there are new and ominous signs that could destabilize the entire mechanism, the process of coalition formation has matured. It is precisely the democratic nature of the state of India that has been most effective in providing political and social mobility to the ever-expanding number of individuals and groups and consolidated the legitimacy of the state as the authoritative intervenor in group conflicts. The struggle for political power among social groups is carried out substantially in the elections. India's functioning democracy confirms that state institutions and structures do matter. They do not simply reflect social relations, they also help to shape the political outcome of social conflicts.

Democracy thus lends procedural legitimacy to the struggle for political power. But whereas in the Western democracies agreements have been reached on the great issues of distributive allocations, in India the failure to realize the distributive values enshrined in the Constitution have caused an erosion of substantive legitimacy despite the continuance of procedural legitimacy which still authenticates the collective decision-making process.

According to Tatu Vanhanen India is not a deviating democracy because its degree of resource distribution is already high enough to support democracy, but its level of democracy deviates from the perspective of the development paradigm that connects success of democracy with a high-degree of socio-economic development and national wealth.

5. Doubts About Indian Democracy

Doubts have been cast earlier about democracy in India and it has been considered a sham or an illusion. Regarding democracy in India, it is alleged that there is constant friction between the center and the state functions both at the national and state levels.

5.1. Cash, Crime and Corruption

The election system on which democracy rests according to the Chief Election Commissioner (CEC) Mr. T.N. Seshan is suffering due to "cash, crime and corruption". To begin with, the electoral rolls and polling booths are imperfect. The ceiling on election expenses is easily circumvented. The candidates spend lakhs and crores of rupees for wining their elections, but their official declarations on expenses show the expenditure within the legal limits. This happens because the law does not prohibit the friends or the political party to provide any amount for election of the candidate. A woman candidate in the Delhi Assembly Election in January 1994 told the CEC, that she spent 60 lakh (6 million rupees). "But it is a matter of happiness that she was defeated", informed the CEC. The common man is the worst hit as social, political and economic justice is bent by a privileged few. The yardstick of social morality has undergone a profound change in the last few decades. Finances attained through illegal means can buy anything. The poor under trials languish in jails, sometimes without even first information reports (FIRs) registered by the police. The CEC said the situation for the common man is grimmer as the civil service has also become "corrupt, collusive and committed."

Coming from the Chief Election Commissioner, the above criticism assumes a special importance. But commenting on a general rot that has set in the system, the CEC does not absolve the common man from the blame. There is no dearth of good laws, but good laws can be implemented only in good atmosphere. The erosion of social and political values[22] has led to a corresponding decline in credibility of the state apparatus. The erosion of credibility has led to the frustration of the common man and a 'sense of alienation from the political set-up'. The impact of such events on the voter is that he loses faith in the government machinery. The political parties face a corresponding loss of credibility in the public eye. According to Schumpeter's conception of manufactured will,[23] many voters will accept their leaders' advice because they trust them without bothering to examine their argument. In India the electoral scene is far from this situation.

However, the participation of the Indian electorate in the electoral process since 1951 has left none in doubt about their concern on the issue of governance in the country. When the chance presents itself, the people involve themselves in the democratic process. In the 1994 by-elections in Nakodar[24] constituency of Punjab state the voter turnout was estimated at 69 percent. But the election scene became marred by allegations and counter-allegations. An example is reproduced below (during the Nakodar by-election) - Akali Dal polling agents claimed that their complaints against bogus voting were not being heard by presiding officers.[25] On the other hand, Congress workers criticized Akali Dal activists for making false allegations. They alleged that the Akalis were trying to browbeat genuine voters.

5.2. Horse-trading and Violence

Various remedies ranging from funding of elections to a presidential form of democracy have been suggested to overcome the menace of horse-trading and corruption. Three factors may be distinguished as the cause of corruption (Ghosh, 1996) [26]:

1. the erosion of India's traditional ideal of simple living and high thinking. In the absence of such an ideal the acquisition and possession of more and more material wealth has become a status symbol. Within this framework, a race for living beyond one's means becomes a forceful drive. Corruption is the inevitable result.
2. the adoption of parliamentary democracy unsupported by participatory democracy at the village and block levels and,
3. the choice of a model of industrialization based on high complexity technologies. The need of the kind of industries in vogue is questionable. There is also a need to disallow certain types of industries and limit some others. Village-level industries should be encouraged so that no one has to beg for food and also de-urbanization becomes easy.

But for this legislators are required who have a poor-friendly perception i.e. very different from the urban elite or the rural-rich-oriented perceptions of today.

The assassination of two Prime Ministers (Mrs. Gandhi in 1985 and Mr. Rajiv Gandhi in 1991) is only the tip of the iceberg. The violence in society finds reflection in the political life. Tampering with the electoral process is one such indicator, the use of muscle power, money power and alleged rigging continues in the different elections held in India. As a result of these malpractices a large number of repolls have to be conducted.

5.3. Center-State Relations

In the recent past the center-state relations have passed through stress. India's democratic set-up provides special relations between center and states. The provision in this regard in the Constitution had a deliberate bias towards the center in order to cope with the multi-regional, multi-cultural and caste-ridden society of India. Till 1967, this arrangement was a success with the Congress Party ruling both at the Center and in the State governments.

After 1967 the center-state relations ran into rough weather especially when some governors exposed themselves rather too markedly in their partisan approach, e.g. in 1967 Dr. Sampuranand, the Governor of Rajasthan, refused to count Independents because they were in the non-Congress camp. But his counterpart in Ultar Prudesh, Bishwanath Das, counted the Independents because they were the Congress party and with their help a Congress Ministry was installed in office.

Other issues[27] of center-state tensions include: Dismissal of Chief Ministers, reservation of bills for consent of president, dismissal of State Governments under Article 356, non-implementation of central laws and gheraos, deployment of Central Reserve Police Force (CRPF), alleged discrimination of States regarding allocation of central projects, allocation of foodgrains, grants and loans.

A *National Emergency* was declared by Mrs. Indira Gandhi in June 1975. Thousands of members of opposition parties were arrested, censorship on press imposed, 26 political organizations were banned (including militant groups of ex-right and pro-Peking left), the holding of public meetings was illegal, and the constitution was amended to limit the powers of the judiciary. The government accused Jayparkash Narayan (a leading opponent of the Prime Minister) of aiming to *incite* the police and armed forces to commit acts of indiscipline. The Government also banned the opposition for seeking to 'disrupt the economy' through a nation-wide railway strike. Mrs. Gandhi's critics considered the declaration of national emergency more as an act to meet the challenge to her own power. In June 1975 the Allahabad High Court had found Mrs. Gandhi guilty of violating the Representation of Peoples' Act in the 1971 election campaign.

5.4. Charge of Incompetence

The critics contend that the art of government is subtle, especially in the modern age of highly technical, political and administrative managerial operations. Democracy is charged as the government of amateurs. The ordinary citizen has neither the time, the intelligence nor the will to participate actively in the affairs of the state. The maximum voter turn-out has been in the 1967 General Elections at 61.33 percent.

Besides, it is argued that democracy degenerates into demagogy, thereby making way for the moneyed class which manipulates politics to serve its own selfish ends. It breeds corruption in politics and administration and erodes standards of morality in society. An opinion poll conducted by Marg[28] (a leading market research company) for India Today on an all - India basis indicated corruption as the major problem faced by the people, only second to inflation.

6. Prospects of Indian Democracy

Of the major events of 1998, few were predicted and some were regarded as unthinkable.

1. Japan collapsed into the deepest recession since World War II. None predicted in 1997 that this would be one of the consequences of the troubles in South-East Asia.
2. Russia collapsed. Earlier analysts had assumed that Russia was too big to fail and that it would be kept afloat at all costs by the West because of its nuclear importance.

If predictions could not be made in this regard, it is almost impossible to predict the prospects of a large democratic country like India. Economic pressures are such at times, that political systems are forced to sacrifice democracy and even human rights. But in favor of India's democracy one can only say that it has fared satisfactorily for herself.

In the modern world, 'democracy' is first and foremost a normative word: it does not describe a thing, it prescribes an ideal.[29] Democracy is a way of saying no to inequality, injustice and coercion. But once the enemy is defeated, the problem becomes to specify what ought to be, i.e. to identify equality, justice and freedom in a positive fashion. Modern democracy is based not on participation but on representation. It presupposes not the direct exercise of power but delegation of power. It is not a system of self-government but a system of control and limitation of government.

The obstacles faced by the democratic process in India are sought to be solved by galvanizing the people through the process of *integration*. Where does Indian Democracy stand today and what exactly does its horoscope predict? How far can the Indian democracy take these discrepancies within its fold? This question that is yet to be answered. Indian democracy is clearly on trial. But, perched at the end of the twentieth century, it seems, that the romance of democracy has begun to fade even in countries who swore by democracy in the past.[30] The pattern of liberal democracies is shifting and perhaps once the tide is over,[31] it would have turned a new leaf - newer formations would crystallize. India hopefully, is likely to remain within the parameters of democracy and not to follow the example of its immediate neighbors (Afghanistan, Pakistan, Myanmar (formerly Burma), Nepal, Sri Lanka) who have been in and out of democracy.

A broad consensus on the national scene on major issues will go a long way in the process of transition to real democracy. In this, the task of opposition as also that of unbiased media is important. Both the opposition parties and the media need to keep the welfare of the people and merits of the issue in view instead of indulging in undue criticism. Gandhi's *'Compromise'* may sound an idealism in today's world but the hope for the future lies in such ideals alone. Gandhi's compromise expresses a willingness to adjust to realities and avoid conflicts, even at the cost of sacrificing some position taken initially. Efforts in this direction are likely to lead to humanizing relations between man and man, groups and groups.

All religions have the same noble objective of enabling their followers to become good human beings. This message is often corrupted by those who wish to exploit religion and use it for their own political or personal needs and power. In the game of buying and selling religion, secularism (enshrined in the Preamble of the constitution of India) has been relegated to the background. It is so, because in modern India, society is largely 'cleansed of religion' and instead the society is now involved in a cut-throat competition where there is decline of public morality in the country due to all-round decline in religious sensibilities.[32]

In other words, what is needed is not rejection of religion but rejection of discord created by religion. Only a new social control can be harnessed towards an effective political system. In this context, the issue of discipline assumes importance. In India, there is a need for adoption of discipline in public life. That nearly all political regimes throughout the world style themselves as democracies and claim adherence to democratic principles speaks for the basic appeal of democracy. Democracy seems to bestow an aura of legitimacy on modern life - laws, policies seem more justified if they are based on democratic principles. It has a universal appeal to human beings. Democracy has the dimension of an inner ocean[33] offering any number of opportunities to individuals to realize their aims - personal, social, political. Adoption of Democracy as a way of life in India seems to be a feasible path through which it can reach its goals.

That India's democracy has not bent under the pressure of internal and external factors speaks for the strong political set-up that has emerged slowly. Stressing the democratic full involvement of the people in the development of the country, the Prime Minister, Mr. P.V. Narsimha Rao[34], asserted "that the rights of minority groups must be protected vigorously under the rule of law. Our Constitution provides for this, our people demand this and our heritage requires this". India is a developing country. It has been usual in the west to say that developing countries can either not afford democracy or that democracy is counter-productive to economic development. But India's Prime Minister, imparting a developmental dimension of democracy described India as one of the developing countries in which the process of development is firmly established. We have realized that no quick fixes are possible and that there is no substitute for hard work with full involvement of the people. The results achieved in India are commended by some, divided by others, on the basis of physical statistics. In all these appraisals, however, one crucial element that has not figured as it should is the fact that India's progress has been achieved in a democratic set up".

Considering the odds against democracy (no background of democracy, multi-cultural, multi-ethnic, multi-regional and caste-ridden society) Indian democracy has tried honestly towards a fairly satisfactory performance.

Notes

1 Total population 838.58 million according to 1991 census.

2 In the recorded history of India, there is no definite pattern followed for the Panchayatas. In the *Manusmriti* and the *Shanti Parva* of the Mahabharata, there are many references to the existence of *gramsanghas* or rural communities. A description of this rural community is also found in the *Arthashastra* of kautilya who lived in 400 BC. In the *Ramayana* of Valmiki, we read about *Ganapada,* which was perhaps a kind of federation of the village republics. An account of village commonwealth during the seventeenth century is found in Sukracharya's *Nitisara.*

3 Per capita income is Rupees 4525/- at current prices (1991-91) Source: Ministry of Information and Broadcasting, Government of India, New Delhi.

4 National Average Literacy Rate: 52.2 percent, according to 1991 Census.

5 Quoted in Thakur, Ramesh (1995): 'India as Literated-Democratic State' in THE GOVERNMENT AND POLITICS OF INDIA, MacMillan, p.337.

6 Dankwart Rustow's seminal 1970 article on "Transitions to Democracy: Towards a Dynamic Model" quoted in Kreiger, Joel: OXFORD COMPANION TO POLITICS OF THE WORLD (OUP) 1993, p. 224.

7 Weiner, Myron: THE INDIAN PARADOX, Essays in Indian Politics, Sage, 1989, p.21.

8 Inhospitable weather conditions subsist on the Indian sub-continent. For more than six months, there is unnerving heat with the temperature going up to 49°C.

9 Mitra, Subrata; 'Crowds and Power, Democracy and the Crisis of Governability in India' in CRISIS AND CHANGE IN CONTEMPORAY INDIA: Baxi, Upendra and Parekh, B (eds.) Sage 1995 p.216.

10 For an account of recruitment, training and operation of All-India services see, Maheshwari SR (1992): PROBLEMS AND ISSUES IN ADMINISTRATIVE FEDERALISM, Alloted, ND.

11 For uses and abuses of bureaucratic power, see Dvivedi OP and Jain RB (1985): INDIA'S ADMINISTRATIVE STATE, Gitanjali ND. Also Sahay S; "Ethics and openness, Straws in the wind", The Tribune, 26 Nov, 1996.

12 Mark Tully, "A Look At India", Special Lecture at Panjab University, 22 Oct 1998.

13 Kothari, Rajni: POLITICS IN INDIA, Orient, 1970, pp. 85-86.

14 STATE AGAINST DEMOCRACY, In Search of Humane Government Ajanta, 1988, p.163.

15 Gandhi, M.K.: MY PICTUE OF FREE INDIA (edited by Hingorani, A.T.) Pearl Publishers, Bombay, 1965.

16 Lijphart, Arend: DEMOCRACY IN PLURAL SOCIETIES, A Comparative Exploration, Popular Prakashan, 1989.

17 For details see Srinivas, M.S.: CASTE IN MODERN INDIA, Media Promoters, Bombay, 1962, pp. 1-15.

18 Vanhanen, Tatu: POLITICS OF ETHNIC NEPOTISM, India as an Example, Sterling, New Delhi, 1991.

19 The Statesman, 4 June 1978, p.11.

20 For details see Carey, John M (1997); "Institutional Design and Party Systems" in: CONSOLIDATING THE THIRD WORLD DEMOCRACIES: Diamond L and others (eds.) John Hopkins University Press.

21 Sh. GMC Balyogi; Speaker of Lok Sabha in The Times of India, 11August 1998, p.13.

22 See Kothari, Rajni: STATE AGAINST DEMOCRACY, In Search of Humane Government, Ajanta, 1988, p.(ii). 'The state and weilders of power'. The need to find individual and local solutions has grown among the people.

23 Plamenatz, John; DEMOCRACY AND ILLUSION, pp. 122-3.

24 The Tribune, Chandigarh, 27 May, 1994, p.1.

25 Ibid.

26 Ibid.

27 See Raghavulu, CV and Bose, BPC; "Centre-State Relations in Disaster, Mitigation and Preparedness," Indian Journal of Political Science, July-September 1992, pp. 314-331.

28 India Today, 15 September, 1990, p.30.

30 Sartori G; 'Democracy' in Int. Encylopaedia of Social Sciences, Shils, David (ed.) Macmillan NY, 1972, pp.116-17.

31 Time, 17 January 1994, p.52.

32 That is, after dust has settled on the erstwhile communist world.
Nandy, Ashish; "Paradox of Secularism, The buying and selling of Religion, "The Times of India, 21 May 1994, p.12.

33 Kateb George in THE INNER OCEAN, Individualism and Democratic Culture (Cornell 1992), draws a picture of the democratic individual, whose personal and political rights, arising within the parameters of a constitutional democracy engender a moral and social climate of respect, dignity and mutuality.

34 Address to the Joint Sitting of the US Congress. From the text of Prime Minister Narsimha Rao in The Tribune, 24 May 1994, p.9.

A Critical Reflection on the Reform of the Kim Dae-Jung Government

KIM KWANG-WOONG

1. Preface

On 28 February 1998, the Kim Dae-jung administration announced the amendment of the "government reform" bill. The nomination of Kim's candidate for Prime Minister, Kim Jong-pil, from the ruling coalition, however, was rejected by the major opposition party (Grand National Party) and eventually failed to be approved in the parliament. This tough political environment in the beginning of Kim's administration was reflected in the deliberation of the government reorganization bill. In the end, the original provisions of the bill were rather distorted. The first stage of drafting the bill was led by the Government Reorganization Council (GRC), in which unbiased experts from various social fields participated, whereas the second stage, the parliamentary deliberation, was highly politicized. This two-tier process inevitably placed many constraints on the bill. It has been argued that difficulty in administrative reform was a product of the structural characteristics of the state (Chong, 1998). In line with this approach, it has also been maintained that structural consistency and political-economic conditions embedded in the administrative system should receive a great deal of attention as significant factors in the pursuit of reform (Kim Pyong-sop,1998).

This article provides a critical reflection upon how the new government reorganization bill was debated to produce such results, from the perspective of a participant in the first stage. The reorganization bill was completed after many complications. To understand the reasons behind the complications, an analysis of the process of the bill's passage is necessary. But it is even more important to understand how such political reforms are made amidst power struggles. This amendment included Presidential Decrees on reorganizing offices which will also be discussed. Moreover, it must be noted that governmental officers actively lobbied.

This chapter will discuss not only the contents of the amendment but also the ideological basis of the reform, its distortion in the process, and finally, the validity of the process. As to the ideological basis of the reform, this essay will focus upon factors such as the relationships between state and civil society and the role of the state, which defined the direction and character of the reform. Also, the differences in the logic of the state and market deserve attention. The matter of procedural validity of the GRC as an advisory agency to the President was questioned on legal grounds. However, political will tends to exceed legal principles. In John Luke's terms, "political power is valid in so far as it is used to further the common good" (Kang Chong-in & Mun Chi-yong, 1996). Nonetheless, various approaches should be taken into consideration if we are to secure an unbiased estimate of ideological perspectives, processes, and outcomes.

The government reorganization bill will probably undergo further amendment. This bill, born out of political negotiation, is likely to be revised through change of office or through political self-review. It is reasonable to think that the administrative inconveniences and irrationality of this reform may necessitate its revision. Moreover, scholars in this field who have come to understand the course and contents of the amendment process need to contribute further criticism.

2. The Formation and Background of the Government Reorganization Council

For about fifty days from 7 January to 24 February 1998, the task of government reform was carried out by a government reform deliberative committee and implementation committee. The former consisted of 14 members from political circles, administration, law, press and academic fields. The latter consisted of 9 members, mainly professors, members of the state research center, the special assistant to the President of National Congress for New Politics (NCNP), and bureaucrats. In addition, the Office of the Prime Minister, the Ministry of Government Administration, and the Korean Legislative Studies Institute provided assistance.

In order to describe the deliberation process, we must clearly understand the legal character of the Government Reorganization Council. Simply put, as mentioned above, the GRC was not an organization with official, legal status. Responding to the demands of the candidate (Kim Dae-jung), it was merely characterized as an affiliated organ of the Government Transferring Council (GTC) with its budget provided by the GTC. However, the fact that a bill drafted by an organization without clear legal status became the bill for a State Council meeting, which was eventually able to change the Government Organization Act, shows the relationship between law and political powers. It must be admitted that the launching of the new government with the temporary appointment of the Prime Minister that precluded the consent of Parliament may continue to spark debate concerning the constitutionality of these proceedings. However if we consider the GRC simply as an assisting organization of the GTC where discussions take place to build the foundations for a reform bill, this debate holds little relevancy.

Establishing the GRC was not a hard task. The GRC was initially established to follow the government draft made by the Minister of Government Administration and submit the final draft to the State Council meeting.

3. The Characteristics of Reform

This government reorganization had very different characteristics from previous ones in terms of the scale of reform and the process. Below is a summary of distinguishing characteristics.

First, it was not the current ruling power but the incumbent political power which played the leading role. However, in January 1993, the Democratic Justice Party (DJP) passed a bill which merged the Ministry of Culture with the Ministry of Sports, and the Ministry of Trade and Industry with the Ministry of Energy and Resources. Still, this was accomplished through a ruling political group, not through a power shift between ruling parties. In most cases, government reform had been planned by a commission for administrative reform established by the government at that time.

Second, it was the first time that government reform became public. When the merger between the Economic Planning Board and the Ministry of Finance, and the Ministry of Construction with the Ministry of Transportation took place on December 1994, some of the members in the Administrative Renovation Council participated "unofficially" but were excluded in the final process. The task was kept confidential at the final stage and the council was denied participation during this stage.

Third, popular demand for government downsizing made reform easier. The unprecedented foreign exchange (or "IMF") crisis helped to build popular support for the restructuring of whole sectors, which helped to overcome any comprehensive resistance to reform. Yet lobbying was quite strong because it proved to be an effective survival strategy at times. At any rate, the appropriate compliance of systemic logic to historical context might have resulted in this outcome of reform (Kang Shin-t'aek, 1997).

Fourth, the GRC did not merely have a superficial role of approving a prepared plan. In fact, all discussions in the council started at ground zero. In newly established departments, the working staff were delegated separate tasks of designing the organizations. The Ministry of Health and Welfare, which underwent many changes in its functions, provides a good example of this phenomenon. In past debates ratification followed the opinions of an organ such as the Blue House, however, this is no longer the case.

Fifth, it is generally assumed that such a reform bill based on political interest is likely to perpetuate contradictions that might later induce another reform. This reform set forth the precedent that governmental organizations may be changed if necessary. The restructuring of government organizations previously regarded as "Untouchable" now became possible. Frequent reforms, however, can also be harmful in that they may destabilize the administration.

4. The Process and Major Contents of the Reform

The deliberative committee adopted the rules to examine issues in the implementation committee meetings held daily. The council convened a public hearing on the first draft on 16 January 1998. After completing the second draft on 6 February, it continued to deliberate upon the second draft until 18 February.

While deliberating on the bill, the implementation committee considered proposals from the administration, the KDI (Korea Development Institute), and the KPPA (Korean Public Policy Association). It also consulted each party's reform proposals issued during the previous presidential election as well as opinions from various sectors of society. In cases where the council determined that the input from these sources was insufficient, it called on the administrators of relevant organs for further reference. Of course, behind these deliberations was an outline of reform that had been accumulating in the academic arena for a long time (Kim Kwang-Woong et al., 1993).

4.1. The First Draft of the Government Reorganization Bill

The points of the first draft are as follows: First, the council established the Civil Service Commission and the Office of Planning and Budget under the control of the President. Second, all 'Chung' (an organizational level slightly lower ranked than that of the ministry, or 'Pu') of the central administrative agencies except that of Science and Technology were downgraded to the vice-ministry level under the control of the Prime Minister. Included as a vice-ministry level organization was the Ministry of Government Administration. Third, the Ministry of Home Affairs changed its name to the Ministry of Government Administration and Home Affairs. Fourth, the Ministry of Trade and Industry was consolidated with the Small and Medium Business Administration and was changed to the Ministry of Industry with the condition that the role of "trade negotiation" be entrusted to the Ministry of Foreign Affairs. Fifth, the Ministry of Maritime Affairs and Fisheries was merged once again with the Ministry of Agriculture and Forestry.

There was considerable difference of opinion over whether the President should possess direct oversight powers and whether it would be appropriate to strengthen the power of the Office of the President under the drive to downsize. The conflict was most severe between assemblymen of the NCNP who wanted to enhance the Office of the President and those of the ULD (United Liberal Democrats) who aimed to enhance the Office of the Prime Minister.

Regardless of political interest, however, most council members maintained that the Office of Planning and Budget and the Civil Service Commission should be kept under the control of the Office of the President. They argued that establishing the Civil Service Commission was necessary to secure fairness without being political and to refrain from "office hunting" (Pak Tong-so, 1998). However, council members' perception of the role of this agency was not very accurate, in addition, they did not feel that it was very important. At most, council members with academic backgrounds in public administration felt that it was necessary for various measures to prevent discrepancies in personnel management. As for the Office of Planning and Budget, some argued that such a powerful organization should not be under the control of the Office of the President. Still, it was agreed that presidential power over the budget should be secured under a presidential system. Moreover, the expectation that the reform bill could prevent the Ministry of Finance and Economy (MOFE) from doing damage as it had done previously, was a major consideration in the development of the reform. However, if the Office of Planning and Budget proves to be another MOFE, or administrative superpower, the validity of the reform must be called into question.

4.2. Opinions from the Public Hearing

There was great interest in the public hearing, in relationship to the importance of the reforms, in that this was the first time ever in the history of government reorganization that public hearings were held. The ten people who testified provided useful opinions, especially blaming MOFE for its responsibility for the foreign exchange crisis. The criticism was also directed toward the Ministry of Foreign Affairs, saying that it was absurd for this organization to assert that it managed trade negotiations while it showed such poor administration in diplomatic affairs. Many council members made the mistake of believing that the Ministry of Foreign Affairs would take away the management of "trade" from the Ministry of Commerce, Industry, and Energy. In fact, the Ministry of Foreign Affairs would take responsibility of the "trade negotiations". In reality, "trade" and "trade negotiations" usually overlap, so that "negotiations" without the actual knowledge of the trade would be difficult to achieve.

Another opinion expressed at the public hearing was that the proposal made by the GRC was rather passive and a more active proposal was required. It appeared that some of the participants were playing the role of "agents," representing the interest and concerns of the administrative agency they belonged to. The range of calls for reform varied from those with progressive attitudes, calling for more radical reform, to others who maintained a conservative stance, worrying about a shake-up in the administration with the launching of a new government.

More than 1,000 people filled the halls of the public hearing. There was even an implicit protest of the downgrading of the Patriots and Veterans Administration Agency. Among ordinary participants, 127 people requested the right to speak, but only ten of them received the chance due to the time limit. In fact, up to 2,700 opinions from various sectors were delivered to the council. The staff attempted to oversee and clarify them so that they could be accurately reflected in the final draft.

4.3. The Second Draft of the Government Reorganization Bill

On 5 February, the second draft was completed with each administrative agency providing its opinion through public hearings. The Ministry of Home Affairs and the Ministry of Government Administration were to be merged into the Ministry of Government Administration and Home Affairs. The Ministry of Government Policy Coordination, previously under the Office of the Prime Minister, was upgraded to the ministry level, while the name of the Ministry of Industry was to be changed to the Ministry of Commerce, Industry, and Energy. Not many drastic changes were made in the final draft. In contrast to its contents, the process of deliberation was not so simple. Until the conclusion of the final draft, the council was characterized by active debate, although quite similar conclusions were often reached. It cannot be said that no political negotiations had occurred by the completion of the second draft.

4.4. Parliamentary Deliberation

The parliamentary deliberation of the reform bill focused upon the issue of "strengthening" presidential power and "weakening" the power of the Prime Minister. The main point of contention was the proposal to center all power and responsibility on the President, providing him with direct control over the budget and personnel.

However, greater responsibility for personnel management did not necessarily mean the enhancement of presidential power, which most parliamentary members failed to realize. Parliamentary members urged that each minister should be granted the right of personnel management over public officials in each administrative agency. They argued that even when an institution was required for personnel management, it should be placed under the Office of the Prime Minister or the Ministry of Government Administration and Home Affairs. Members in parliament also maintained that it was possible for the Office of the President to constrain each minister's personnel management. At the same time, however, they misunderstood the independence of personnel power as an expression of lack of faith in the Prime Minister and ministers, and worried about possible impairment to the power of approval exercised by the Prime Minister. Certainly, they were well aware of the drive of the reform to weaken the possibility of political intervention, which had infected much of the personnel management system. In the end, the ruling party (NCNP) in the process of negotiations withdrew this proposal. This proposal for the establishment of the Civil Service Commission was the only measure proposed that would check the unlimited presidential control of personnel management in order to promote fairness in personnel affairs. The defeat of this measure was quite disappointing, and it consequently nullified the raison d'etre for this council.

As to the control of budget, in the words of assemblyman Kim Yong-chin, it would not be appropriate to leave "the implementing function to the Office of the President. Instead, strict surveillance would be more desirable while entrusting that power to a related agency." Still, in a strong presidential system, it would not be unusual for the agencies charged with management and budget to be placed directly under presidential control, as in the U.S. Another argument, however, is that the Korean presidential system differs from that of the U.S., and the exercise of budget control does not make much difference in a country with such strong presidential power. However, the real intent of the reform proposal was to link the budget with the function of planning and reform with the assumption that the reform would be continued. Thus direct presidential control would be suitable considering the considerable weight of its importance. In the end, a rather odd outcome was produced with the Planning and Budget Commission remaining as a part of the Office of the President, next to the Office of National Budget. Although it was formerly an advisory organ, an agency called the Administrative Reform Council was established as an affiliated division.

Another long-standing issue in parliament was the establishment of the Ministry of Government Administration and Home Affairs. The merger of the previous Ministry of Home Affairs with the Ministry of Government Administration triggered the question of which administrative agency would have the authority to countersign affiliated governments' documents, a job then belonging to the head of the Ministry of Government Administration. Even after the Minister of Government Administration and Home Affairs was assigned to deal with it, the same problem occurred with the establishment of the Planning and Budget Commission. (The relevant law is Article 82 of the Constitution which says that the acts of the President performed in accordance with law shall be executed by written document, and such documents shall be countersigned by the Prime Minister and the apropos members of the State Council.)

The other changes which occurred during the parliamentary deliberation are as follows: the Ministry of Maritime Affairs and Fisheries was restored to its original assignation and the Ministry of Culture was changed to the Ministry of Culture and Tourism. The task of administering broadcasting functions was originally assigned to the Ministry of Information and Communication on a temporary basis until the establishment of the Broadcasting Communication Council, but this responsibility was transferred to the Ministry of Culture and Tourism during parliamentary deliberation. Agencies such as the Supply Administration, the Military Manpower Administration, and the Rural Development Administration were upgraded to the vice-ministry level, and Korean Food and Drug Administration under the Ministry of Health and Welfare was upgraded to an "administration." The competition and rivalry over bureaucratic jurisdiction was quite severe, revealing that the process of devising a reform bill had become extremely political. Administrative reform is often termed "a process of re-writing the contract between elected politicians and bureaucratic officials" (Haggard, 1995). In Korea however, strangely enough, the reform appeared to comply with bureaucratic interest, although the political sector constrains the bureaucratic power in most other countries.

4.5. The Amendment of the Government Reorganization Bill

The government reorganization bill passed by the parliament was characterized by the following:

1. The Planning and Budget Commission (PBC) was established to deal with the long-term financial planning and further administrative reform. In addition, the Administrative Reform Council was established to advise the chair of PBC.
2. The Government Legislation Agency and the Patriots and Veterans Administration Agency were absorbed as vice-ministry level agencies under the Office of the Prime Minister. However, the amount of pay of the heads of these agencies was to be decided between the Minister and the Vice-Minister on 24 February, when the bill was to be passed at the State Council meeting. The Office for Government Policy Coordination became a ministry-level agency and the Office for Public Information was entrusted to act as the "spokesman" of the government.
3. The First and the Second Ministry to the President for Political Affairs were abolished. Instead, the Second Ministry to the President for Political Affairs was transformed into the secretariat of the Presidential Commission on Women's Affairs.
4. The Board of Finance and Economy was converted into the Ministry of Finance and Economy and under it, the Office of National Budget was established and designed to cooperate more closely with the Planning and Budget Commission. This rearrangement appears to be rather inappropriate, considering that it is the Minister of MOFE who addresses the parliament with the budget statement. Despite a lack of direct accountability to parliament, the PBC was designated as the organization for developing basic budget policy and lead reform.
5. The Ministry of Foreign Affairs assumed the task of trade negotiation with the launching of the Trade Negotiation Center, and changed its name to the Ministry of Foreign Affairs and Trade.
6. The Ministry of Home Affairs and the Ministry of Government Administration were merged together to form the Ministry of Government Administration and Home Affairs.
7. The Ministry of Trade and Industry changed its name to the Ministry of Commerce, Industry, and Energy.

In the end, the number of the members of the State Council was decreased from 21 to 17.

4.6. The Reorganization of Offices

Immediately following the passage of the government reorganization bill through parliament, the GRC turned to the work of reorganizing the office. Amending the Presidential Decrees was a more controversial issue than the reorganization of government under the reform, since some posts were abolished and some officers were transferred, which directly affected personnel. As a result, each department engaged in desperate lobbying. Reducing some offices, bureaus, and departments was not a simple task. The higher rank they were, the more desperately each minister and politician lobbied in order to avoid being affected by the measure. At the same time, this reform reduced the number of public officials, which generated other problems.

Eventually, the number of offices, bureaus, and divisions of the central administrative agencies was reduced quite substantially. In the central administrative agencies, 14 of 97 public officials in the political affairs, 14 of 138 first-rank officials, 65 of 713 second- or third-rank officials (Bureau Head level), 163 of 2,118 third- or fourth-rank officials (Department Head level), and 17,186 of 156,040 fifth-rank and lower-level officials decreased in number. About 10.9% or 17,442 of 159,806 total positions were to be cut. Political affairs includes the Office of the President, Presidential Security Service, and the Board of Audit and Inspection. Public officials engaged in foreign affairs (except those in foreign embassies) were removed; 12 of 72 special first or second rank, 2 of 68 first rank, 31 of 355 second or third rank, 17 of 470 fourth rank, and 99 of 1,081 fifth rank and lower-level officials. About 7.8% or 160 of a total of 2,049 positions were cut under this measure.

This plan was to cut the number of officials by 10.9%, or 17,597 out of the total of 161,855 public officials (90,501 from central agencies and 71,354 from state institutions). The 286,000 public officials in educational affairs and 112,000 in security-related jobs were unaffected, along with the Office of the President, the Presidential Security Services, and the Board of Audit and Inspection.

5. The Ideological Evaluation of Governmental Reorganization

There is a fundamental question that is raised whenever government reorganization is discussed. The first question concerns the ideology of the reform and the definition of the role of the government: In other words, what is the proper relationship between the state and society, between the state and people, and the state and market?

If civil society is so mature that the state need not closely intervene, the role of the state should be decreased. If the reverse is the case, the state must take a more active role. This would be so in case of market failure, which has often been suggested by Keynesian scholars. However, the failure of the state is also common, which poses another question of "what should be done?"

There has not yet been an adequate discussion of the range and characteristics of reform, as it relates to reality, that depend upon the answers to the aforementioned questions. The debate is the dialectic between the micro-economic approach and the neo-institutional economic (NIE) view. According to the latter, all human beings are selfish and their behavior is rational. Hence, there is little room for the state to intervene. Therefore, formal or nonformal institutions work together to maximize interest as a whole. What is required is the formation of a system which is autonomous and spontaneous. Even when this emphasizes the necessity of such a system, which seems to necessitate a role for state intervention, the formation of such a system must take place autonomously from the perspective of neo-institutional economics (Ostrom et al., 1994).

Recently in Japan, this issue is being seriously debated. The so-called bureaucratic perspective is fighting the market-economy view for dominance. Japan, like Korea, has bureaucratic officials who claim to have contributed to economic development after the War, in the face of the private sector crying for freedom and deregulation as the only way to survive. However, Japan sided with those supporting its bureaucracy by increasing the consumer tax rate from 3% to 5% to put the bureaucracy on a more secure financial footing. However, this measure ended in failure. Also it was not as easy for the Japanese to pursue deregulation as it was for Korea. The proportion of the sector regulated by the state amounted to 6.6% in the U.S. in 1988 (17.0% in 1977) compared to 42.3% in Japan in 1994 (40.8% in 1988). The tension between the state and market or society over the scope of regulation has always existed.

What was the position represented in this reform? Apparently, it aimed to minimize state intervention in line with reforms pursued by the previous administration. It intended to leave to the private sector as much room as possible for what could not be efficiently managed by the state. Within the Administration, the notion gained ground that the central agency need not intervene in everything and it would be better to entrust responsibility to the local government and to further decentralization thereby encouraging localization of power. Since the previous government reorganization had postponed the issue of local government autonomy, the decentralization process was not fully debated. However, the impending issue of downsizing ad hoc authorities such as local small and medium business administrations became a troublesome task due to pressure from the central government. At the same time, the fact that private organizations, including academic ones, opposed subordinating cultural properties or local museums to the local government proves that even intellectuals were still siding with centralized authority.

Thus, many barriers had to be overcome to increase commissions, decentralize authority, and decrease central intervention through government downsizing. It is also doubtful that, as neo-institutional economics maintains, the private sector could construct the formal and nonformal system and manage it autonomously. Home nursery schools are a typical example of the practice of private contract. The problem is, however, that the managers can exploit consumers by setting a much too high price on education. As this example shows, private contract is not the only and the best solution.

Thus, when an individual citizen acts selfishly and irrationally, the role of the state and its boundary with civil society becomes very difficult to define. This is a dilemma that reform cannot avoid. In addition, the size of government cannot be determined solely by ideological standards. Since reform is a response to historic calling, the size of government should be related to it (Kim Kwang-woong, 1997).

The second question is how to perceive the nature of the state. Among many aspects of the state, government officers should make a choice between governmental "administration" and business "management" styles. This choice actually poses a very fundamental question. In other words, if the latter is chosen, people oriented towards economics and business administration would be qualified to become government officers in the government reform group. Even the President emphasizes managerial administration and high productivity. Most government officers take "entrepreneurial government" for granted.

Thus, a very serious problem ensues. Both in the private and public sector, it is important to increase productivity and to maximize utility on the basis of economic principles. It is claimed that governmental service does not differ from that of business. If so, how can we explain the conscription system for national defense? What is the validity of the state's request for private aid in the face of natural disaster? What about "publicness" as the basis of governmental administration?

The government actually tries to satisfy the people as consumers by rearranging the administrative apparatus, reducing its payroll and budget. This is exactly like a company that tries to satisfy its consumers by producing high-quality products. However, the state, or the government as the agent of the state, cannot take the role of a business since it is responsible for advancing the development of each person, the equity between different classes, and providing justice. The nature of the state should be rooted in morality and the common good. Therefore, a paradigm which equates the state with business endangers the principles of reform and risks a surrender to materialism with adopting an orientation towards extreme economic development. In short, calls for an easy transfer to "decentralized market coordination" from "authority-centered coordination" are naive in that they ignore the bureaucratic mechanism. This idea also threatens the very academic identity of scholars in public administration.

Third, it is necessary to ascertain whether the ideological ground of the reform is rooted in liberal democracy or neo-liberalism. It is even more important to ask the question "who is this reform for?" It would be very shocking indeed if the reform merely succeeded in promoting bureaucratic interests. That is, if the ruling coalition that includes the bureaucratic class adopted and continues to adopt reform in name only, while keeping the components of the coalition the same.

The world today has been transformed from state monopolistic capitalism under Fordist Keynesianism to that of post-Fordist neo-liberalism (Kim Song-ku & Kim Se-kyun, 1988). Open markets, liberalization, and privatization are all based on this view of neo-liberalism. It presents a big problem if neo-liberalism deepens the inequality between administrative agencies and between state and civil society. If government reorganization is equal to a "game of power expansions of massive organizations," the reform would merely promote quarrels for territory between administrative agencies. The commitment to "small but efficient" government is nullified when the state is weak toward capital and strong only against the small and powerless.

Therefore, the new administration needs to clearly set its foundation for reform. Simply setting a goal of simultaneously realizing democracy and economic development is not enough. The opposition party's transformation to the ruling party may provide a great chance to rewrite the history of politics. Yet, the unconditional call for economic recovery may allow materialism to trap the reformist spirit, resulting in an administration with few differences from its predecessors. It is still likely that the officialdom will be haunted by consumer-capitalism. For example, cultural items and cultural events, which are temporally and suddenly promoted to merely stimulate short-term profits, would make culture the slave of business. The establishment of the Ministry of Culture and Tourism clearly has demonstrated the intention to degrade culture to the point of for-profit commercial culture. If we choose to ignore these changes, we will witness the sinking of the ship of reform.

It is time to address the ideological basis for the reform. Responding to global changes, the government should establish a flexible structure to promote the sort of multi-item, small production suggested by post-Fordist scholars. Through a deepening of liberal democracy, where the interest of the people is recognized before that of the government, through self-reflection by the bureaucrats, and efforts at downsizing government, the real objectives of the reform will be achieved. Even with a change of regimes and the drive for government reform, the only temporary reform will occur if the basic prototype and principle of the ruling structure does not change and if asymmetric relationships, inequality, and materialism persist.

Fourth, the reform of government structure only marks the beginning. Financial and personnel reform should be accompanied by reshaping the attitudes of bureaucrats. Structural reform cannot be completed by only decreasing the number of administrative agencies and rearranging offices. It will be complete only when it provides a new perspective on the organization corresponding to a new era. Disappointingly, although on this occasion a measure to contract with private specialists was partly introduced (in the Planning and Budget Commission) in restructuring the organization, change of perspectives relating to organization is not found in the reform.

A new perspective of organization is that of New Science or "quantum society," which differs from the views that primarily see the world in material reality. In contrast to people-centered perspectives, this view puts the emphasis on the "relationship" between people, the "weblike association which is invisible" (Wheatley, 1992). Respect and faith are cherished in this kind of organization. It is not the cage but the space between bars that pens up the lion, and it is not notes but the silence between the notes that makes the music. With the same logic, an invisible "unified whole" links our experiences together. So, adhering to the survival of each department rather than considering the government as a whole would make reform meaningless. The same logic should be applied to the reform of leadership. Setting melody, tempo and key, and casting the players can be entrusted to anyone, but the music comes from a place we cannot see, and the players together create "the unified whole," which goes beyond the independence of particular units. If everything works out, the only thing left for critics is to sit back and enjoy the music. Thus, we only have to adjust to the pattern through the axis of time – rhythm, flow, direction, and shape. Light (1997), who maintains that the philosophy of reform is scientific management, banishment of waste, supervision, and liberal management, sought to view reform as a rhythmical ocean tide.

The chairmen of companies in the U.S. are not likely to isolate themselves from employees. At companies like Intel and Hewlett Packard, presidents and vice-presidents are served by one secretary and the office is not spacious while having a simple open ceiling. Furthermore, in many U.S. companies, the president, general managers, managers, and employees freely discuss problems in one space. No gap between ranks can be found which is a sharp contrast to the Korean type of administration where chiefs and directors each have their own rooms, creating hierarchy between ranks.

This present reform did not introduce new perspectives on organization. Certainly, there is room for the ministers to play a leading role in mending the system. For example, the Minister of Labor reduced his office size to 20 pyong and the offices of the Minister and the Vice-Minister of the Ministry of Foreign Affairs and Trade were redesigned. The momentum for future organizational reform can be provided by more concern from high-ranking officials.

6. The Process and the Outcomes of Government Reorganization

In evaluating the process, what we should judge depends on the question of how objectively and fairly the bill for government reorganization has been established. It is clear that the participation of specialists was different from politicians. The criteria for evaluating the implementation committee and the deliberative committee is different since their characteristics are different. Moreover, we should accept the fact that the basic idea about government reform has been obscured by political intervention in the parliamentary deliberation process.

As mentioned above, the reform process encompassed several steps. It was not easy for the implementation committee to do the basic work, but it achieved relative success with the help of the working staff. Still, it is doubtful that the implementation committee considered the reform as a whole. There is no evidence on how much the original plan has been distorted by administrative intervention in the form of intensive lobbying. But it is assumed that school ties or regional ties exercised a considerable influence. It was also easy for the committee to be biased since it was required to consider data from each administrative agency, and the location of the committee was known and open for many public officials to visit. The basic ideas behind the reform –downsizing of an over-magnified and solidified organization, improvement of the quality of life, consolidation of national competitiveness, decentralization, invention in the administrative system to promote responsible management – were sustained.

The deliberative committee's case is quite different, however. Each party's representatives were included as members of the deliberative committee. So it was natural that each of them were more concerned about their own party's interest. It seemed that they were more interested in how much power they were able to obtain than in solving the basic problems themselves. Some members sided with particular agencies. But we cannot be certain that a member's familiarity with a related administrative agency led him/her to represent the interests of that agency. Whatever may be the case, discussions of the deliberative committee cannot help but include more political factors than that of the implementation committee.

Regarding distortion in the parliamentary deliberation process, it can be expected that a governmental reform process under opposition control of the parliament would generate this kind of outcome. It is natural that the opposition party would be critical of concentrating too much power in the President after it had just lost the presidential election. This situation resulted in the malformation of both the Planning and Budget Commission and the Office of National Budget. There was also a power dispute in the deliberation process. As was pointed out earlier, the broadcasting authority was reallocated from the Ministry of Information and Communication to the Ministry of Culture and Tourism. The power of the Ministry of Agriculture and Fisheries led to its incorporation of the Forestry Administration as opposed to the formation of the Ministry of Environment, as originally planned.

Also it is difficult to precisely estimate the role of the media and civil organizations. In fact, media editorials and the opinions expressed in the public hearings were expected to be reflected in each draft. It was quite easy to reach agreement where there was already much consensus. However, considering the time and scale of the reform as well as conditions of the period, the conflicts among each different group were quite unavoidable.

Lastly, there is one point that should be examined about the deliberative committee itself. It is true that the committee lacked sufficient time to coordinate their opinion, as a sub-deliberative committee was established in the final stage to suggest various opinions contrary to that of the implementation committee. The sub-committee had a commission, but only one or two members represented all the others.

Next is the evaluation concerning the results. Although the number of members of the State Council was only slightly decreased from 21 to 17, the governmental structure itself faced a major reform. All the organizations which were directly controlled by the Office of the Prime Minister were transformed and the Deputy-Prime Minister system was abolished. Redundant organizations were the target of further trimming. One administrative agency was no longer able to control another through its organization, personnel, and budget. This reform focused on providing the minister of each ministry with an individual autonomous budget, organization, and personnel. Now, the government more than ever resembles a president-centralized structure.

It presents a big problem, though, that this integration and dispersion created a dinosaur-like organization in the end. The Ministry of Government Administration and Home Affairs, the Planning and Budget Commission, the Ministry of Finance and Economy, and the Office of National Budget are perfect examples. The cases of integration ignored trends for localization and drives to downsize supportive organizations, while the cases of dispersion produced crippling political power games. For instance, Han Seung-Soo, a member of the National Assembly, insisted upon the importance of the existence of a strong Deputy-Prime Minister or Senior Secretary to the President for Economic Affairs which could control economy-related affairs. He also emphasized that this government reform failed to consider the relationship between the President and the Administration (interview with Han Seung-su on 16 April 1998). The Ministry of Maritime Affairs and Fisheries was not abolished due to political reasons and the elimination of the Civil Service Commission also resulted from a political compromise. Also, appending tourism to culture, with the superficial argument that culture is commercialized by tourism, is in fact worse than frivolous.

It is possible to understand this reform in many ways. But the most damning question is: For whom was this reform undertaken? According to one bank officer, the reform has not resulted in weakened government intervention at all, and the number of economic agencies had not been reduced. There was also no change in the Board of Audit and Inspection, the Public Prosecutor's Office, the National Police Agency and the National Tax Administration. For whom was this reform introduced? If the ruling coalition has gained more power and the lot of the administrative class has not been reduced, the people's share must have remained the same. Then the true task of reform will be assigned to the next regime.

There is more to be said pertaining to future reform. It would seem ideal to introduce the principle of "accountable management" to administrative institutions, for example, as in the "Next Step" system at the Driving License Bureau in the U.K. But what we should keep in mind is that reform must conform to the traditions and the origin of the Korean administrative structure itself. It would seem natural to start with the paradigm identifying the government as a form of business. However, even the same tree might not be able to grow well in different soil. If we follow that model, we will probably encounter such a difficult situation that we will be forced to accept trade unions in the public sector. I wonder whether proponents of the reform have clear solution for this or not. With regards to local government reform, the rearrangement of the administration of the provincial system is more crucial than anything else now. The only thing the provincial governments are supposed to do is to delegate tasks and powers to lower local organizations. Administrative reforms should not be reviewed in such a micro-perspective. Moreover, it should be noted that financial reform has been ignored. It is important to reform administrative organizations, but it is more important and urgent to reform the budget system itself to prevent extravagant use of the national budget.

7. Conclusion

So far I have introduced the content, process, and critical analysis regarding the reform of Kim Dae-jung's early administration. There are more problems, which usually appear after the reform has been carried out to a considerable extent. These problems will be the task of the next reform and deserve to be addressed in the closing comments.

The major task of the last administrative reform was downsizing. The jobs that the government did not necessarily have to do were passed to the private sector, while excessive intervention and regulation were reduced. This is ideal in itself, but if we call it the "first wave," we need a "second wave" for the next reform. This should be to rebuild institutional and administrative capacities. It should be our next objective to bring about the realization of "good government" with reconstructed institutional and administrative capacities (Heredia and Schneider, 1998). While this reform sought to achieve a more competitive economic and political market, it is doubtful that it will lead to good government. Maybe we will have to provide a second chance for the next reform to achieve "good government."

For this to happen, academics and progressive organizations should lead the reform of the central government, as is done in other developed countries. It is desirable to build an organization like the Alliance for Redesigning Government (REGO) in the U.S. in order to continue our reform process. A recent reform group entitled "Study Group for Ideal Government," an Internet-based organization, has called for reform of the central government along with other academic groups. The reform made this movement possible and shows us the lessons we may gain from it.

References

Chung, Yong-tok. 1998. "Kukka kigu-ui chedojok t'uksong-gwa haengjong kaehyok (Institutional Characteristics of State Agencies and Administrative Reform). Paper presented at Korean Politics Seminar II–Korean Political Economic Crisis and Response, 21 March.

Haggard, Stephan. 1995. "Reform of the State in Latin America." Unpublished paper.

Heredia, Blanca, and Ben Ross Schneider. 1998. "The Political Economy of Administrative Reform: Building State Capacity in Developing Countries." Unpublished paper.

Kang, Chong-in, and Mun Chi-yong, trans. 1996. T'ongch'iron (Government Theory). Seoul: Kkach'i.

Kang, Shin-t'aek. 1997. "Chongbu kaehyok-ui nolli" (Principles of Government Reform). Paper presented at the Conference of KAPA, 22 October.

Kim, Kwang-woong. 1997. "Munje-rul ponun shigak-kwa hyonjae-ui chongbu mosup" (Perspective for Problems and the Current Feature of Government). Paper presented at the Seminar of KAPA, 20 March.

Kim, Kwang-woong, Chong Chong-kil, and Pang Sok-hyon. 1993. "Sae chonbu-ui chonbu hyongt'ae-wa chongbu chojik" (New Government Structure and Organization). In Haengjong chojik kaehyok–sae chongbu-ui pang-an (Administrative Organization Reform–Perspectives for Restructuring New Government). Graduate School of Public Administration, Seoul National University.

Kim, Pyung-sub. 1988. "Yoktae chongbu-ui haengjong kaehyok p'yongka-wa hyon chongbu-ui kwaje" (Evaluation of Previous Government Reforms and Current Tasks). Paper presented at the Seminar of KAPA, 20 March.

Kim, Song-ku, Kim Se-kyun, et al. 1998. Chabon-ui segyehwa-wa shin chayujuui (Capital Globalization and Neo-Liberalism). Seoul: Munhak Kwahaksa.

Light, Paul C. 1997. The Tide of Reform: Making Government Work, 1945-1995. New Haven: Yale University Press.

Ostrom, E., et al. 1994. Rules, Games, and Common Pool Resources. Ann Arbor: University of Michigan Press.

Pak, Tong-su. 1998. Han-guk haengjongnon (Korean Administration). Seoul: 398. Bobmun Sa.

Wheatley, Margaret J. 1992. Leadership and the New Science: Learning about Organization from an Orderly Universe. San Francisco: Berrett-Koehler Publishers.

List of authors

Pami Aalto	Bradford University (Great Britain)
Dirk Berg-Schlosser	Philipps-University of Marburg (Germany)
Jane L.Curry	Santa Clara University, California (USA)
Stephen Fisher-Galati	Editor, "East European Quarterly" (USA)
Scott Gates	Michigan State University (USA)
Nils Petter Gleditsch	International Peace Research Institute, Oslo & Norwegian University of Science and Technology (Norway)
Artur Gruszczak	Jagellonian University (Poland)
Havard Hegre	International Peace Research Institute, Oslo (Norway)
Gabriella Ilonski	Budapest University of Economic Sciences (Hungary)
Kim Kwang-woong	Seoul National University (Korea)
Algis Krupavicius	Kaunas University (Lithuania)
Christoper Marsh	University of Connecticut (USA)
Irena Panków	Institute of Political Studies (Poland)
Lenka Rovna	Charles University, (Czech Republic)
Jüri Ruus	Tartu University (Estonia)
Laslo Sekelj	University of Kassel (Germany)
Surinder K.Shukla	Panjab University (India)
Tatu Vanhanen	University of Helsinki (Finland)
Raivo Vetik	Institute of International and Social Studies (Estonia)